ın

Impact of Managed Care on Psychodynamic Treatment

Impact of Managed Care on Psychodynamic Treatment

Editors

James W. Barron, Ph.D.
Harry Sands, Ph.D.

International Universities Press, Inc.
Madison ● Connecticut

Copyright © 1996, International Universities Press, Inc.

INTERNATIONAL UNIVERSITIES PRESS and International Universities
Press, Inc. (& design) ® are registered trademarks of International
Universities Press, Inc.

Library of Congress Cataloging-in-Publication Data

Impact of managed care on psychodynamic treatment / editors, James W.
Barron, Harry Sands.
    p.   cm.
   Includes bibliographical references and index.
   ISBN 0-8236-2542-7
   1. Psychodynamic psychotherapy—Effect of managed care on.
  I. Barron, James W., 1944–   . II. Sands, Harry.
   [DNLM: 1. Managed Care Programs. 2. Psychotherapy. W 130 AA1 I3
1996]
RC489.P72I47 1996
616.89'14—dc20
DNLM/DLC
for Library of Congress   96-9118
                            CIP

Manufactured in the United States of America

To those individuals who grapple creatively with the realities of healthcare and who struggle to keep the range of psycho-dynamic treatments accessible to patients who need them

Contents

*HISTORICAL, ETHICAL, AND LEGAL DIMENSIONS OF
MANAGED CARE*

INTERNATIONAL PERSPECTIVE

    National Health Insurance Plans Around
    the World
    Brent Willock, Ph.D.   281

    Epilogue
    James W. Barron, Ph.D.   297

    Author Index   303

    Subject Index   309

Contributors

Daniel J. Abrahamson, Ph.D. Administrative Director and Partner, Traumatic Stress Institute/Center for Adult and Adolescent Psychotherapy_{L.L.C.} South Windsor, Connecticut

Martin G. Allen, M.D. Clinical Professor of Psychiatry at Georgetown University School of Medicine; Utilization Review Consultant, Principal Behavioral Health, Integrated Behavioral Care, and the American Day Care Treatment Centers; private practice, Washington, DC

Thomas F. Barrett, Ph.D. Director, Cleveland Center for Research in Child Development, Cleveland, Ohio

James W. Barron, Ph.D. Past-President of the Division of Psychoanalysis, American Psychological Association and of the International Federation for Psychoanalytic Education; Faculty member of the Psychoanalytic Institute of New England, East and of the Massachusettes Institute for Psychoanalysis; private practice, Brookline, Massachusetts.

Fredric Neal Busch, M.D. Lecturer in Psychiatry, Columbia University Center for Psychoanalytic Training and Research; Instructor in Psychiatry, Cornell University Medical College

Shirley Ann Higuchi, J.D. Staff member, American Psychological Association, Washington, DC

Paul M. Lerner, Ed.D. Private practice of psychoanalysis, psychoanalytic psychotherapy, and psychological testing in Ashville, North Carolina.

Beth Meehan, C.S.W., B.C.D. Faculty member, Psychoanalytic Psychotherapy Study Center, Cochair, Alliance for Universal Access to Psychotherapy; private practice, New York City

Jerry A. Morris, Jr., Psy.D. Staff member, Community Mental Health Consultants

Russ Newman, Ph.D., J.D. Staff member, American Psychological Association, Washington, DC

William S. Pollack, Ph.D. Director of Continuing Education (Psychology) at McLean Hospital, Belmont, MA, and Assistant Clinical Professor, Department of Psychiatry, Harvard Medical School; Past President of the Massachusetts Psychological Association and candidate, Boston Psychoanalytic Institute

Karen W. Saakvitne, Ph.D. Clinical Director, Traumatic Stress Institute / the Center for Adult and Adolescent Psychotherapy$_{L.L.C.,}$ South Windsor, Connecticut

Harry Sands, Ph.D. Training Analyst, Postgraduate Center for Mental Health, New York City

Norma P. Simon, Ed.D. Former Chair, New York State Board for Psychology; former President, Association of State and Provincial Psychology Boards; former Chair, Ethics Committee for the Division of Psychoanalysis of the American Psychological Association; Vice-Chair Ethics Committee, American Psychological Association; Supervisor, New York University Postdoctoral Program in Psychoanalysis; Director, New Hope Guild Training Programs; private practice, New York City

Gerald Stechler, Ph.D. Professor of Psychiatry, Boston University School of Medicine; faculty member, Massachusetts Institute for Psychoanalysis and the Boston Psychoanalytic Society and Institute

Josef H. Weissberg, M.D. Associate Clinical Professor of Psychiatry, Columbia University, New York City; Faculty Member, Columbia Psychoanalytic Center; Training Analyst, New York Medical College Psychoanalytic Institute; Former President, American Academy of Psychoanalysis

Joshua Williams, Ph.D. Director, East Tennessee Children's Hospital Integrated Psychiatric Services, Knoxville, Tennessee

Brent Willock, Ph.D. Chief Psychologist, C. M. Hincks Treatment Centre, Toronto, Ontario

Preface

James W. Barron, Ph.D.,
Harry Sands, Ph.D.

Alluding to attacks on the efficacy of psychodynamic treatment, Hans Loewald (1974), presenting the Rado Lecture at the Columbia University Psychoanalytic Clinic for Training and Research, commented: "I myself have no doubt about its therapeutic value and potentialities, although I do question whether we can expect general or ready recognition of its therapeutic worth and effects—given the anti-individualistic tendencies and simplistic behavior-modification trends in our culture" (p. 352).

Loewald was prescient. In the ensuing decades, the tendencies he observed have become dominant forces in our culture. The growth of biological psychiatry with its arsenal of psychotropic medications has captured the public imagination with explicit or implicit promises of magic bullets offering instant cures. The proliferation of therapies and specialized support groups has fragmented the field, leaving the public, as well as many mental health professionals, confused and searching for the quick fix. This fragmentation is also evident in the prevailing diagnostic system which relies heavily on signs, symptoms, and numerical rating scales of level of stress and degree of adjustment. Not surprisingly, these various tendencies have found their organizational expression in the growth of the managed care industry.

Managed care did not develop de novo. Aspects of managed care go back to the turn of the century. Despite some superficial similarities between those early plans and contemporary managed care systems, there is a critical difference. The early experiments did not congeal into an oppressive model. They were not driven primarily by market forces and the profit motive. In "The Greening of the HMO: Implications for Prepaid Psychiatry," which appeared in the *American Journal of Psychiatry*, Bennett (1988) observed:

> There has . . . been a change in the organizational mission and its derivative, system values: yesterday's HMO was designed to organize and deliver health care; today's is likely to be a product line, one activity of an organization seeking to prosper in the marketplace. Ginzberg [1984] has termed this "the monetarization of medical care," i.e., increasing domination of health care by those whose primary business is the preservation and increase of capital. These changes create a crosscurrent that threatens to confuse and inundate those who work in such settings [p. 1546].

The changes which Bennett cited continue unabated. In 1994 for-profit health maintenance organizations overtook nonprofits as the dominant force in managed care. This shift of ownership to the for-profits, along with the largest insurance and managed care companies consolidating and purchasing hospitals and provider networks, form the dominant features of the health care landscape.

These transformations have created a practice environment which is increasingly hostile toward psychodynamically oriented clinicians who value meaningful psychotherapeutic treatment of the individual as opposed to amelioration of a symptom fragment; who desire real engagement with their patients; who understand the significance of unfolding developmental processes in themselves, in their patients, and within the therapeutic encounter; and who appreciate the complex layering of personality organization and the simultaneity of experiencing at different levels of awareness. This book came into being because of the strongly felt need of the editors, the contributors, and their colleagues seriously to question basic premises of managed care; to examine which treatment modalities are truly cost effective (as opposed to cost-shifting) when health benefits are studied over time; to place managed mental health care in its proper historical, economic, and sociopolitical context; to analyze the legal, regulatory, and ethical dilemmas associated with managed care; and most importantly to take a careful, sustained look at the impact of the policies and procedures of many managed mental health care companies on critical aspects of clinical process. The contributors examine the influence of managed care on a broad spectrum of patients at different stages of the life cycle, presenting with a variety of serious psychological disorders, and treated by a wide range of psychodynamic approaches. Although several contributors acknowledge that managed care has led to some useful innovations, most have found that managed care places formidable obstacles in the path of treatment responsive to their patients' needs.

References

Bennett, M. J. (1988), The greening of the HMO: Implications for prepaid psychiatry. *Amer. J. Psychiat.*, 145:1544–1549.

Ginzberg, E. (1984), The monetarization of medical care. *New England J. Med.*, 310:1162–1165.

Loewald, H. W. (1974), Psychoanalysis as an art and the fantasy character of the psychoanalytic situation, In: *Papers on Psychoanalysis*, ed. H. W. Loewald. New Haven, CT: Yale University Press, pp. 352–371, 1980.

Therapeutic Relationship
and Process

1

Psychoanalysis and Dynamic Psychotherapy, the Mental Health Provider and Managed Care

Harry Sands, Ph.D.

The Growth of Managed Care

Network-based managed care[1] evolved from Health Maintenance Organizations (HMOs), which were established in the 1940s. They were created to reduce the cost of health care (U.S. General Accounting Office [GAO], 1993). Since then costs have escalated in the United States to an estimated $1 trillion or 14.6 percent of the gross national product.

Managed care, including utilization review, is well established within the health care industry, the third largest in America (Stone, 1995). This is reflected in the continued growth of HMOs. In mid-1993, HMOs enrolled 18.5 percent of the total U.S. population, and the number of corporate preferred provider organizations (PPOs) increased by 17 percent in 1992 (*Marion Merrill*, 1993). Today nearly 90 million individuals are covered by managed care (U.S. General Accounting Office [GAO], 1993). President Clinton's proposed Health Security Act, which was not enacted into law

---

[1]The terms *managed care, insurance company, utilization review entities*, and *third-party payer* are used interchangeably in this paper.

3

by the 103rd Congress, included managed competition as a
form of managed care, and under Title III funding was to
provide training in managed care (Health Security Act,
1993). The 1994 appropriation mandating the Department
of Defense "to implement a managed care program within
three years" (Dunivin, 1993) is further evidence that managed care is firmly established.

To control the costs of Medicaid benefits, state governments have also turned to managed care systems. In New
York state, for example, the Department of Social Services
is moving away from fee for service and has instituted managed care to oversee the control of Medicaid costs (Surles,
1994).

How Managed Care Influences Patient Care

Insurance companies indemnify insured persons for the cost
of their health care. The managed care company contracts
with the health benefits plan of the insurers, employers, or
union trusts to administer the program and to pay for clinical services for a fixed fee. If costs are greater than this fixed
amount, the managed care company absorbs the loss. If the
costs are less, the company makes a profit. Because managed
care companies, like the insurance firms which often own
them, are in business to make money, they have an incentive
to lower the cost of clinical services (Shueman, Troy, and
Mayhugh, 1994, Allen, see chapter 2), and their operations
are directed at enhancing the plan administration and
profits (U.S. General Accounting Office, 1993, p. 4). Stone
points out that "Mental health care has always been the step-
child of health insurance. . . . [the] Plan's cost containment
objective . . . is always to take shortcuts and to go with less
expensive treatment (which may not be the best treatment
or treatment of choice) . . . . (Thus,) the big picture, . . . is

about *money* and not ideology or communitarian principles (1995, pp. 5-6; emphasis added). In the psychotherapeutic area, there are a number of ways to lower costs. One method is to limit the number of therapy sessions or to cap the dollar cost of treatment. Another way is to limit the number of practitioners the companies enroll into their provider panels. According to the GAO report, keeping the number of members in the network small enables the company to provide each member with a large number of referrals. This then gives the company leverage to negotiate lower fees with these providers (U.S. General Accounting Office, 1993). A third way to reduce cost is for the carriers to select providers who practice short-term, focused, or strategic therapy (Shueman et al., 1994) and drop those who do not. Still another method is for companies to stop payments for additional sessions before treatment has been completed, usually after the reduction or removal of symptoms (see Barrett, chapter 8), but before optimal functioning has been attained.

The latest mechanism used by managed care companies is not to authorize payments when psychotherapy or psychodiagnostic testing is carried out by interns and residents, even those receiving close supervision in accredited programs at universities, medical centers, community mental health clinics, and training institutes (Sanderson, personal communication, 1994). In effect, Health Care Finance Agency (HCFA) also takes a similar position when it requires the clinical supervisor to establish a relationship with the patient and to be present when the resident or intern is doing the testing or providing the psychotherapeutic service (Wiens, personal communication, 1994).

By establishing their own practice protocols as a standard for their representatives to review the appropriateness of the providers' clinical decisions, managed care companies are setting standards and criteria for treatment (U.S. General Accounting Office, 1993, p. 31; Shueman et al., 1994), which up to now, have been determined by research, clinical literature, and the accepted practices of peers. The companies also become de facto qualifying agencies by choosing which licensed providers to accept, reject, or drop from their panels.

Issues for Practitioners

Managed care has spawned a vast number of nearly insurmountable issues for psychoanalysts and psychoanalytic treatment. These range from patient confidentiality to ethics, from legal responsibility to the technical requirements of the psychoanalytic process.

The dyadic psychotherapist–patient relationship is seriously breached by this addition of a third party, as are technical requirements such as the neutrality stance or establishing a structural frame. The structural frame is essential for psychodynamic treatment to take place. However, managed care companies neither understand nor have regard for this requirement. As a result, Lerner (see chapter 7) asserts that managed care's impact is devastating. Analysts are "placed in a position of having to negotiate with the [managed care] company to allow for additional therapy sessions for their patients" (Higuchi and Newman, see chapter 13). The courts have ruled that health care providers who accede without protest to the treatment determinations of insurance/ managed care companies are, along with the companies themselves, liable for harm caused to their patients.

As the gatekeeper of treatment, the managed care company poses an additional problem: neither the therapist nor the patient knows when, during the course of psychotherapy, the company will stop authorizing further payments. This uncertainty interferes with the patients' establishing a therapeutic alliance which is an essential condition for therapy to take place. Also, Stone holds that "A continuing psychotherapeutic relationship may be the only way to achieve [treatment] compliance" (Stone, 1995). Also, for patients who depend on their insurance reimbursement as the only source to pay for their treatment, this can be severely traumatic. In group psychotherapy, too, payment approval is a special and serious concern. Group psychotherapists carefully choose group members who differ on a number of parameters: diagnosis, defenses, age, gender, ethnic and cultural background. Heterogeneity is an essential requirement for the operation of a dynamic psychotherapy group. A patient's unplanned departure changes the group's composition and dynamics. "Patient turnover," Williams observes, "destroys cohesiveness and continuity in group therapy" (see p. 170). It is understandable that providers are reluctant to place in group individuals who are under the purview of a managed care company, even in cases when conjoint individual and group psychotherapy would be the treatment of choice. While some psychotherapists maintain that such untoward events can be used as "grist" for the analytic mill, such incidents should be seen as destructive to analytic treatment, not, as managed care companies contend, as furthering quality care.

It is also deeply troubling for mental health practitioners that managed care companies use medical condition as a basis for authorizing payment. For example, insurance companies often deny payment for psychotherapy in the case of individuals diagnosed as having a depression. They do so on the grounds that this is a psychological condition, not a medical condition. If it *is* medical, then they deem the treatment inappropriate because antidepressant medications are not being prescribed as part of the treatment regime. Companies also use this argument to avoid paying for "longer-term services aimed specifically at the treatment of personality disorders" (Shueman et al., 1994). It cannot be ascertained whether this means that companies are more likely to approve treatment by psychiatrists than by psychologists or social workers. If such data exist, they are inaccessible. However, Stone contends that whenever possible, to achieve economies, managed care companies replace psychiatrists with psychologists, psychologists with social workers, social workers with nurses, and nurses with mental health workers or counselors (1995, p. 7).

Managed care and utilization review companies make constant and inordinate requests for information, including the providers' full case records. This goes beyond what is required to authorize payment for psychotherapy and is a severe challenge to a mental health provider's adherence to ethical codes of conduct. In fact, by satisfying such requests, a psychoanalyst or psychotherapist violates patient confidentiality.

Managed care entities often use provider profiling as a basis for rejecting qualified mental health practitioners or dropping them from their panels. The purpose of the profiling is to determine how well practitioners meet the company's cost-cutting objectives and to refer patients to the providers who meet these criteria (U.S. General Accounting Office, 1993; Shueman et al., 1994). Also, those providers who are accepted to be on their provider panels are required by most managed care companies, according to Bertram P. Karon, "to sign a contract including an agreement never to make any statements critical of care under that managed care plan" (personal communication, 1994). It is understandable that rejections, even on these grounds, may raise doubts about the practitioner's qualifications. These doubts can spread and impugn the practitioner's reputation in the community.

The many issues raised by third-party payers seriously compromise the psychoanalytic treatment process and are excessive burdens on it. They can cause psychoanalysts to deviate from the course of the treatment process and thereby diminish its efficiency, and, at times, even impair its effectiveness. These issues overwhelm and confound the treatment with excessive transference and by what Lerner (see chapter 7) refers to as indirect countertransference reactions.

The Importance of Mental Health Care

Psychoanalysts and psychotherapists are aware of the necessity for medical cost containment. But they also recognize the dangerously high cost of emotional and mental disorders, and of the psychopathology of violence and sexual and child abuse in the community.

In 1978 the President's Commission on Mental Health noted in its report that many people disabled by mental illness "received deplorably inadequate assistance" (see p. vii). A major goal was to remedy this situation by 1988. In 1995 the goal remains unmet.

In a recent study, researchers found that although almost half of the respondents "reported at least one lifetime mental disorder, . . . less than 40% of these" had ever received treatment (Kessler, McGonagle, Zhao, Nelson, Hughes, Eshleman, Wittchen, and Kendler, 1994). In another study 54 percent of subjects with defined mental health disorders who do receive treatment are seen only by nonpsychiatric physicians (Borus, Olendzki, Kessler, Burns, Brandt, Broverman, and Henderson, 1985).

President Clinton's proposed health care reform legislation embodies many of the recommendations of President Carter's Commission on Mental Health. It would presumably make mental health care more accessible to everyone. Yet by limiting psychotherapy to thirty sessions annually, this legislation, in the words of the Commission, offers "deplorably inadequate assistance" (p. vii). Abused children, battered women, and others who have experienced severe trauma cannot be appropriately treated in thirty sessions. Removing the proposed limit would not unduly increase the cost of the Clinton proposal. At 50 percent copayment, it is estimated that health care cost would increase by only 3.2 percent (Bryant Welch, personal communication, 1994).

It is time to stop putting obstacles in the way of consumers' access to appropriate treatment and choice of providers. The latter is consistent with the Commission's report, which calls for freedom of choice of providers by people seeking mental health services (President's Commission, 1978, p. 30). Interference with access and freedom of choice are not problems only in the United States. In varying degrees these barriers are found in national health plans of countries throughout the world. Brent Willock's survey (see chapter 15) clearly documents this and also shows how these impediments impact on the practice of dynamic psychotherapy.

The Cost Effectiveness of Psychotherapy

Contrary to the position held by the insurance/managed care industry, psychotherapies are highly cost effective. A large number of studies in diverse settings have found a reduction in the use of medical services as a result of mental health care (Hankin, Kessler, Goldberg, Steinwachs, and Starfield, 1983; Mumford, Schleisinger, Glass, Patrick, and Cuerdon, 1984; Jacobs, 1987; Massad, West, and Friedman, 1990). Lechnyr (1993) notes: "Mental health care can reduce medical overutilization by up to 75%," and Shemo (1985–1986) reports that the cost offset increases over time.

Psychological interventions not only reduce the overuse of inpatient and outpatient medical services but substantially lower absentee rates and increase productivity in the workplace. For example, in 1990 major depression accounted for an estimated $23 billion in lost work days. Minor depression, by affecting more people, may be even more expensive (accounting for 51 percent more disability days than major depression) (Practice Directorate, 1991).

For maximum effectiveness, the situation requires the use of appropriately trained personnel. This is borne out in a study by Lechnyr (1993), who found that mental health professionals correctly diagnosed depression 86 percent of the time, family physicians paid on a fee for service basis detected 54 percent of depressed patients, and physicians working in managed care programs recognized only 42 percent. In addition, Lechnyr notes that "depressed patients treated by general physicians have poorer physical functioning and experience more pain and more days in bed than patients treated by a mental health professional." These findings support the recommendation of the Report of the President's Commission that "appropriate mental health professionals . . . be available [to provide the care] where . . . needed" (p. viii).

Studying changes in health care costs and utilization associated with mental health treatment of Ætna Insurance Company beneficiaries, Holder and Blose found:

> A decrease in total health care costs can be expected following the start of mental health treatment—even when the costs of this treatment are included. . . . This . . . supports a conclusion that the initiation of mental health treatment by self-motivated patients can yield positive reductions in health care utilization and costs for a large insured population [1987, pp. 1074–1075].

The converse is also true; failing to provide psychological interventions increases costs (Practice Directorate, 1991).

In sum, to reduce the cost of overall medical care there must be an active outreach, a removal of barriers, and access to mental health services.

In addition, treatment interventions with individuals who have personality and character disorders that manifest themselves as social pathologies (for example, violence) also reduce medical costs and therefore should be included as cost offsets.

The health indemnity policy of the insurance industry does not take these findings into consideration. This shortcoming, along with the evidence that patients rate the "care they receive from managed care providers lower than [do patients] visiting fee-for-service physicians," may be reflected in employers' disappointment with the cost of managed care. The latter is not refuted by the Health Insurance Association of America, which "acknowledges that few rigorous analyses exist of the cost effectiveness of managed care" and "most data on PPO cost savings are anecdotal and cannot be generalized" (U.S. General Accounting Office, 1993, p. 39).

Accordingly the GAO concluded that there is "little empirical evidence . . . on the cost savings of managed care" (U.S. General Accounting Office, 1993, p. 3).

Psychoanalysis and other appropriate psychodynamic interventions, without the barriers imposed by managed care companies, could do much more to prevent costly mental and physical illness from developing and thereby result in real major cost savings.

References

Borus, J. F., Olendzki, M. C., Kessler, L., Burns, B. J., Brandt, U. C., Broverman, C. A., & Henderson, P. R. (1985), The "offset effect" of mental health treatment on ambulatory medical care utilization and charges. *Arch. Gen. Psychiatry*, 42:573–580.

Dunivin, D. (1993), Opportunities for psychology and social work, fiscal year 1994, appropriations. *Memorandum to Senator Daniel Inouye.* December 13:1–45.

Hankin, J. R., Kessler, L. G., Goldberg, I. D., Steinwachs, D. M., & Starfield, B. H. (1983), A longitudinal study of offset in the use of nonpsychiatric services following specialized mental health care. *Med. Care,* 21:1099–1110.

Health Security Act (1993), S. 1757/HR 3600.

Holder, H. D., & Blose, J. O. (1987), Changes in health care costs and utilization associated with mental health treatment. *Hosp. & Commun. Psychiatry,* 38:1070–1075.

Jacobs, D. F. (1987), Cost effectiveness of specialized psychological programs for reducing hospital stay and outpatient visits. *J. Clin. Psych.,* 43:729–735.

Kessler, R. C., McGonagle, K. A., Zhao, S., Nelson, C. B., Hughes, M., Eshleman, S., Wittchen, H.-U., & Kendler, K. S. (1994), Lifetime and 12-month prevalence of DSM-III-R psychiatric disorders in the United States. *Arch. Gen. Psychiatry,* 51:8–19.

Lechnyr, R. (1993), The cost savings of mental health services. *EAP Digest,* November/December: 22–27.

Marion Merrill Dow Managed Care Digest/PPO Edition (1993).

Massad, P. M., West, A. N., & Friedman, M. J. (1990), Relationship between utilization of mental health and medical services in a VA hospital. *Amer. J. Psychiatry,* 147:465–469.

Mumford, E., Schleisinger, H. J., Glass, G. V., Patrick, C., & Cuerdon, T. (1984), About reduced cost of medical utilization following mental health treatment. *Amer. J. Psychiatry,* 141:1145–1158.

Practice Directorate (1991), *The Costs of Failing to Provide Appropriate Mental Health Care (a fact sheet).* Washington, DC: American Psychological Association.

The President's Commission on Mental Health and Illness, (1978), *Report to the President from The President's Commission on Mental Health,* Vol. 1. Washington, DC: U.S. Government Printing Office, stock no. 040-000-00390-8.

Shemo, J. P. (1985–1986), Cost-effectiveness of providing mental health services: The offset effect. *Internat. J. Psychiatry in Med.,* 15:19–30.

Shueman, S. A., Troy, W. G., & Mayhugh, S. L. (1994), Some questions and answers about managed behavioral health care. *Register Report: The Newsletter for Health Service Providers in Psychology.* Washington, DC: Council for the National Register, 20:1–28.

Stone, A. A. (1995), Psychotherapy and managed care: The bigger picture. *Harvard Ment. Health Newsletter,* 11:1–8.

Surles, R. C. (1994), Managed care is coming. Albany, NY: NY State Office of Mental Health.

U.S. General Accounting Office (1993), Managed health care: Effect on employers' costs difficult to measure. *Report to the Chairman, Subcommittee on Health, Committee on Ways and Means, House of Representatives.* Washington, DC: GAO/HRD-94-3.

2

Understanding and Coping with Managed Care

Martin G. Allen, M.D.

History

For thousands of years doctors have treated patients without third-party coverage. In the 1930s health insurance began when a group of doctors organized Blue Cross and Blue Shield. It was only thirty years ago that mental health coverage was introduced. Yet now, both we and our patients focus on insurance coverage. Right now, with the medical care debate, there are basic relevant questions being raised in this country (Cummings, 1986; Relman, 1987; Sharfstein, 1990; Tischler, 1990; Office of National Cost Estimates, 1990; Schwartz and Mendelson, 1991; Austad and Hoyt, 1992; Jellinek and Nurcombe, 1993). Is insurance and health care a basic right? Is it a privilege? Or is it simply a contract as to what is covered and what is not covered?

Most health insurance is a contract between an employer, an individual, or a group and the insurance company as to what is or is not covered. Insurance companies are businesses. Their purpose is to make money, and one way to do this is to limit costs; that's a reality of the business

15

world. In contrast, mental health professionals and their patients are very concerned with limitations and discriminatory coverage for mental health. Mental illness is not covered to the extent of other medical illnesses. There are differences in coverage; there are differences in policies; there are differences in patients' incomes.

Another historical fact is that in the 1950s, the *Diagnostic and Statistical Manual of Mental Disorders* (DSM-I) presented diagnoses as reactions. Schizophrenia was considered a "reaction." Mental illness was due to the effect of environment on a vulnerable individual. Psychoanalytic and psychodynamic diagnoses were defined with attention paid to psychic conflict. In contrast, DSM-III, DSM-III-R, and DSM-IV have focused on signs and symptoms for reliability of diagnosis in treatment and research (APA, 1994). This change has evolved over thirty years.

The *Diagnostic and Statistical Manual of Mental Disorders* also has the global assessment of functioning (GAF) score on a scale from 0 to 100. Each ten points on the scale is defined by what a patient can or cannot do in terms of life functioning. As a result, insurance companies, as well as the mental health profession, now focus on signs, symptoms, and functioning.

Increasingly, in much of our culture, there is a focus on the "quick fix." Similarly, in mental health care, there is an increase in treatment oriented toward quick symptom relief, and less motivation (and payment) for more lengthy and intensive therapy directed toward the working through of intrapsychic conflicts.

Additional factors impinging on mental health treatment are:

1. Health care is an increasing percentage of gross national product and of corporate expenses (Office of National Cost Estimates, 1990).

2. There is increasing competition for limited health care dollars.
3. The government is talking of capping or reducing Medicare. The number of aged patients is expanding, but the amount of money the government plans to pay for their health care will contract or stay the same.
4. There is increasing medical review, which started with Medicare in the late 1960s. Private insurance, the government, and corporations are increasingly demanding more control over their dollars spent on health care. As a result, utilization review or managed care has developed (Cummings, 1986; Kuzmicki and Penner, 1987; Allen, 1988; Scharfstein, 1990; Tischler, 1990; Austad and Hoyt, 1992; Mattson, 1992; Jellinek and Nurcombe, 1993). And in the last five years, managed care/utilization review activities have increased.
5. Whatever is not tangible or visible is less understandable to people. A broken leg or a bullet wound, something that we can see or touch, is more comprehensible than something like anxiety or depression which is not visible or touchable. For most people—including government and insurance policy makers—psychiatric signs and symptoms are less comprehensible, less real.
6. There is a belief that psychiatry, especially psychoanalysis, deals with the "worried well." Patients who can work effectively in psychotherapy and analysis are precisely those individuals who may appear to function well in the external world. And the DSM-III, as just mentioned, focuses on signs, symptoms, and the global assessment of functioning.

Basic Concepts of Utilization Review

There are three basic terms in utilization review. The first is *medical necessity*. Is care medically necessary? Determination of medical necessity requires a medical diagnosis, specifically defined by DSM-IV in terms of signs and symptoms that need treatment. Consequently, treatment is defined in terms of symptom relief.

The second term is *medically appropriate*. Is the treatment appropriate for the illness? It is a reasonable question. Does the treatment fit the illness?

The third term is *least costly alternative*. Is the treatment "cost effective"? From a management point of view—for a corporation, HMO, or insurance company—there are a limited number of dollars. In determining allocation of resources, management asks: Is there an illness which needs to be treated? Is the treatment appropriate for that illness, and is it "cost effective"? Effectiveness is defined by asking: Are the illness and the patient being treated in the least costly way? Is the treatment likely to result in improvement or at least stabilization? You may not like the concept of "cost effective," you might disagree with it, you might want to fight it, but it is one of the three basic concepts in managed care. To understand these three terms is to comprehend the fundamentals of utilization review and managed care.

There are additional concepts to discuss: The first is "certification" for payment. Utilization reviewers are careful to use the words *certify* or *denial* of certification. There is obviously a lot of power with a denial, since the presence or absence of payment will affect treatment. Both for legal and ethical reasons, utilization review is not telling doctors how to treat patients, they are saying what they'll pay for. However, managed care is more specifically directing the form, frequency, and type of treatment. Organizations are moving from reviewing utilization of care to actively "managing" care. Therefore the previous terminology "utilization review" is changing to "managed care."

In managed care there is more active involvement by the review organization in directing and influencing patient care. Based on developed criteria of care, review organizations are now limiting certification to specific treatment approaches (e.g., insisting on the use of medication for acute symptoms; directing referrals to certain treatment centers for specific problems such as substance abuse, or residential treatment of adolescents).

When I meet with a patient in my practice, I take the reality of managed care into consideration. I decide what treatment to recommend for the condition. We might want to treat patients for free after their insurance runs out; we might want to reduce the fee; we might do neither. If managed care says it is "not certifying" after a certain date, it is similar to saying "the 20-visits-a-year limit is over; now you and the patient work it out."

The patient needs to know about the existence of utilization review, and therapist and patient need to talk about it. Are we going to embark on treatment that has a likelihood of being aggressively reviewed? Where are things going to stand subsequent to that review? I recommend that with the existence of managed care review, the information which will be requested in the review process, and the possibility of denial of reimbursement, be discussed initially with the patient. It is going to be a factor, a "parameter" in the therapy. As a third party, utilization review may be viewed by the patient as an oedipal intruder, sibling rival, an authoritarian domineering parent (Gabbard, Takahaski, Davidson, Bauman-Bork, and Ensroth, 1991). In any case, when certification is denied, it doesn't mean treatment must necessarily end. It means that the doctor and patient need to negotiate an arrangement for payment.

Another important concept is that of "review by a peer." Most review organizations are required to have a review process at several levels. Sometimes a request is made for a subspecialty—an adolescent psychiatrist may want to speak to an adolescent psychiatrist; an analyst may want an analyst. Generally speaking, the insurance industry and the courts have said that a peer is a person with the same professional degree who is certified in the same specialty (Allen, 1988; Sederer, 1992; Goodman, Brown, and Deitz, 1992). How far does this apply to the subspecialties? That is a subject of debate and has not really been clarified. In any case, one can usually have three levels of review, if not more. The first is usually with a nurse or MSW, the second is with a psychologist or psychiatrist, and the third is that if the case is denied, it can be appealed. But before appealing the decision, the therapist should clearly understand what the basis is for the denial, and what the reviewer's thinking is about the denial. Some employers also have their own appeal board.

A California case went to court, and the doctor was judged liable because he had not appealed his case. The court said he still had professional responsibility to the patient (Sederer, 1992). So legally, as professionals, we are always responsible for the patient. In addition, many preferred provider organizations and managed care networks have a "hold harmless" contract with providers of mental health care. These clauses typically absolve the utilization review/managed care company from any professional/legal responsibility in the decision-making process of patient care. As review organizations become more active in influencing the type and intensity of professional care, the degree to which these "hold harmless" clauses will protect managed care companies is open to some question. To my knowledge, these legalities have not yet been tested in the courts (Sederer, 1992). Theoretically, the reviewer is not telling us how to treat the patient. They are consultants (for the insurance company or the employer or both) who render judgment as to whether the care is medically necessary, appropriate, and cost effective.

We may experience utilization review as an insult to our integrity and professional judgment; we may view it as intrusive. But insurance companies, the government, and corporations want to control health care costs, and they are paying the bills. In any review process, we should present a strong clear case, colleague to colleague. Ideally utilization review provides the opportunity to discuss a case with a fellow professional—a peer—as opposed to an arbitrary limit in the number of sessions or amount of dollars per year.

Case Examples

Utilization review can serve a positive function when it identifies instances of inappropriate or inadequate treatment. Here are some actual examples:

1. A psychiatrist was hired by an insurance company to review a patient in analysis. The patient and the analyst were notified by the insurance company. The insurance contract specified there could be review for medical necessity. (Even if the patient has not signed directly, the employer has signed a contract with the insurance company, and usually buried in the fine print of the contract is "payment for care which is medically necessary.") So the insurance company asked a psychodynamic psychiatrist (not an analyst, but someone knowledgeable about medications) to review the case. The patient was alcoholic, but his active drinking had not been addressed in the analysis. The patient was also depressed, with significant family history and vegetative signs, but had never been treated with medication. Also this patient sometimes came to sessions drunk. The report to the

insurance company was that a trial of medication was indicated and that the alcoholism needed to be addressed. Psychoanalysis for this patient was judged not medically appropriate or useful until the alcoholism and the biological depression were addressed.

2. A patient was judged acutely suicidal by an employee counselor. Nevertheless, he traveled alone hundreds of miles to the hospital unaccompanied by anyone. The hospital staff also said he was acutely suicidal, yet the medical records revealed that the day after admission he was given an unaccompanied pass off the hospital grounds. Such discrepancies raise serious questions which need to be explored.

3. A 65-year-old man had troubles in his second marriage. His wife wanted to leave him. His only previous history was that in his forties he had been depressed and treated as an outpatient for grief after a divorce. He never had vegetative signs, and was never suicidal, homicidal, or psychotic. His wife took him to a hospital, and the hospital recommended a lengthy inpatient treatment. The reviewer questioned: "He isn't homicidal, suicidal or psychotic. Why couldn't he have outpatient therapy—maybe couples treatment if there is a marital problem? Why does he need to be an inpatient?"

Unfortunately, a reviewer may be very arbitrary or judgmental. The following is an example:

4. A 10-year-old had been in outpatient treatment with both male and female therapists at different times. A variety of medications had been tried. He had set fires and tortured pets. The boy had climbed on a ledge of a window of his apartment building, threatening to jump. He was brought to the hospital, but the psychiatrist reviewer said, "I don't think he would have jumped, he was probably bluffing. I think this kid would do just fine on five to six times a week outpatient treatment." In my opinion, this decision was

grossly unreasonable. Another example is the arbitrary reviewer who feels everybody should be on medication. Nevertheless, in each case we can and should try to explain our rationale and thinking.

With a patient in three or four times a week intensive psychodynamic treatment, the utilization review guidelines of the managed care company may specifically limit treatment to twice weekly sessions unless there is a clear medical emergency. So the case may not be denied completely. The reviewer may say "I don't see the medical necessity for four times a week treatment. But I can and will certify twice weekly treatment, based on the history and clinical presentation." Such a decision (a reduction in frequency) may be based on the policy that the company does not certify more than twice weekly treatment under any circumstances, or it might be that the patient never had a trial of once or twice weekly treatment. In such cases, the concept of "least costly alternative" is operating; that is, the reviewer's judgment that there is medical necessity for some treatment, but not more "intensive" than once or twice a week psychotherapy. In such a case, there is a "partial certification." Then there is always the option of working out self-payment with the patient for the additional sessions.

As a reviewer, I am influenced by a reasonable, thoughtful, articulate colleague who is not angry, argumentative, and threatening but rather is clearly conceptualizing the case (Goodman et al., 1992). I'll conclude with an example:

A borderline, anorexic, and suicidal college girl was previously hospitalized for about eight months. She regressed and was rehospitalized. The case was referred to the physician reviewer, because she was given passes to go out to class. The treating psychiatrist said, "I am concerned about her regressing in the hospital. She used outpatient therapy productively, and I'm hopeful that she can again. So I would like to limit this hospitalization by keeping her focused on the outside. I or the nurses will have the power to cancel her passes at any time. I would like to get her stabilized, keep her going to classes, and hopefully have her out soon."

References

Allen, M. G. (1988), Psychiatric peer review: A current perspective. *Psychiatric Annals*, 18:487–491.

American Psychiatric Association (1994), *Diagnostic and Statistical Manual of Mental Disorders*, 4th ed. rev. (DSM-IV). Washington, DC: American Psychiatric Press.

Austad, C. W., & Hoyt, M. F. (1992), The managed care movement in the future of psychotherapy. *Psychotherapy*, 29:109–118.

Cummings, N. A. (1986), The dismantling of our health system. *Amer. Psychologist*, 41:426–431.

Gabbard, G. O., Takahaski, T., Davidson, J., Bauman-Bork, M., & Ensroth, K. (1991), The psychodynamic prospective on the clinical impact of insurance review. *Amer. J. Psychiatry*, 148:318–323.

Goodman, M., Brown, J., & Deitz, P. (1992), *Managing Managed Care*. Washington, DC: American Psychiatric Press.

Jellinek, M. S., & Nurcombe, B. (1993), Managed care, mental health, and the marketplace. *JAMA*, 170:1737–1739.

Kuzmicki, K. V., & Penner, N. R. (1987), Cost containment: The American Psychiatric Association's psychiatric case management program. *Qual. Rev. Bull.*, 13:21–25.

Mattson, M. R., Ed. (1992), *Manual of Psychiatric Quality Assurance*. Washington, DC: American Psychiatric Press.

Office of National Cost Estimates (1990), National health expenditures, 1988. *Health Care Finance Rev.*, 11:20–33.

Relman, A. S. (1987), Editorial: The changing climate of medical practice. *N. Engl. J. Med.*, 316:333–334.

Sharfstein, S. S. (1990), Utilization management: Managed or mangled psychiatric care? *Amer. J. Psychiatry*, 147:965–966.

Schwartz, W. B., & Mendelson, D. N. (1991), Hospital cost containment in the 1980's: Hard lessons learned and prospects for the 1990's. *N. Engl. J. Med.*, 324:1037–1042.

Sederer, L. I. (1992), Judicial and legislative responses to cost containment. *Amer. J. Psychiatry*, 149:1157–1161.
Tischler, G. L. (1990), Utilization management of mental health services by private third parties. *Amer. J. Psychiatry*, 147:967–973.

3

The Impact of Managed Care on the Therapeutic Relationship

Karen W. Saakvitne, Ph.D.
Daniel J. Abrahamson, Ph.D.

The increasing prevalence of managed care and insurance review for mental health benefits has changed the frame of psychotherapy. As psychoanalytic psychotherapists, we are challenged to bring our theoretically informed analysis to understand and incorporate these developments into our treatments. The authors propose that managed care impacts psychotherapy, and specifically the therapeutic relationship, at two levels: at a practical level through actual changes in the therapeutic frame, and at a relational, meaning level through effects on transference, countertransference, and the understanding of reenactments.

The growth of the role of managed care in third-party reimbursement has outpaced our ability to develop a theoretical understanding of the structure and meaning of the presence of managed care in the therapeutic relationship. While everyone cites the economic and social factors that have contributed to the proliferation of managed care, we rarely examine how our own training and practice have contributed to our unreadiness to respond in a systematic and thoughtful way. Most psychoanalytically trained clinicians have very little training in practice management. While psychoanalytic practitioners are skilled and practiced in understanding and interpreting the meaning of events and boundaries, we have only recently utilized those skills to understand the impact of managed care.

The authors' concern about the impact of changes in health care reimbursement on the practice of psychoanalytic psychotherapy is informed by their particular context of practice. As clinical director and administrative director of an independent Boulder-model[1] mental health organization, we deal on a daily basis with the challenges of balancing quality of care and commitment to excellence in clinical practice with cost containment and the reality of keeping an outpatient practice fiscally viable.

As a Boulder model organization, the Traumatic Stress Institute and its clinical division, the Center for Adult and Adolescent Psychotherapy (TSI/CAAP) strive to integrate multiple aspects of psychological practice. Our clinical work is informed by the scientist–practitioner model; thus, we integrate research, education, training, community involvement, and professional development into our organizational work. The organization, comprised of ten doctoral level psychologists, has a dual mission; first, to increase our knowledge of the impact of traumatic stress on individuals' development and functioning, and provide expert treatment for those who have experienced traumatic life events; second, to promote the profession of psychology (Abrahamson,

---

[1] By Boulder model we mean a model of training and practice for clinical psychologists adopted by the American Psychological Association at a conference in Boulder, Colorado, in 1949. The Boulder (also referred to as "scientist-practitioner") model emphasizes the importance of psychologists functioning as well-trained clinicians who combine clinical practice with research methodology that is appropriately suited for a clinical setting.

1992a). We have struggled successfully to maintain the integrity of our clinical standards and to grow as an organization in a time when virtually everyone is sounding the death knell of individual and small-group practice.

Theory and ethics form the foundation of effective psychotherapy. Psychoanalytic theory provides a rigorous theory not only of personality, but of the process of psychotherapy. Integrative theories such as constructivist self development theory (McCann and Pearlman, 1990a) allow us to build on the sophistication of psychoanalytic theory and integrate social learning and trauma theories. An ethical treatment is one conducted by an appropriately trained therapist, practicing within his or her level of expertise, and within an identified theoretical orientation that informs the therapeutic frame, technique, and conceptualizations. The ethics of psychotherapy include our commitment not only to do our best to help our patients in their personal struggles, but further, "to do no harm," that is, to refrain from knowingly participating in interactions that serve to meet our needs over those of our patients, from intentionally misleading patients, violating boundaries, or engaging in "therapeutic" activities that are not in our patients' best interest.

Just as theory and ethics are necessary to effective psychotherapy, it is essential to have a framework from which to evaluate managed care and its impact on psychotherapeutic practice. Many of the dilemmas posed by the impact of managed care on clinical practice are conceptual and ethical. This paper examines the impact of managed care on the therapeutic relationship by examining the specific impact on the therapeutic frame and the therapeutic relationship, specifically transference and countertransference responses. These two realms, structure (frame) and meaning (transference and countertransference), reflect the integration of theory with practice in psychoanalytic psychotherapy.

THE IMPACT OF MANAGED CARE ON THE
THERAPEUTIC FRAME

DEFINITION OF THERAPEUTIC FRAME

While typically we may think of the therapeutic frame as it surrounds the therapeutic dyad, the frame defines the relationship of outsiders to the therapeutic dyad as well as the relationship between the therapist and patient.

> The therapeutic relationship is contained by the therapeutic frame; this frame creates the uniquely bounded intimate relationship that defines psychotherapy. The frame reflects the shared framework in which the relationship and therapeutic work will occur. It is the interpersonal manifestation of the theoretical model of the psychotherapy and defines the tasks, role, structure, and boundaries of both the therapy and the therapeutic relationship. Within the therapeutic frame is established the safe context for the unique shared intimacy of the therapeutic relationship which then allows the creative potential of the relational space to emerge [Pearlman and Saakvitne, 1995, p. 147].

Therapeutic frame includes issues of confidentiality, accountability, and choice as well as the traditional components identified above.

There are several specific components of therapeutic frame, both internal and external, that can be altered or disrupted by the presence of managed care in the treatment. Historically, the therapeutic frame has defined an anticipated progression of treatment such that the therapist and patient together could establish and predict their frequency of appointments, and the overall length of treatment. The addition of the managed care reviewer changes and adds complexity to the negotiation of these aspects of the therapeutic frame. When a case manager becomes actively involved in the treatment, the therapeutic relationship now involves three people. Zuckerman (1989) warns of a potential danger then that "all of our accumulated knowledge of how to develop, understand, and utilize the therapeutic alliance becomes obsolete" (p. 122), or at least incomplete.

IMPACT ON THE THERAPIST

Any change in frame is likely to evoke resistance from the therapist. A central source of this resistance is the therapist's affective response to what is often perceived as an "assault" on his autonomy of practice, his identity and ego ideal as a therapist, and his theoretical training. The presence of managed care reviewers requires significant shifts in our beliefs and expectations about autonomy in practice. In addition to concrete logistical adaptations, we are challenged to integrate a new paradigm, no small task for psychoanalytic therapists who practice within a clearly defined theoretical paradigm.

Managed care systems are unabashedly atheoretical. Because their evaluative systems are symptom based, managed care systems rely on descriptive modalities, specifically symptom lists and diagnoses drawn from the DSM-IV, a manual that defines itself as descriptive, atheoretical, and generally indifferent to etiology (American Psychiatric Association, 1994). This descriptive paradigm contrasts fundamentally with the meaning-based premises of psychoanalytic theory and practice. It is extremely difficult to incorporate two such divergent paradigms into one consistent treatment.

Thus, the impact of managed care on therapeutic frame includes the clash of paradigms and the collaboration of individuals with very different agendas and frameworks. Personally, the therapist may feel his knowledge and training and the complexity of his clinical thinking are devalued by a review process that is simply interested in symptoms and considers meaning and interpretations irrelevant. Often, the reviewer herself has not only different, but less clinical training, experience, or sophistication. Even when a reviewer's training is similar, however, her task and framework are different from that of the analytic practitioner. The reviewer will be following guidelines that emphasize acuteness of need as defined by symptomatology, rather than clinical appropriateness. Thus, resolving these various clashes of paradigms, tasks, and frameworks is inherent in the process of accommodating managed care into psychoanalytic practice.

IMPACT ON PATIENT

Many people struggle with the implications of entering into psychotherapy in the first place. The decision to access one's mental health benefits is already fraught with uncertainty and anxiety. The added effect of the managed care system of case review can increase the obstacles to treatment. The system itself communicates to the patient the societal valuation and devaluation of mental health services and thus of mental health itself. The use of benefits carries with it a belief and expectation that one's mental health is as important as one's physical health. Patients are often acutely attuned to messages that criticize and shame them for their experiences of pain, emotional distress, or behavioral symptoms. The system can participate in cultural denial and stigmatization of these patients which further impedes their progress toward health. As one patient said, "It is one thing to be battling this terrible illness. It is another when the culture tells you it is a non-illness."

Within the therapy, the presence of managed care can invite passivity and regression because the patient is invited to be a passive recipient of decisions made for her by others. As such, the process can contradict the therapeutic goals of psychotherapy.

COMPONENTS OF THERAPEUTIC FRAME IMPACTED BY MANAGED CARE

The therapeutic frame incorporates several specific issues in the structure and negotiation of the therapy. Each component is associated with aspects of meaning in the therapeutic relationship. Below we examine specific components of the therapeutic frame and discuss the impact of managed care on each frame issue.

Fees and Money. First, obviously, managed care impacts on frame issues about fees and money in the treatment relationship, specifically how much the clinician gets paid, whether the clinician gets paid, and what the clinician has to do to be paid. At a societal level, the transformation of insurance review to managed care review reflects a societal devaluation of the mutuality of the psychotherapy process. Shulman (1988) suggests that as society pays increasing attention to corporate concerns about cost, we make the economic system and not the patient the true subject of therapy. He warns that systems established to address large-scale cost concerns do not adequately address the needs of the individual patient. These competing needs can raise a danger to patients when a therapist's business relationship with or financial dependence on the payer supersedes the therapist's relationship with his patient.

It is widely accepted in analytic literature that the therapy fee is a rich vehicle for transference enactments and the working through of intrapsychic and interpersonal conflicts. It is a common perception that any payment plan that requires nothing from the patient runs the risk of inherently devaluing the therapy (Halpert, 1973; Herron and Welt, 1992). Yet too many psychoanalytic therapists ignore or overlook issues of money in treatment, experiencing fees as an

"unpleasant necessity" (Herron and Welt, 1992, p. 3). Psychotherapy has always involved money and payment; our
failure to integrate the meaning of the cost of our services
into the theoretical framework has deprived practitioners of
the understanding and knowledge necessary to take an active
role in the dialogue about and negotiation of these issues.
Our denial on a microlevel with individual patients sets the
stage on a macrolevel for our sense of powerlessness and
loss of control regarding the politics of financing mental
health services.

The therapist's conceptualization of the meaning of
fees and money in the therapy may reflect his own ongoing
conflicts. Yet, our reluctance to examine the meaning of
money to the therapist can lead to overuse of projection in
clinical interpretations of fee issues. When Halpert (1985)
writes of insurance payments in psychotherapy that, "protection against castration and depletion of body contents, as
well as the need for control are central unconscious fantasies
that accompany the use of insurance to pay for analysis" (p.
937), he could as easily be speaking of the therapist's fantasies as the patient's. Each therapist must be familiar with his
beliefs and conflicts about payments and fees.

Third-party payers and managed care systems, however,
can complicate the process of payment so that the interpretation and therapeutic negotiation of fee issues can be compromised. Both the client and therapist need to be clear
about the particular financial frame for the therapy. To date,
the literature has addressed the meaning of insurance and
third-party payment far more extensively than the meaning
of a managed care system of review. Zuckerman (1989), in
his review of the literature on the fee in psychotherapy and
the role of insurance, describes the range of viewpoints on
the issue, with some believing that the use of insurance and
resistances associated with it can be interpreted. Others see
intrusions by the third party into the therapeutic process or

relationship as potentially destructive. Still others believe that any use of insurance corrupts the therapy altogether (Langs, 1979).

Even those who hold most strictly to a highly defined frame would undoubtedly recognize the qualitative difference between interpretable fantasies about having one's insurance pay for a treatment, and the meaning of a managed care reviewer refusing or strictly limiting payment. Thus, previous attempts to understand and incorporate the meaning of third-party payments in psychoanalytic psychotherapy are insufficient to address the more intrusive and interactive nature of a managed care system.

Uncertainty about insurance reimbursement can undermine or stalemate the progression of a treatment. When payment issues continually resurface, yet cannot be resolved in the context of the therapeutic relationship, they serve only as an unproductive disruption to the treatment. Unresolvable preoccupation with insurance issues takes time and attention away from significant treatment issues. Even in cases where treatment is not prematurely terminated, uncertainty about authorization for continued treatment may have an adverse impact on the treatment process (Melnick and Lyter, 1987).

Clearly concerns about cost effectiveness in mental health must include assessment of clinical need and efficacy. If we emphasize cost effectiveness without incorporating our clinical knowledge and standards, we create a system that is not only short sighted, but potentially iatrogenic.

Confidentiality. A second major aspect of the therapeutic frame impacted by managed care systems is therapeutic boundaries, specifically confidentiality, an essential component to any psychotherapy. Confidentiality provides the safety necessary to invite a patient to engage in the challenging process of "saying whatever comes to mind," free association. The assurance of confidentiality establishes respect for the patient and serves to enhance trust in the therapeutic relationship. Managed care inherently alters the contract of confidentiality. It has become standard for insurance and managed care companies to require a blanket authorization to release information when a consumer purchases the insurance policy. Yet such an open-ended, unlimited release of detailed clinical information is both inappropriate and compromises the task of the psychotherapeutic process. The presence of the listening ear of the managed care reviewer in psychotherapy sessions introduces a nonneutral third to the therapy dyad which if unlimited will alter the meaning of therapeutic communication.

Current managed care practices do not represent the first occasion of alterations in therapeutic confidentiality; peer review systems introduced in the 1970s represented an early effort on the part of the mental health professions themselves to provide quality assurance. However, peer review systems originated within the mental health system and as such tended to be respectful of the therapist's role and the confidential nature of the therapeutic relationship. Zuckerman (1989) asserts that the movement from retrospective peer review to managed concurrent reviews has fundamentally altered the nature of the therapeutic relationship by opening the active management of an ongoing therapy to a third party. Because managed care review emerged in response to the call for health care cost containment, it reflects the norms and values of medical and economic models and is far less concerned about confidentiality and not at all concerned about the meaning of interpersonal or therapeutic events.

Autonomy of Practice. The third area of frame altered by managed care is in the arena of freedom of choice and autonomy of practice. The field is reeling from the profound changes in the private practice of analytic therapy. We have experienced and were trained in a model of full autonomy and complete privacy of practice. For some, that autonomy and privacy are what drew them to the practice of psychoanalytic psychotherapy. The inevitable limitations posed by a managed care system will have different meaning in particular therapies, with particular therapists, patients, and combinations thereof.

Many issues that arise in this context are related to the autonomy and control needs of the therapist. When we need to depend on others to monitor or approve our patients' therapies, we are invited into regressive dynamics. The terminology of the managed care system can invite struggles that have both current and historical contexts of control and competition. For example, the term for the reviewer's decision is *authorization* for treatment, a provocative term that implies the authority of the reviewer in the treatment. This language invites both anal and oedipal transference dynamics between reviewer and therapist, and parallel countertransference dynamics between therapist and patient. Additionally, these conditions influence the unfolding therapeutic relationship by potentially diluting the transference, and creating actual reenactments outside the control of the therapy.

CHRONOLOGICAL EMERGENCE OF FRAME ISSUES

In the clinical situation the frame is established early in the treatment relationship and maintained through negotiation and boundaries throughout the psychotherapy. How does the presence of managed care impact on this aspect of the therapeutic relationship across the course of the therapy?

The first contact is normally by telephone. Relevant information about frame includes the exchange of information about fees, insurance policies, and provider status, that is, whether the therapist is eligible according to the insurance company to be reimbursed by that company. This communication brings the financial aspects of the therapy relationship and the presence of an evaluative other into the therapy from the outset in a way that is radically different from the therapist's simple statement of his fee. To the patient, the therapist's inclusion or exclusion from a particular provider panel may be falsely equated with the therapist's competence. The presence of fantasies about money in the therapeutic relationship is not new; patients and therapists have always had fantasies about the meaning of money, the worth of the therapist and the patient, and the value of the psychotherapy process. What is new is the presence of an influential other who also has power in the now triadic system.

In the first sessions during the initial consultation process, it is common for the therapist to have a more active role and stance. This process of mutual evaluation of therapist–patient fit allows both parties to ask questions and the therapist to provide information about the therapeutic frame (Greenson, 1967). Discussion about the frame must now include the role of the insurance or managed care component of the treatment. Alterations in confidentiality and clarity about frequency, quantity, and content of information sharing need also to be clarified at this point.

Often here the length and goals of treatment are addressed. For many psychoanalytic therapists, this approach differs from their stance of allowing the process of therapy simply to unfold, or from assuming all therapies will be long-term treatments. Thus, the influence of managed care is to change structurally the way we practice. It necessitates that we negotiate the goals of treatment more actively with our patients than we have done in the past. We then must ask how these shifts are useful clinically and how they hamper the unfolding of the therapy.

Early in the work of psychoanalytic psychotherapy the major task is the establishment of a therapeutic alliance. The building of trust, a shared language, mutual knowledge, and a safe respectful context for the examination of transference, fantasy, conflict, and meaning is the goal. Managed care can influence this process in a variety of ways. If the managed care contract is one that requires frequent reevaluation of treatment with little guarantee of continued approval or authorization, the therapy occurs in an unsafe, unpredictable context of impending loss and disruption. If the therapist is required to release detailed information when a patient is just beginning to have the trust to reveal this information, the therapist's trustworthiness becomes suspect.

Alternatively, the presence of a threatening outsider can initially cement a therapeutic alliance, albeit in a potentially problematic way. Gabbard, Takahashi, Davidson, Bauman-Bork, and Ensroth (1991) recognize that with certain patients the development of the therapeutic alliance may be facilitated through joining forces against a mutual enemy. Insurance reviewers become easy targets since their involvement in the treatment process has direct implications on the patient–therapist dyad. An alliance based on this type of foundation, however, is unsteady at best and certainly too precarious to withstand the later negative feelings that must emerge in the therapeutic relationship.

The phase of therapeutic working through—in many therapies, the bulk of the therapy—involves the elaboration of intrapsychic and interpersonal themes and patterns with the potential resolution in the transference of intrapsychic conflicts, object relational reenactments, and identity development. Managed care can influence this process in several ways. To begin with, the premise of many managed care review systems is not the creation and understanding of meaning, but the resolution and eradication of symptoms.

The working through phase of therapy has as its goal intra-psychic change, specifically to solidify the relinquishment of symptoms by alleviating the need for symptoms as compromise formation and in doing so prevent mere symptom substitution. Thus, the eradication of symptoms is insufficient evidence of transformative and effective change for many patients. Again, these standards of clinical effectiveness need to be incorporated into conceptualizations of cost effectiveness.

As stated earlier, these goals come from different paradigms. Managed care reviewers do not have a place on their symptom checklist for transference enactments. Further influences emerge in the transference. The insurance company that authorizes treatment can be seen as a transference manifestation of, for example, a gratifying all-giving mother which makes up for years of emptiness (Zuckerman, 1989). The managed care reviewer can be seen as the cruel depriving parent. This transference can be manifest in associations, wishes, and fears, but the ability to interpret this material is compromised when it is influenced by strong intrusions of reality. Clinically the analysis of transference assumes symbolic meaning. Yet, when the reality is outside the therapeutic relationship and not neutral, it is difficult to separate transference from real events.

The final phase of a therapy is termination. Clearly, managed care can have a significant influence on the timing, pacing, and processing of this phase. Traditionally, termination is mutually negotiated between the therapist and patient based upon the therapeutic process and progress. There has always been the influence of resources; however, in the climate of managed care, this influence is embodied in the reviewer and the review process. Often, this external representation of loss becomes the focus of the patient's and therapist's conflicts about separation, autonomy, and other developmental conflicts. This externalization, both real and transferential, can impede the necessary processing for both patient and therapist of these important transference and countertransference issues. The presence of managed care often merges different phases of treatment by creating an undercurrent of anxiety throughout the treatment. When unplanned termination is a continuing threat, both therapist and client must work under the cloud of uncertainty. This mimics powerful early anxieties, including castration anxiety, invoked by the fear of retributive loss of power, separation anxiety invoked by the constant threat of loss of an essential object of dependency, and annihilation anxiety invoked by the threatened loss of a selfobject at a crucial point in a patient's development of identity and esteem.

The Meaning of Managed Care to the Therapeutic Relationship

TRANSFERENCE AND COUNTERTRANSFERENCE

We have discussed the structural impact of managed care on the frame of a psychotherapy. Additionally, the impact of managed care is felt in the realm of meaning and interpretation. The goal of psychotherapy is to understand the complex meaning of psychological and interpersonal events, largely through the creation of meaning in the therapeutic relationship. Our psychotherapeutic task is now made more complex as we strive to incorporate and elaborate this meaning within the context of managed care. The authors believe the explicit naming and discussion of these levels of meaning is essential within the psychotherapy. It is not enough for the therapist to understand the implications; we must name them as part of the therapeutic relationship of which they have now become a part.

The creation of meaning is necessary for both patient and therapist and as such is influenced by transferential and countertransferential dynamics in the therapy. The managed care company and reviewer represent authoritative, potentially depriving others to the therapy dyad. For both patient and therapist, old conflicts about authority, giving and depriving parents, and conflicts about dependency, autonomy, and control will be activated.

A second arena of meaning is reflected in the standards of review. As stated, managed care standards emphasize symptoms not meaning, and illness not growth. Implicit in these standards is the message that a patient needs to be symptomatic and ill to deserve or earn the right to treatment (Zuckerman, 1989; Gabbard et al., 1991). If no immediate progress is made due to the severity and complexity of the treatment, the reviewer may insist upon termination or drastically limited treatment or insist upon alternative or ancillary treatment modalities. A corollary of this premise is that when the patient does show improvement there is the threat that treatment will no longer be seen as necessary or justified. These meanings are potentially dangerous to the health of the patient, and need to be addressed directly in the treatment relationship. When a patient feels she has to maintain or create symptoms in order to get approval for treatment, the therapist not only has to explore that belief, but also the corollary fantasies about the role of the therapist in that system.

This dynamic invites another common scenario, the split between the good therapist and bad reviewer. Managed care reviewers may act in ways that make them easy targets for anger from and devaluation by the patient (and also the therapist). It may be difficult then to work on the anger in the context of its transferential implications. When anger that might have relevance to the patient's problems and history, and as such needs to be explored in the transference, is displaced toward the reviewer, the work of the therapy is detoured. This problem is compounded by the fact that the patient may in turn idealize the therapist as a hero who will save the day against the intrusive and sadistic insurance company. This dynamic may encourage and intensify the patient's inability to hold ambivalent objects. Consequently, the managed care reviewer becomes the recipient for all bad-object projections and the therapist the recipient of good-object projections. If unchallenged, this stable split can result in a therapeutic stalemate. It is antithetical to the goal of psychoanalytic psychotherapy; the goal of therapy is the successful integration of devalued and idealized parts of objects (Gabbard et al., 1991) and self representations.

When the therapy context invites such a split, the patient is also invited to reenact in the therapy object relational paradigms from the past (Halpert, 1973; Zuckerman, 1989). Ideally, the therapeutic space is one in which reenactments are transferential and symbolic and therefore available to interpretation and reworking. With many patients, reenactments in the therapy provide crucial opportunities for insight and healing. When the patient feels deceived by the system as she learns that her benefits are not what she expected, her earlier experiences of betrayal and deceit will be reinforced. The therapy then serves to support rather than alter basic beliefs about trust and mistrust (McCann and Pearlman, 1990a).

With trauma survivor populations the danger of reenactment of betrayal and disrespect is particularly toxic. The task of creating a therapeutic alliance and developing trust in the therapeutic relationship is extraordinarily challenging in these treatments (Courtois, 1988; McCann and Pearlman, 1990a; Herman, 1992; Waites, 1993; Pearlman and Saakvitne, 1995). These therapies can be especially vulnerable to the malevolent reenactments invited by a system that can at any point deprive the patient of the resources she believes she needs in order to survive. When a child was failed by a society and its agencies who ignored or denied her needs and abuse, the failure of the external review system to facilitate her healing repeats that societal abandonment.

One specific arena for reenactment is in the interpretation of dependence. Commonly, managed care reviewers take a stance that dependence is pathological and patients should not be encouraged or allowed to develop dependence in the therapeutic relationship. Psychotherapists, however, know that developmentally an individual must experience dependence in order to develop independence. Shulman (1988) raises concerns about models of treatment that deemphasize or totally negate the importance of the therapist's role in the treatment process. He feels that by pushing patients to take total responsibility for their treatment and to solve their own problems, we unwittingly foster the kind of counterdependent thinking that brought the person to treatment in the first place. Paradoxically, when managed care interrupts a treatment prematurely, it can block a patient's progress toward independence by depriving them of the resources needed to develop independence. Gabbard et al. (1991) elaborate this dilemma with hospitalized patients who are discharged prematurely because of insurance limitations.

It is easy for us to lose sight of the developmental process of the psychotherapy and participate in a countertransferential enactment of "victim blaming." When we get angry at our patient for not improving in a "timely" manner, we join with her punitive internalized introjects and superego in a destructive (and often familiar) way. If we join with the managed care reviewer out of countertransferential motives, we can unconsciously participate in a reenactment.

The denial of psychotherapy benefits can tap into a patient's feelings of unworth. When a patient has struggled to take the courageous step of seeking psychotherapy, the message that her problems are insufficient to warrant insurance payment may reinforce long-standing negative self-concepts and poor self-care. Additionally, psychotherapy should offer opportunities for the patient to achieve mastery; when this fails, the patient is left feeling hopeless, helpless, and without resources to meet her own needs. This danger underscores the necessity of frank thoughtful discussion in the therapy of the limits and reality of each patient's benefit package.

SPECIFIC TRANSFERENCE DYNAMICS

When we are called upon actively to justify the patient's need for treatment, there is an open invitation for complex transference dynamics. We are the hero, the partner in crime, the protective parent, the corrupt schemer who gets the system to work for him, and when it fails, the perpetrator, the nonprotective bystander, or the victim. Thus a whole arena of transference is created by the presence of managed care review. When a managed care company pays the therapist a lower than normal fee, the transference is altered. Below we will discuss some representative transference paradigms elicited by the presence of managed care in a treatment.

Zuckerman (1989) writes:

> The analysis of the transference works effectively as a therapeutic tool because no matter how persuasive the patient's feelings are, both patient and therapist understand that they are cultivated as a creative and symbolic process, an "as if" process. When third parties with goals of cost-effectiveness become active participants in the treatment, deviations from the exclusive commitment to introspection necessary for a therapeutically manageable transference process becomes reified. The result is technical changes in the unfolding treatment that compromise the curative effect of the entire process [p. 128].

Specific transference identities are attributed to the therapist as she is perceived within the triadic relationship among patient, therapist, and reviewer. One such identity is the therapist as perpetrator. The therapist is seen as the one who seduces the patient into the relationship, then deprives her of what she needs and abandons her. The therapist is seen as joined with the managed care reviewer as a malevolent, sadistic villain. The patient feels victimized and betrayed. The countertransference response to this transference is often one of anger, hurt, futility, and negation. When the therapist is herself angry at the managed care process, she can feel deeply wronged and simultaneously silenced in her own anger. Alternatively, a patient may feel gratified by a generous insurance policy, and contrast that with her experience of her therapist as withholding (Halpert, 1973).

A second transference paradigm centers around the therapist as a colluder, or a nonprotective witness. For patients who have suffered abuse that was witnessed and not stopped by others, strong feelings toward those others are readily available. When a patient feels betrayed, wounded, or destroyed by a threat to his therapy, he looks to his therapist for protection and support. When the therapist cannot single-handedly protect the patient's benefits and thus his treatment, he may feel rage, bitter disappointment, and deep grief. He may want the therapist to make it up by lowering or eliminating her fee so the patient can continue therapy without benefits. A patient may feel the therapist is colluding or joining with an unfair, unjust system, and thus launch a superego assault on the therapist. These transference responses can evoke difficult countertransference responses. A therapist can feel guilty and be moved to change her frame in response to the guilt, potentially then disparaging her worth and needs in the process. She can feel resentful about the unfair burden of being held responsible for a third-party payer system by which she may also feel victimized. To the extent that she has a countertransference wish not to repeat childhood abandonments with this patient, she may unrealistically wish or try to rescue the patient and herself from this process. To the extent a therapist may find that her language and clinical formulations do not translate to a managed care review process (i.e., they are not sufficiently symptom or behavior focused), she may feel that she has failed her patient and perhaps herself.

A third transference identity a patient may attach to a therapist is that of victim; a patient may see his therapist as also a victim to a powerful and abusive other. This transference can evoke feelings of sympathy, identification, contempt, despair, and at times guilt. It can initially strengthen a therapeutic alliance as it evokes a sense of therapist and patient in it together against a malevolent, hurtful world. Over time, however, the patient can experience the therapist as helpless and weak, and therefore devalued. When a patient maintains a stable transference that is unmodified or unmodifiable by interpretation, the treatment can be stalled. If the therapist accepts the transference as actuality, she will be unable to interpret it. In reality, the therapist is neither a victim nor a creator of the system, but to the extent that the therapist herself shares this belief, she will join with it and not interpret or work through the genetic factors in the transference. That dilemma stems from a countertransference response to the transference. An alternative countertransference response is for the therapist to wish to disprove the identity by taking extraordinary action or expressing rage to overcompensate for the limits of her power in the situation.

SPECIFIC COUNTERTRANSFERENCE PARADIGMS

There are a host of countertransference responses and enactments invited by managed care. As therapists, we are in the middle of a changing therapy climate. Individually, we struggle to make sense of a system that is changing as we speak. It can be difficult to maintain equilibrium in the face of our patients' responses, as we struggle with our own. In that situation we are likely to bring our struggles to our therapies in countertransference responses. This situation puts us at risk unwittingly to use a managed care situation to justify unanalyzed countertransference responses, or to act out our feelings about managed care in our countertransference.

We all carry an ideal of what it means to be a good therapist. In order to maintain our professional self-esteem, we behave in ways that are consistent with a certain identity. A common identity wish for any therapist is the wish to be a good parent, a good-enough mother, an adequate protective father. Out of a need to be a good therapist, a clinician can easily move into a defensive posture similar to that of patients in which he projects all the problems with the treatment process onto the insurance reviewer. This defense robs the treatment of opportunities for a more complex examination of the therapeutic relationship, including countertransference reactions.

This projective process may also reflect the therapist's need to rid herself of uncomfortable feelings of helplessness, frustration, or shame. She can overidentify or wrongly identify a patient's experience of victimization. In fact, the therapist may experience a sense of relief when the patient's hostility is directed toward some other object, outside of herself. Alternatively, the therapist may need to make the patient bad to protect herself from these feelings.

Therapists can become more emotionally involved and reactive to the reviewer and the review process and unconsciously abandon both the patient and the therapeutic process. Treatment limitations imposed by managed care reviewers can lead the therapist to develop an unrealistic expectation for the patient. Therapists may unwittingly shame their patients by expecting a level of change that is not possible. If therapists want to be reviewed favorably by managed care companies they may become more invested in patients showing demonstrable improvement than are the patients themselves (Melnick and Lyter, 1987; Gabbard et al., 1991). This dynamic can force us to reenact from our patient's childhood the imposition of unrealistic developmental expectations, by expecting them to achieve maturity before they are developmentally prepared.

In this vein, when we join with the paternalistic model offered by managed care review that we or a managed care reviewer can know what is best for our patients, we undermine the goal of psychotherapy to empower and enhance our patient's self-determination. Alternatively, if we accept the reviewer's frame of reference and identify the reviewer as the expert, we abandon ourselves and our clients. Often insurance reviewers can act as though they are supervising a case when they have neither the data nor the mandate to do so. If we fail to maintain a clear frame about our roles and knowledge, we can lose the boundaries of the now more complicated therapeutic frame. This new framework can move the therapist to collapse into passivity and despair in the face of the powerful review process and system of third-party payment. If we are so coopted, we can reinforce our client's negative identity, childhood context, or worst fears.

These transference and countertransference dynamics are simply examples of the many complex ways the meaning of a managed care system of clinical review can emerge in the psychotherapy process and in the therapeutic relationship. Our clinical attunement and interpretive formulations must be enlarged to accommodate these new contextual realities for our work. In the final section of this chapter, we will discuss specific implications for the psychoanalytic practice of psychotherapy.

Conclusion and Implications for Practice

The presence of managed care systems of treatment review has and will continue to impact the therapeutic relationship in psychoanalytic psychotherapy. Its impact is both structural and meaningful. A managed care review system affects the structure through its impact on the therapeutic frame. It affects the interpretive process of the therapy through its emergence in the realms of meaning, specifically transference and countertransference dynamics in the therapy.

In presenting this discussion, it is our hope to help the reader incorporate into practice a more complicated understanding of the impact and meaning of managed care. To this end, what follows are specific recommendations for practice.

Herron and Welt (1992) clearly summarize the issues:

> Practitioners are sophisticated about what psychotherapy can do and with whom, but the value of psychotherapy may have to be sold and resold. In terms of fees as barriers, the current situation appears to be that psychotherapists can expect patients to have limited amount of support from insurance. Therapists can try to reduce the barrier by lobbying the third-party payers, their regulators, and their employers to provide more support. This has been carried out effectively in the past but it is clear that it continues to be necessary. It is useful to demonstrate some of the effects of psychotherapy in cost benefits, but others require educating the payers to a value system that embraces a broad definition of health. At the same time, psychotherapists need to get their own house in order, meaning in particular a real concern with cost effectiveness for the payers. That does not automatically mean following the accountability models that at times are now visited on therapists, but it does mean having a demonstrable model for effectiveness [p. 67].

The above quote suggests a tripartite template for effective management of managed care on clinical practice, one that occurs at the clinical level, the organizational level, and the policy-making level.

CLINICAL IMPLICATIONS

As we have noted throughout this paper, these new aspects of the therapeutic context must be included in the ongoing discussion of the therapeutic relationship and therapeutic process. Fundamentally, this means that the managed care review process needs to be treated like other events in the therapy, noticed, named, examined in its relational context, and understood in terms of present, historical, interpersonal, and intrapsychic meaning. For example, the patient who is ready to hand all power over to the therapist to negotiate his benefits with a managed care reviewer, might be asked to plan with his therapist what information seems relevant and to discuss personally with the reviewer what the process entails and what can be expected in the patient's particular case.

Psychoanalytic tradition recognizes the complexity and difficulty of achieving excellence in clinical work. Good clinical work is grounded in theory, specifically personality theory, that allows an understanding of the whole self in a developmental context, rather than treating a patient as a cluster of symptoms and disorders. The theoretical orientation of the TSI/CAAP is generally psychoanalytic. Specifically, we utilize the integrative, trauma-oriented, constructivist self-development theory (McCann and Pearlman, 1990a) and emphasize the therapeutic relationship as the context for healing. Thus, our clinical and interpretive focus is on the relational, transference, and countertransference paradigms that emerge in psychotherapy.

Our emphasis on theory-based treatment recognizes that any psychotherapy that is not theoretically grounded will be reactive and inconsistent, either forcing the patient into the therapist's mold, or responding alternately only to disconnected aspects of the patient as they emerge in symptoms. This danger is particularly clear with trauma survivor patients who present a wide range of compelling symptomatology.

If a therapist is aware of the sometimes subtle invitation to abandon her frame and paradigm for that of the review system, it is useful to state or reiterate her frame and identify how it differs from that of the reviewer. When reviewer and clinician can acknowledge their different premises and languages, they can begin to work together to create a shared communication that is respectful of all three parties.

To negotiate the above parameters, we recommend a clearly defined consultation period prior to the formal beginning of the exploratory and interpretive work of the psychotherapy. We are reminded of Greenson's (1967) assertion that the frame must be articulated before variations from it can be interpreted. His model of responding to questions in the analytic situation first with an explanation of therapeutic silence, and subsequently with therapeutic silence reflects the respectful acknowledgment of the joint venture of psychotherapy; our patients can work with us when we share our framework with them. When we include our patients in an open and frank discussion of the logistics and boundaries of managed care review, we widen the therapeutic frame to include this process and thus protect the frame from assault by managed care review processes.

Early in a treatment when a therapist and client are discussing reimbursement, boundaries of confidentiality are established. When a client brings in her insurance form and signs *both* the insurance company and the therapist's authorization to release information, the therapist must clearly identify the extent and limit of the release. For example, we commonly clarify that the general release allows us to divulge the patient's name, dates of sessions, and diagnosis code. If further information is requested, we will discuss it with the patient before releasing it. This establishes from the outset the triadic nature of this process; without that frame, the review process can create two dyads, effectively ostracizing the patient from her own insurance.

For the therapist negotiating with the managed care reviewer, this process includes asserting her needs as well as responding to the needs of the reviewer. For example, as therapists we are bound by very specific confidentiality statutes. We then need to get a more specific authorization to release information, that is, one which specifies the recipient by name and the content in specific terms. In order to meet this standard, a therapist needs to have a particular reviewer identified for a particular patient, and then ask the patient to sign a specific release. This process itself educates the reviewer to the therapist's standards and reasserts the rights of the patient to respectful boundaried consideration. Toward this end, we recommend the explicit articulation of policies and procedures for interacting with managed care personnel.[2]

ORGANIZATIONAL IMPLICATIONS

As noted earlier, the authors' organizational context is an independent mental health organization with a clinical, research, and training specialization in the psychoanalytic and constructivist treatment of traumatic stress. Abrahamson (1992a) identifies how this organization's identity and structure, quality assurance program, and research program contribute to our ability to negotiate effectively with managed

---

[2]See Appendix for a sample of a policy and procedures statement for routine contact with managed care reviewers.

care. The "Practice Model" (Abrahamson, 1992b) is a model we have developed to describe the integration of clinical work with other components of psychological practice. This model identifies eight facets that uniquely define a practice as psychological (using the acronym P-R-A-C-T-I-C-E as a mnemonic). This model further serves to empower practitioners and offset the creeping malaise of angry helplessness that many psychoanalytic practitioners feel in response to managed care and their insurance policy.

A key aspect of the organizational structure is interdependence with one another. We interact on a daily basis and provide collegial support in a variety of ways, including individual and group clinical supervision and vicarious traumatization consultations (McCann and Pearlman, 1990b; Pearlman and Saakvitne, 1995).

When any of our staff interact with managed care companies, we define our training and expertise and ask the reviewer about his or her experience and areas of expertise. This process serves not to challenge the reviewer, but to clarify the mutual dialogue that will ensue.

We recognize that many psychoanalytic psychotherapists continue to practice within a solo private practice model that does not afford some of these organizational opportunities. Yet, as a community of psychoanalytic psychotherapists there are many ways for us to collaborate and support one another.

ADVOCACY AND POLICY-MAKING IMPLICATIONS

Finally, what is increasingly clear is that we all need to have our voices heard and our knowledge incorporated into the current policy debates. We are at a critical turning point in the politics of mental health care. The decisions made over the next several years will set the stage for our professional lives well into the next millennium; we have a responsibility to ourselves and our clients to have a voice. As a profession, psychoanalytic psychotherapists have not been encouraged to think of our spheres of influence as extending beyond our consulting rooms. This belief is disempowering. We have knowledge, information, and clinical data necessary to influence policy development.

In Connecticut members of the Connecticut Society for Psychoanalytic Psychology have been actively lobbying with policy makers on the need for and cost effectiveness of long-term psychotherapy. One of the early and empowering victories for the Practice Directorate of the American Psychological Association (APA) was to ensure the inclusion of psychologists in psychoanalytic training institutes. Psychoanalytic psychologists, including Bryant Welch, Ph.D., J.D., and James Barron, Ph.D., have been leaders in the campaign to have clinical voices heard in health policy debates, both within and outside the APA. Every psychoanalytic practitioner can have a voice by working with APA and by individually contacting legislators and policy makers.

Our organization was active in getting legislation passed in the state to regulate the managed care industry. While the legislation is not perfect, it is an important step toward assuring that managed care practices are in line with community standards of care. Shapiro (1994) writing on the impact of managed care on a long-term psychoanalytic hospital (Austen Riggs Center) highlights the necessity of keeping our clinical principles and vision clear while recognizing economic reality. "The world of increasingly limited resources is real. But the meaning of an individual patient's life cannot be obliterated by social expediency" (p. 16). There are many other examples of how psychoanalytically oriented therapists and organizations have combined their resources to have a voice. We must all do our share.

Psychoanalytic practitioners have a compelling vision of a theory-based transformative psychotherapy process. Joined together we can have a powerful voice in the future of psychotherapy. We must find ways to both modify and expand the role for psychoanalytic conceptualizations of behavior in our society. Just as psychoanalytic concepts have been applied to history, culture, and organizational dynamics, we can bring our theoretical knowledge to bear on the development of health care policy by integrating our understanding of the complex relationship between psychology and health, the psyche and the soma.

References

Abrahamson, D. J. (1992a), A scientist–practitioner organization responds to the challenges of managed mental health care. *Psychother. in Priv. Pract.*, 11:21–27.

_____ (1992b), Managed care and psychological P.R.A.C.T.I.C.E.: An acronym for our future. Paper presented at the American Psychological Association 100th Annual Convention, Washington, DC.

American Psychiatric Association (1994), *Diagnostic and Statistical Manual of Mental Disorders*, 4th ed. (DSM-IV). Washington, DC: American Psychiatric Press.

Courtois, C. (1988), *Healing the Incest Wound: Adult Survivors in Therapy*. New York: W. W. Norton.

Gabbard, G. O., Takahashi, T., Davidson, J., Bauman-Bork, M., & Ensroth, K. (1991), A psychodynamic perspective on the clinical impact of insurance review. *Amer. J. Psychiatry*, 148:318–323.

Greenson, R. R. (1967), *The Technique and Practice of Psychoanalysis*, Vol. 1. New York: International Universities Press.

Halpert, E. (1973), A meaning of insurance in psychotherapy. *Internat. J. Psychoanal. Psychother.*, 1:62–68.

_____ (1985), Insurance. *J. Amer. Psychoanal. Assn.*, 33:937–949.

Herman, J. L. (1992), *Trauma and Recovery: The Aftermath of Violence—From Domestic Abuse to Political Terror*. New York: Basic Books.

Herron, W. G., & Welt, S. R. (1992), *Money Matters: The Fee in Psychotherapy and Psychoanalysis.* New York: Guilford Press.

Langs, R. (1979), *The Therapeutic Environment.* New York: Jason Aronson.

McCann, I. L., & Pearlman, L. A. (1990a), *Psychological Trauma and the Adult Survivor: Theory, Therapy, and Transformation.* New York: Brunner/Mazel.

—— —— (1990b), Vicarious traumatization: A framework for understanding the psychological effects of working with victims. *J. Traumatic Stress,* 3:131–149.

Melnick, S. D., & Lyter, L. L. (1987), The negative impacts of increased concurrent review on psychiatric inpatient care. *Hosp. & Commun. Psychiatry,* 38:300–303.

Pearlman, L. A., & Saakvitne, K. W. (1995), *Trauma and the Therapist: Countertransference and Vicarious Traumatization in Psychotherapy with Incest Survivors.* New York: W. W. Norton.

Saakvitne, K. W. (1994), The Traumatic Stress Institute: A model for psychoanalytic psychological practice. *Psychologist Psychoanalyst,* 14:11–12, 45.

Shapiro, E. (1994), Adjusting to new realities. *Berks. Bus. J.* Business Report. January:

Shulman, M. E. (1988), Cost containment in clinical psychology: Critique of Biodyne and the HMO's. *Prof. Psychol.: Res. & Pract.,* 19:298–307.

Waites, E. A. (1993), *Trauma and Survival: Post-traumatic and Dissociative Disorders in Women.* New York: W. W. Norton.

Zuckerman, R. L. (1989), Iatrogenic factors in "managed" psychotherapy. *Amer. J. Psychother.,* 43:118–131.

Appendix:
Sample Policy and Procedures for Routine Contact with Managed Care Reviewers

RELEASE OF INFORMATION

Get a release of information that specifies a particular person (the one case reviewer) to whom information may be released and that specifies what information will be released. This means having the managed care company identify a single reviewer at the outset before you release any information. Let your client and the managed care company know that these are the only conditions under which you will release any information.

CONSIDER THE FRAME

Do not accept the managed care company's assumption set automatically and note inaccuracies in assumptions. Their assumption set often includes a belief that they are entitled to any and all information, that they do not need to get specific release of information, that they can redefine the treatment, that they are supervising you. Remember you are a professional and the clinician in charge of the treatment, and the one who knows your client best. They can refuse to pay your client, but they do not have any right to direct the treatment. Although you may have a contract with the managed care company, you also have a contract with your client, and are legally and ethically bound to his or her interests first. Also, you have seen and interacted with your client in person over time and your assessment is more valid (and defensible legally) than that of someone who has never seen the client. The reviewer is there for quality control, to make sure you are qualified and practicing within your expertise, but he or she is not your supervisor or the case manager.

You and the reviewer can work together to ensure quality control standards are met.

WHEN SPEAKING TO THE REVIEWER

1. Ask for his or her professional credentials and training.
2. Ask about his or her expertise and experience working with the patient or problem or population being treated (be specific if appropriate, e.g., incest survivors, panic attack, etc.). If it is insufficient, ask for a different reviewer or to speak with a supervisor.
3. Identify yourself, including a brief overview of your training, experience, and expertise.
4. Briefly describe your treatment philosophy and relevant information about the structure of your practice. Include appropriate information about other aspects of your professional work (e.g., supervision, research, specialty programs, teaching, etc.). If you have information about your practice, offer to send it to the reviewer so he or she can become more familiar with your work. If you have thought about your approach to quality assurance and risk management, put it in writing and offer to send any reviewers you deal with a copy.
5. Underscore the importance of confidentiality and note that your release is to him or her only. Suggest that you hope to establish an ongoing working relationship with the reviewer around this client.
6. Request to know questions to be asked in advance. It is usually a good idea to request the questions be sent to you in written form. If they use the same format for ongoing review, they only need send the request for specific information once. Ideally, you should review these with your client first and discuss what will be disclosed. Do not open yourself up to open-ended questioning.

7. Write down, in note form at least, what you plan to say as discussed with the client, and stick as closely as possible to those notes in your conversation with the reviewer.

8. If the reviewer gives you feedback about evaluation, approval, etc., comment on its appropriateness (i.e., the evaluation process is not one way). If the reviewer approves ten sessions and requests another reevaluation, you can state this is a burden to the treatment and note the countertherapeutic aspect of introducing uncertainty into a therapy relationship for which consistency, predictability, and stability are critical factors.

9. Before ending the contact, clarify when the next contact will be and the information that will be requested, and who is responsible for making the contact.

10. Document the contact; write a note indicating date, reviewer's name and credential, information reviewed, recommendation made, and your recommendation to them. Document instances of misinformation, unclarity, unprofessionalism, and your responses.

11. Inform your client before and after contacts.

APPEALS

Establish a policy or protocol for appealing decisions by managed care companies when there is a disagreement.

POSITIVE FEEDBACK

Remember managed care reviewers are people too. When you have a positive interaction and feel that a case was handled particularly well, recognize this to the reviewer. They usually only have complaints, so an occasional compliment can go a long way toward helping to establish a positive working relationship.

4

The Impact of Managed Care on the Psychotherapeutic Process: Transference and Countertransference

Fredric Neal Busch, M.D.

Most clinicians believe that psychodynamic psychotherapy proceeds most effectively with as little outside interference as possible. Freedom from external factors, along with the standard technical guidelines of anonymity, neutrality, and abstinence, allow the patient the fullest opportunity to develop and work through a transference neurosis. Therapists attempt to use occasional unavoidable interferences positively in the therapy as "grist for the mill," but these intrusions can be counterproductive, especially if the patient is not yet prepared to work with them. Social changes in the way that psychotherapy is being delivered have led to a significant increase in the complexity of the therapeutic task. Managed care injects a third party into the therapeutic situation in a way that almost always disrupts and sometimes derails the therapeutic process. This paper catalogues a variety of disruptions of the process that can occur and discusses how therapists can best proceed under the auspices of a managed care program.

Some therapists are still able to avoid managed care systems through having a group of patients who are able to afford the treatment on their own. Most therapists, however, are increasingly entering into managed care contracts to maintain a flow of patients into their practices and to accommodate existing patients whose employers or insurance plans adopt such a system. This trend is likely to continue over the next several years as increasing numbers of patients enter into managed care systems. Although managed care systems have been touted as allowing some individuals previously unable to afford psychiatric care to obtain it, and as providing some form of quality control, the overall reduction in the availability of long-term psychotherapy engendered by these systems has also been noted (Sederer and St. Clair, 1989; Austad and Berman, 1991; Rosenblatt, Adler, Bemporad, Feigelson, Michels, Morrison, and Offenkrantz, 1992; Hartmann, 1992). Managed care programs become marketable to employers and more profitable by encouraging shorter term treatments. As one managed care psychiatrist recently stated to this author: "Characterological change is not a service that we cover."

Managed care forces a number of unwelcome intrusions into the therapeutic situation for therapists. For example, the managed care program almost always sets the fee which therapists can charge. Typically this is below the fee that therapists consider their baseline and removes the important fee negotiating system, which often provides valuable information about the patient's conflicts, from the hands of patients and therapists. Additionally, therapists usually must send in reports requesting further therapy visits for the patient. Many therapists consider these reports, for which they are not compensated, to be unproductive for their thinking process. Some managed care programs require that therapists discuss their patients' clinical situations regularly with a managed care agent. Therapists may feel uncomfortable

describing intimate details of their patients' care with someone outside the therapeutic process. Individual managed
care agents vary widely in their training and knowledge
about therapy, and the therapists' task is more difficult with
a less knowledgeable agent. Therapists can experience significant frustration with the many obligations that they are
required to fulfill to maintain funding for their patients'
psychotherapy.

Patients may also experience frustration with tasks required by managed care. Varying amounts of time must be
spent in psychotherapy sessions dealing with managed care
issues, such as how many visits the managed care company
has currently approved for treatment. This takes time away
from patients' discussion of their problems. Patients may
become angry at bureaucratic snafus that delay approval of
further sessions or payments to their therapist. In addition,
programs have varying requirements about contacts patients
must have with managed care agents or psychiatrists. Some
programs require that the patient speak regularly with a
managed care agent to discuss the progress of the therapy.
Other programs require that patients be evaluated by a psychiatrist either at the beginning or during the course of
therapy. Patients may view this not only as an unnecessary
expenditure of their time but also as a tremendous intrusion
on their relationship with the therapist.

Although on occasion a consultation with a managed
care agent can provide useful information for therapist and
patient, for the most part these consultations interfere unnecessarily with an established therapeutic process. At times
the results can be disastrous. Aronson (1992) describes a
patient with unacknowledged murderous rage toward his
son. The patient had been involved in an accident in which
a young man was injured, after which the patient developed
guilt, depression, and irritability. Although the therapist was
aware of the connection between the patient's difficulties

with the accident, in which he was not at fault, and his anger at his son, he realized that the patient was unable to hear this interpretation at that time. A consultant from the managed care program told the patient he feared his death wishes with his son had come true. This interpretation precipitated a serious suicide attempt.

In addition to the intrusions described above, the managed care situation can have a significant impact on the therapeutic milieu. The constant need to obtain "approval" for funding of further sessions adds an element of insecurity to the therapeutic situation: therapies are often on the verge of significant disruption. In many cases patients are allowed a certain number of visits per year, for example thirty, after which they are granted no further funds for psychotherapeutic treatment. Other programs require approval for funding of every five, ten, or twenty sessions. Therapists who are accustomed to the slow progress of psychotherapy in treating characterological issues can find it difficult to understand why they are required to report on "progress" and "goals" so frequently. At any point funding can suddenly be terminated upon the decision of the managed care agency. Since many of these patients are unable to afford psychotherapy without managed care benefits, both therapist and patient proceed with treatment knowing that at any point continuation of the treatment may be significantly affected.

Managed care decisions can also affect the patient's perception of himself and the therapist. As noted in a report by the Group for Advancement of Psychiatry (Rosenblatt et al., 1992), patients may conclude that there is something wrong with them when they are unable to respond in the number of sessions recommended by the managed care agency. Patients will also respond to a reduction of funds in ways consistent with their character pathology. For example, a narcissistic patient can view the loss of funds as a rejection and a blow to their feelings of self-importance. The therapist is often seen as devalued and at the mercy of the forces of others: he does not set his own fee or make the determination of what treatment is necessary. For example, one patient saw his mother as constantly devaluing and demeaning his father. He had always wished that the father would stand up to the mother and struggle with her. He viewed the therapist as subject to being "pushed around by managed care" in the same way as his mother dominated his father. Patients who are in a state of resistance to exploring frightening unconscious fantasies may use a managed care company's suggestion for decreased frequency of visits in the service of this resistance. Although at times patients may feel that therapists are not adequately in charge of the case, patients may also view therapists as agents in withholding treatment that patients need.

Typical therapists' reactions to these conditions include feelings of humiliation and rage at being forced to submit to limitations of their autonomy. Instead of functioning as independent agents, clinicians are acting at the behest of others who are deciding what treatment funding is appropriate for their patients. Frustrations are intensified with having a third party making decisions, often someone who has not even seen the patient and who may not be as well qualified as the therapist to make a decision about what treatment is necessary. As noted above, therapists may also be angry at the fee limitations and the unpaid time spent dealing with the managed care company. The angry feelings can lead to a countertransference in which the therapist displaces feelings about the managed care company onto the patient. Patients and therapists may share transference reactions to the managed care agency, which can be viewed, for example, as the depriving, withholding mother. Patients and therapists may experience wishes to collude in order to "get around" the managed care system.

Therapists may also feel demoralized or experience "burnout" as a result of constant struggles to keep funding for psychotherapy available. They may feel a constant pressure to reduce the frequency of visits to a level that they feel is inadequate. Therapists must wrestle with how much to reveal to patients of their own feelings about what the managed care company is recommending. If treatment funds are discontinued, therapists are placed in very difficult positions. They are forced either to significantly reduce the fee, cut back treatment, or terminate treatment and refer the patient to a community mental health clinic. Therapists must struggle with issues such as how much of a fee reduction they are willing to accept and whether patients would be better off at a mental health clinic or in a less intensive treatment with their therapists. Incidentally, managed care companies often send a letter when funds are cut off or reduced, to the effect that they are not dictating treatment, even though patients often depend on these funds to pay for therapy. Therapists' difficulties with these pressures can interfere with their ability to achieve the highest quality of care with their patients.

Case Report

The following is a case report of a patient treated by a provider who joined the patient's managed care company.

Mr. J, a 44-year-old married white male, had a history of sociopathy and depression, and a past history of polysubstance abuse. He had recently been involved in criminal activity and had become depressed and anxious when he realized his behavior was going to be discovered. In this context he made a suicide attempt, cutting his wrists, and was psychiatrically hospitalized. He was diagnosed as having a Major Depression, which responded to fluoxitene, and a mixed personality disorder with narcissistic, antisocial, and borderline features. After discharge he was referred to the therapist for outpatient therapy.

Under any conditions this patient presented a difficult treatment case. The therapist recommended two times per week psychotherapy as essential to address this patient's characterological difficulties. The patient was associated with a managed care company, which the therapist joined in order to help the patient pay for his treatment. Ongoing psychotherapy revealed that the patient was highly intolerant of any negative affects, had trouble identifying them, and tended to act out impulsively when uncomfortable. His chronically low self-esteem was countered by a maniclike grandiosity with a lack of regard for certain consequences of his behavior. This included the criminal behavior referred to above and limited homosexual contacts.

Over time, the patient's financial condition became more problematic, as he was having difficulty obtaining employment, making him dependent on the managed care company for payment of his treatment. The managed care program required that the therapist be in regular contact with a managed care agent. Initially the agent was very cooperative with the patient's need for intensive psychotherapy. The patient became very engaged in the psychotherapeutic process, and despite his severe characterological impairments, was highly motivated to change and gained increasing insight into his conflicts.

After initially being cooperative, beginning about two months into the treatment, the managed care agent began to question the patient's need for twice weekly psychotherapy. The therapist provided what he believed to be an adequate explanation of the necessity for this intensive treatment, especially given the patient's tendency to dangerous acting out. The agent then indicated that the patient might require a switch to clinic treatment because his treatment was too expensive. She implied that if the therapist did not reduce his fee the managed care agency would cut off funds for the patient's treatment. The therapist felt angry and manipulated by the managed care agent, making it difficult for him to decide what was best for the patient. He experienced an initial impulse to terminate the treatment. Ultimately, because he felt that the patient benefited greatly from the treatment and was already deeply involved in it, he agreed to a small fee reduction.

However, this only represented the beginning of the managed care program's efforts to reduce the treatment. For example, the agent stated that she wished to have bimonthly discussions with the patient. This was discussed extensively with the patient, who was willing to tolerate these calls if they were not too personally invasive. In addition the agent increased the frequency of contacts with the therapist from once a month to once every two weeks. At each discussion the agent would react with surprise that the therapist felt the patient still required twice weekly visits, asking the therapist to explain in detail why this frequency was necessary. Finally, the managed care agent stated that a review on the case would be required by the managed care company's psychiatrist. After the therapist discussed the case in detail with the managed care psychiatrist, the psychiatrist made the decision to reduce the managed care company's payment for the patient's visits to one time per week. The therapist was highly frustrated because he felt the description made it very clear that the patient required twice weekly psychotherapy. The reviewing psychiatrist asked no questions and made the decision without having met with the patient.

An increasing proportion of time in therapy sessions was spent discussing the managed care situation. As the treatment progressed the patient felt increasingly vulnerable due to the managed care agency's threats to his treatment. He had become aware of the severity of the damage that his problem had created for him and had become increasingly attached to the therapist. The patient spent more time focusing on his fears of disruption of his treatment. The therapist attempted to use this experience as it related to feelings of emotional disconnection that he had experienced with his parents. However, the threat of real disruption made this a less serviceable area of interpretation.

More useful in therapy was the patient's difficulty with intrusion by the managed care agent, whom he considered incompetent. His reactions clued the patient into his feelings of intrusion by his mother. He described his mother as always walking into his room when he was an adolescent: on one occasion, for example, he was "making out" with a girl friend. In a later incident the mother infuriated him and his wife by insisting on accompanying them on a vacation and then not leaving them alone. The patient had intense difficulty with his rage at his mother's behavior, and would become silent and withholding in an attempt to control his rage. The same behavior also occurred with his wife, who became more frustrated when the patient would lapse into silence. His criminal behavior appeared to represent a displacement from the rage at his mother, which he was unable to articulate in any way other than action. The patient's rage at the managed care agent provided opportunities to explore how the patient could better manage his angry feelings.

The therapist's countertransference threatened his treatment of the patient. The therapist felt enraged at the agent for the time she required and for her incredulous response to the therapist's treatment plan. He had the urge to displace this anger to the patient, seeing the problems as stemming from him. Additionally the therapist felt humiliated because he felt others were overriding his treatment decisions. Increasingly the therapist felt trapped by the treatment, caught between being pressed to not give the treatment he felt was indicated and pressure to refer the patient on to a mental health clinic. The therapist and patient were both enraged at the managed care agent. She became a third party in the treatment, the depriving mother who interfered with the patient's access to needed help.

At the same time that treatment funds were reduced, therapist and patient learned that the patient would be changing managed care companies the following month. Therapist and patient agreed to a fee and frequency for that month and began the process of attempting to grapple with the new managed care company. The situation remained highly uncertain at the time of writing of this article.

Responding to the Managed Care Environment

This section addresses how therapists can best handle managed care issues and maintain a psychodynamic psychotherapeutic process under adverse conditions. Therapists must apply their therapeutic skills and knowledge of transference and countertransference to pursue, as best as possible under the circumstances, the goals of insight into the unconscious and change in character. In the case described above the therapy was successful despite the multiple intrusions into the therapeutic situation which occurred. Although therapist and patient were hampered and distracted by managed care issues, they were able to spend the bulk of the time pursuing the patient's intrapsychic conflicts as they related to his current difficulties and his tendency to dangerously act out.

Therapists must speak straightforwardly about the managed care situation to their patients in a way that minimizes the amount of interference in the therapeutic process. They should make clear to patients the number of visits granted, the times that reviews will be necessary, and the potential reduction or discontinuation of funds for treatment. To reduce a sense of uncertainty about the future of the therapy, therapists and their patients must plan ahead for how they want to handle time and fees should managed care companies withdraw coverage.

Therapists should as much as possible not involve patients in their own frustrations with managed care systems. Therapists' refined attunement to countertransference should help them to recognize the potential to displace some of these feelings onto the patient. Therapists should also be alert to shared transferences to the managed care agency, which can be even more difficult to identify, particularly when therapists feel justified in their anger. Finally, they must be alert to feelings of flagging morale that can so greatly impair their ability to listen to their patients.

In many ways issues remain as available for exploration as prior to managed care. For example, although fee negotiation is often removed from the initial phase of the treatment, feelings that patients have about payment still arise. Additionally, in planning ahead for what to do if funds are discontinued, in some instances patient and therapist can negotiate a fee for when the patient has no further coverage. As in the case above, reactions to the managed care situation can be explored, often providing valuable insight into the patient's dynamics.

Although the focus of this article is not "how to manage managed care" (Goodman, Brown, and Deitz, 1992; Appelbaum, 1993; Lazarus, 1993), therapists must think about how to talk with the managed care agency. The dynamic therapist can attempt to communicate how the patient's symptoms may be integrally connected with the patient's character, necessitating long-term psychotherapy. A brief intervention may well lead to temporary resolution of symptoms, but vulnerability to recurrence will remain. Although many managed care programs or agents will respond negatively to this view, others will understand why a brief intervention will not be enough in a given case.

A new era of medicine has arrived in which therapists are pressured by an outside party to make certain treatment decisions and charge specific fees. Therapists have always had to deal with the "grist," and economic factors have always been involved in therapeutic decision making. They have not, however, been so frequently expected to conduct psychotherapy with a third party always looking over their shoulders, attempting to control the nature of the treatment. Managed care takes a heavy toll on the therapist, patient, and the therapeutic process. As always, therapists must do their best to help the patient understand their internal world, despite the noisy intrusions of the external one.

References

Appelbaum, P. S. (1993), Managing the impact of managed care. *Hosp. Commun. Psychiatry*, 44:525–527.

Aronson, M. J. (1992), Tactics in psychoanalytic psychotherapy. In: *Psychotherapy: The Analytic Approach*, ed. M. J. Aronson & M. A. Scharfman. Northvale, NJ: Jason Aronson, pp. 131–146.

Austad, C. S., & Berman, W. H. (1991), Managed health care and the evolution of psychotherapy. In: *Psychotherapy in Managed Health Care: The Optimal Use of Time and Resources.* Washington, DC: American Psychological Association.

Goodman, M., Brown, J., & Deitz, P. (1992), *Managing Managed Care: A Health Practitioner's Survival Guide.* Washington, DC: American Psychiatric Press.

Hartmann, L. (1992), Reflections on humane values and biopsychosocial integration. *Amer. J. Psychiatry*, 144:1134–1141.

Lazarus, A. (1993), Improving psychiatric services in managed care programs. *Hosp. Commun. Psychiatry*, 44:709.

Rosenblatt, A. D., Adler, G., Bemporad, J. R., Feigelson, E. B., Michels, R., Morrison, A. P., & Offenkrantz, W. C. (1992), *Psychotherapy in the Future.* Committee on Therapy of the Group for the Advancement of Psychiatry. Report no. 133. Washington, DC: American Psychiatric Press.

Sederer, L. I., & St. Clair, R. L. (1989), Managed health care and the Massachusetts experience. *Amer. J. Psychiatry*, 146:1142–1148.

5

From "Comfort" to Chaos: Mental Health Insurance Coverage in the 1990s

Beth Meehan, C.S.W., B.C.D.

Mental Health and Insurance: A Historical Sketch

Insurance reimbursement for psychotherapy and psycho-analysis, as for medical illness, has traditionally been through indemnity insurance plans. In this case an insurance company, which fixes a percentage of coverage and annual and lifetime caps, bases its policy on estimated risk. In gross terms, the more medical services are used by the total insured population the higher the premiums charged to the employer or privately insured individual. Within this system it is profitable for insurance companies to provide service (Winegar, 1992). Benefits are spelled out with an 80 percent rate of reimbursement and a 20 percent copayment a usual but not universal formula. For the insured, benefits are stable and predictable.

Under pressure from employers, insurance companies began to create cheaper insurance packages. They also began to subcontract the administration of benefits to companies whose task it is to curtail utilization. *Utilization management,* or *managed care* are the terms most often used to refer to "any method that regulates the price, utilization, or site of services" (Austad and Hoyt, 1992, p. 110). Managed care companies can be under contract to employers or to insurance companies.

> Preferred Provider Organizations (PPO's) are entities through which insurance companies or employer groups purchase services for their subscribers or employees . . . the purchaser, on behalf of its members, negotiates discounted fee arrangements with the PPO in advance of service delivery. In exchange for this discount, employer groups or insurance companies provide incentives for clients to utilize the PPO providers [Winegar, p. 51].

Independent practice organizations (IPAs) refer to provider groups who organize to contract out their services to PPOs (or to HMOs); provider members of IPAs can also see patients who do not belong to the HMO or PPO plans with which they are affiliated. The PPO is a network model of the traditional staff model health maintenance organization (HMO).

In order to appreciate the current state of the insurance industry, and the inclusion of mental health benefits, it is useful to know something of the history of the HMO. This model, in which care was both financed and delivered by the same organization, was developed in the 1900s to meet the medical needs of those in the lumbering, mining, and transportation industries in the Pacific Northwest (Bennett, 1988). Radical at the time, it strove to respond to a social ideal. The best known and largest staff model HMO is Kaiser-Permanente which originated in Northern California. According to Nicholas Cummings, who was chief psychologist at Kaiser-Permanente, and later executive director of American Biodyne Center, in South Central California, HMO physicians made a startling discovery: they found that 60 to 70 percent of patients who consulted them did not have organically based physical illnesses but instead had illnesses related to stress. At first they assumed that the population they served somaticized more often than others. They found, however, that it was the difference in reporting procedures between HMO and fee-for-service physicians that accounted for this apparent discrepancy in populations. Fee-for-service physicians, unlike their HMO counterparts, had to make a medical diagnosis in order to get reimbursed. Recognizing that psychotherapy would provide cheaper as well as better quality care for those suffering from stress related illnesses, Kaiser-Permanente added therapists to the medical team (Cummings, 1991). The psychotherapist functioning within this model was, like the physician, available as needed, over time. Psychotherapeutic services tended then to be conceptualized as short term and symptom focused, but always available. An HMO act was passed in 1973 and subsequent amendments provided for a minimum of twenty mental health visits per year and referral for alcohol and drug treatment (Austad and Hoyt, 1992, p. 111). Austad and Hoyt acknowledge that with the proliferation of nonstaff networks and the development of "managed health care," that the original idea of a medical team working together in the same setting with the shared goal of meeting the total needs of patients has been supplanted by the "fiscal relationship" of the various off-site models (p. 110).

Research, especially that which studies illness, absenteeism, and performance in the workplace, replicates the findings of the HMO staff (Kennecott Cooper Corporation, 1970; Manuso, 1980; Gaeta, Lynn, and Grey, 1982; VandenBos and DeLeon, 1988). Employee assistance programs (EAPs) can be seen as a development which attempts to (1) recognize the psychological needs of workers; (2) reduce absenteeism associated with untreated mental health needs;

(3) reduce costs associated with the unnecessary utilization of medical services, including hospitalization; and (4) regulate the amount spent on mental health and substance abuse services.

Research has shown that providing appropriate mental health services saves companies billions of dollars (Thakur and Jacobson, 1992). It has also shown that patients typically do not overuse psychotherapy benefits, that in fact only 6 or 7 percent remain in treatment beyond the twenty-sixth session (Stern, 1993).

Thus the current aggressive monitoring of mental health service utilization is puzzling. One of the problems seems to be that insufficient distinction has been made between the costs of inpatient mental health and substance abuse treatment programs where costs have risen enormously, and the cost of outpatient care, which has not risen beyond the rate of inflation. A further distinction needs to be made between the cost and utilization of inpatient substance abuse services and psychiatric hospitalizations where there is no substance use involvement.

The research cited indicates that a very large percentage of individuals (around 60%) need some kind of mental health or substance abuse treatment. The fact that the industry, responding to employers, has steadily developed products offering mental health service supports this conclusion. Yet, with the need clearly established, a method has evolved that has substantially reduced care to patients, is systematically destroying the profession that treats them, and is directing profit to the corporations which manage this system.

Far from the social idealism of the HMO movement of the 1900s, we find ourselves, at the close of the century, "in the unlikely position of having witnessed the accomplishment by business and industry, during a conservative administration, of what had been impossible for the government to effect for decades: the application of business methods to medical care" (Weissberg, 1992, p. 504).

Insurance and Psychotherapy: A Clinical Review

When mental health benefits began to be included in benefit packages offered by for profit insurance companies in the 1950s, psychoanalysts raised concerns about the effect of such coverage on treatment. Like Freud they considered the possibility of increased instinctual gratification or resistance, the tendency to undervalue what is cheap, and, especially in the case of treatment that is provided without charge, the effects of removing the treatment from "reality" (Freud, 1913; Haak, 1957; Halpert, 1972, 1986). Experience has shown, however, that while increased instinctual gratification, or the support of grandiose defenses is problematic in some cases, that these effects are usually analyzable (Chodoff, 1972; Halpert, 1986). Chodoff, reporting again in 1985, points out that the inclusion of nonmedical providers has helped to institutionalize insurance reimbursement procedures, reducing requests for confidential information, for example. He concludes that "whatever third-party influences are present have been accepted and incorporated into the treatment situation, apparently without disruptive effects on results of psychotherapeutic treatment" (p. 120). Halpert believes that removing all responsibility for payment from the patient, as is the case with universal coverage, or where the therapist accepts assignment, is to be avoided. The issue here is not so much of "overgratification" but of separating issues that would come up around money, and payment of fees, from the treatment. He has found, for example, that payment by a relative is less destructive because patients tend to remain in touch with conflicts related to accepting or needing help from family (Halpert, 1972).

Authors who blame universal coverage for treatment failures in the Medicaid population have typically treated few cases and provided no clinical data to support this conclusion. I have treated a number of Medicaid patients and have not found that the presence of this coverage has been destructive to treatment. Typically, such patients are keenly aware of the "quality" of treatment, and form a strong alliance with a therapist who is perceived as being caring, respectful, and allied with their own goals of achieving a better life. Such patients rarely miss sessions and work diligently in treatment. For Medicaid patients, who usually suffer a constant level of distress associated with being poor, and for whom spending carfare for treatment is sometimes a hardship, treatment that is provided "free" is not experienced as "free," and so does not isolate them from concerns about financial reality. What transference gratification there is seems to work in a positive way, furthering the goals of treatment.

In *The Therapeutic Environment* (1979), Langs devotes a whole chapter to the impact of the therapist's acceptance of insurance reimbursement. He maintains that at best, where there is no overt dishonesty on the part of the analyst, that the analyst's participation in this activity creates an "unneeded modification" (p. 477). He states further that because of their own investment in patients' use of insurance, that therapists may not recognize that the signing of insurance forms contributes to the creation of an adaptational context. This creates unconscious responses which need to be analyzed. Case material is used to demonstrate that the analyst's agreement to consider and then accept insurance reimbursement made the treatment situation unsafe, offered a "framework cure," and finally led to premature termination.

Several authors have stressed the social relativity of the treatment frame, and believe that it can absorb routine activity related to insurance reimbursement (Paris, 1983; Raney,

1983; Chodoff, 1985). They point out, in response to Langs, that frame disturbances cannot always be distinguished from other problems related to motivation (Paris), or from other frame disturbances (Raney).

Paris practices in Quebec where all citizens are entitled to no-fee psychotherapy. He reports that difficulties arise not because treatment is "free" but in the special instances where payment is required. These arise when a patient fails to present his insurance card or when he misses a session. In the second instance physicians are not reimbursed by the government; thus the patient is charged. In Sweden, when the patient misses a session the physician is paid but at a greatly reduced rate. Christer Sjödin addresses the specific transference and countertransference pitfalls that result from this system (Sjödin, 1991).

The literature supports the conclusion that insurance reimbursement, whether through traditional indemnity plans or Medicaid coverage in the United States, or the universal coverage provided by national plans such as those of Canada and Sweden, is not in itself harmful to analytic treatment. Analysts need to be attuned to the transference and countertransference reactions evoked by specific policy requirements as well as to the unconscious meaning that coverage has for patients and for themselves.

In my own practice I have been impressed by the way in which insurance reimbursement has provided an important support for the treatment. In some instances, where one member of a couple is in treatment and the other is not, insurance helps to reduce the resistance of a spouse who is threatened by the treatment relationship and resents the expenditure of mutual funds which supports it. Goldensohn, writing about the advantages of psychotherapy coverage provided by an HMO, reports that reimbursement is particularly helpful in the treatment of children, reducing guilt in some children and forestalling premature termination when parents are financially stressed or feel that insufficient progress has been made (Goldensohn, 1986). Issues related to the negotiation of insurance matters, especially for young patients whose financial independence is new, provide opportunities for helping them deal with the anxieties associated with the demands of an authority that is less protective than a parent but no less needed.

The by now institutionalized expectation that insurance coverage for psychotherapy is an entitlement, the degree of social and familial isolation experienced by many individuals, the presence of character issues related to dependence and independence—these make financial and emotional needs for insurance difficult to distinguish. Therapists, dependent on their patients for income, may wish that their patients felt less dependent on third-party reimbursement. Or they may long for the purity of the uncontaminated field that Langs describes. Up to now most have maintained a neutral, or at least resigned attitude toward the prevalence of insurance coverage.

Managed Care: The Destruction of Clinical Practice

Patients and therapists alike have been deeply affected by the changes wrought by managed care. Traditionally, insurance plans have provided for a stable benefit. The benefit amount has been both predictable and reliable, enabling patients to plan financially, and to experience the feeling of security that reliable help fosters. Though patients might experience anxiety related to filling out forms, have a variety of reactions about asking the analyst to sign them, and become both anxious and angry when payments are delayed, the traditional policy provides that benefits *will* be paid. Therapists, who could limit their involvement to the signing of an already completed form, could thus remain neutral and available to help patients deal with whatever reactions matters

related to their insurance evoke.[1] Except for the addition of
the therapist's signature, full responsibility for reimbursement rests with the patient. Though patients are required
to sign a release on the claim form, inquiries from insurance
companies are rare, and primarily limited to checking dates;
I know of no instance where information conveyed to the
insurance company was communicated to a patient's employer. Occasionally a treatment review is requested, and this
necessitates supplying more comprehensive information.
Though therapists have always been concerned about the
breach of confidentiality involved in disclosure of the patient's involvement in treatment, the reporting of a diagnosis, and supplying any clinical material, what has been
required has been limited and the threat to patient confidentiality contained. Finally, fees are set by the therapist,
often with input, and always with the ultimate agreement of
the patient.

When care is "managed" a number of things are different. First, benefits are neither predictable nor reliable. Neither the patient nor the therapist knows how many sessions
will be "certified," or, once certified, whether they will be
"recertified." In order to begin the certification process,
patients must call the managed care company. They are routinely asked whether they are "on medication" and are
sometimes asked why they seek treatment. Some patients
discontinue the process at this point. Receipt of benefits,
whether they go to the patient who has paid the therapist
his fee, or, increasingly, are paid directly to the therapist
who is forced to accept assignment, is almost totally dependent on the activity of the managed care company and the
therapist. The latter must submit all paperwork, and do so
as frequently as every three sessions. Copayment, which has

---

[1]Completion of forms by patients becomes a problem for analysts who believe
that allowing the patient to fill in the analyst's name and address constitutes an
enactment of sexual or aggressive impulses.

had the effect of keeping issues related to the payment of a fee alive in the treatment, is reduced to 10 or 0 percent, thereby further separating the patient from participating in the arrangement of his own care and experiencing the reactions he would characteristically have. Reviews are frequent, and in some cases constant, and often require that the most difficult and personally painful aspects of a patient's life be told so that treatment can be "justified" to someone who does not have the training or motivation to appreciate pain which is less dramatically told. Finally, fees are set by the managed care company. Fees are often lower than what the experienced therapist would charge. Worse than this, the fact that the managed care company dictates the terms of treatment, including whether and for how long it will be provided, completely undermines the professional authority of the analyst and prevents him from establishing the necessary treatment frame. This has important implications for the transference, and for the countertransference.

The case material which follows illustrates the effects of managed care practices on treatment. The first case illustrates the disruptive effect that the intrusion of managed care had on a patient who was in the middle phase of treatment. Already three years later the case is an anomaly; if the patient had depended on managed benefits neither the treatment nor the transference would have progressed to the point it had. The second case illustrates the disruptive effect of managed care involvement on the development of a treatment process.

The Case of Ms. A: The Undermining of "My Comfortable Situation"

Ms. A had been in once weekly treatment for four years when her case was reviewed. "Management" came with her employer's hiring a new insurance company. The review process, relentless once it was begun, took about six weeks. During this period, calls from "Databank," the managed care company, were constant, and demands for multiple verbal reviews insistent. On one day I received three calls. The first two, both from the Southwest, were returned immediately. In the third message of the day the reviewer threatened to cut off benefits "if you do not respond within 40 minutes." Requests to respond to reviews in writing were denied. Misconceptions about diagnosis that have come to be associated with managed care were glaring; though the patient was diagnosed with dysthymia it was expected that she have "problems in daily functioning," that she be evaluated for medication, and that symptoms remit within eight weeks. Not realizing at the time that there was no intent to reimburse, I actually sent one reviewer copies of the DSM-III pages describing criteria for the diagnosis of dysthymia. Finally, there was the quasi-intimate sharing by a "member of your own profession" who told me that eight to ten sessions were the "wave of the future," was "already happening in the West," was "coming down the pike."

The sessions recorded below took place during this period. Ms. A learned that benefits had been denied and quickly dispatched a memo to her personnel department. In it she responded to the manner in which her treatment had been "dismissed" and stated its value to her. She indicated further that had she known that benefits would be denied she would have chosen the company's cheaper insurance option which acknowledged "up front" that it did not cover psychotherapy. With Ms. A's consent I wrote a detailed letter of complaint to the New York State Insurance Department and sent copies to Databank, her personnel department, and the Vendorship Committee of the New York State Society of Clinical Social Workers. Exactly four months after my letter of complaint was received by the New York State

Insurance Department I received a response indicating that
the insurance company had been contacted and it was found
that neither the insurance company nor the managed care
company were subject to state legislation.[2]

As the following material indicates, Ms. A did not want
to discuss the insurance problem in her sessions. For my
part, I handled the insurance matter as briefly and factually
as possible, informing Ms. A of the fact of the review, but
sharing nothing of my experiences with Databank. When
she was denied benefits I shared with her my recommendation that a letter of complaint be written to the New York
State Insurance Department. Though every attempt was
made to protect the integrity of the treatment, the case material illustrates that the experience had a powerful effect on
the patient.

BACKGROUND

Ms. A sought treatment at the point where her job was seriously threatened. An astute businesswoman, with a graduate
level degree, she had helped her boss, Jerry, to successfully
develop his small firm. According to Ms. A things went down-
hill when Jerry hired Eric, who became his confidante, gradually replacing Ms. A in her role as chief advisor. In Ms. A's
opinion the business faltered as a result of this new partnership, and she, feeling she could have prevented the problems
that ensued, was forced to look for another job. In the weeks
prior to her referral to me Ms. A had seen her physician
who prescribed a minor tranquilizer for her feelings of agitation. The patient quickly discontinued this medication,

---

[2]The Employee Retirement Income Security Act (ERISA) of 1974, originally
passed to insure pension equity across state lines, contains a provision allowing
self-insured groups to be exempt from most state regulations pertaining to mandated health insurance benefits and mandated provider requirements (Winegar,
1992, p. 16).

which was prescribed inappropriately and which she had taken irregularly.

RELEVANT FAMILY HISTORY

Ms. A is the oldest of three and the only girl. She had felt supplanted, especially in her relationship with her mother, by the birth of her first sibling when she was $2^1/_2$; she was 9 when a second boy was born. She describes her childhood in a rural suburb as generally happy and secure. Throughout her childhood, continuing to the time she began treatment, Ms. A felt that she had a special relationship with her father who, himself well educated, took pride in her academic achievements. Though proud of her talent as an artist, Mr. A had discouraged Ms. A's interest in attending art school. Neither son attended college. Ms. A's parents separated when she was in college and shortly thereafter Mr. A married a woman with whom he had been having an affair. He informed Ms. A of his intention to remarry, and asked her to keep this a secret for several months. Ms. A's mother works in a supermarket. Following the divorce she was dependent on Mr. A for financial support, and continues to depend on rent provided by her two sons, both of whom live at home. Ms. A describes her mother as a "traditional housewife," a role Ms. A ascribes in part to her mother's ethnic heritage. She is experienced by Ms. A as kind and supportive, accepting and generous, but is seen by Ms. A as weak, dependent and passive in relation to men, and an unsatisfactory role model for herself.

Though Ms. A's entry into treatment was precipitated by the events surrounding the anticipated loss of her job, and the intense feelings of anger and anxiety that were evoked, it soon emerged that Ms. A had a recent history of involvements with married men; prior to this she had been involved with men who were either mentally unstable or alcoholic.

At the time of the review by Databank, Ms. A was in the fourth year of once weekly treatment. Though encouraged to do so at an earlier phase of treatment she had resisted increasing her commitment to twice a week. She had long since successfully changed jobs and held a responsible position as an account manager with a major corporation. Though she remained sensitive to the periodic layoffs and swings of the economy that posed threats to her position, feelings evoked were manageable in their intensity. Though not yet involved in a satisfying intimate relationship, Ms. A had stopped dating married men, and was moving out of a platonic involvement with a married colleague who gave her gifts of art supplies. Her interest in painting, always present, had blossomed during treatment, and had become very important to her, helping her to consolidate a growing sense of personal identity and independence. In the excerpt which follows Ms. A had just returned from a week's vacation and had not yet returned to work.

> I just really like my life right now. I'm glad about it. I'm enjoying my life right now and I'm not fearful of losing it, not sad or depressed. Painting is going well. I spend the weekend in the studio with Pam. I've decided on Life Drawing in the Summer and another one in the Fall. The relationship [with Peter, her art teacher] is very pleasant, almost as if I've got confidence I didn't have before.

The mood in the sessions of this period is thoughtful and calm. Always concerned with having enough money, Ms. A muses about the meaning it has had for her: "My security with money is symbolic." She considers where she is in her relationships with male and female friends, especially the artists with whom she shares studio space. They are "nicer than businesspeople."

The case review was requested around the time of the above report, and I had informed Ms. A of this fact. Several sessions later, during the six- to eight-week review period, Ms. A alluded to a communication from the insurance company, vaguely, in the beginning of the session. "It's not for you. I don't like spending time on it . . . it's a little too much. I really don't care that much. They have another question." Ms. A sounded irritated. My impression was that she experienced the insurance questions as an unwelcome intrusion and was warding off additional intrusion from me. The next day she received a denial of benefits form from Databank. The paragraph which had been checked off read "Maximum benefit of treatment has been reached. Continued treatment at this level is not likely to produce further benefit." Ms. A brought a copy of the denial and the memo she had written to her personnel representative to her next session. One week later she said: "I've been lately in a euphoric like state. Why am I feeling so good? I've lost 16 pounds since January, been following Weight Watchers, decided to stop being a pig." Toward the middle of the session she reported:

> My art is going very well. Last Wednesday night I went to the studio and had a really bad night. People were making such a big deal [telling her what to do with her painting]. Do this, do that. I was just really, like get off my case. I wanted to kill somebody. I really did. People deprecating their own paintings. I don't want to hear that; we all do our own thing. I was in such a good frame of mind, even after talking about the bullshit insurance company. I was upset, so I called up Peter.

Ms. A explained that she did not want her classmates to know of her involvement with Peter:

> I don't want to answer any questions. I don't want anyone to know . . . I want to protect it. I like having a secret type

relationship. But if we were out I would not feel the least bit of conflict. That's progress. And I feel your acceptance . . . I think your acceptance made me able to go over and kiss him [last Wednesday evening] . . . My father would not approve. He would say, "he's too old, not as smooth and educated as you are, not as intellectual; he doesn't make a lot of money." I think, bottom line, my father doesn't like anybody . . . it's nerve-wracking . . . it's more comfortable for me to be viewed unattached . . . I don't want people imagining . . . that kind of piercing, like I'm being totally seen. He'd make me feel like that.

The material reflects Ms. A's feeling of safety with me and with Peter and her enjoyment of these "secret" relationships. The introduction of her father here, the association to his "piercing," to her discomfort with being "seen" as well as the agitation in her affect, can be understood as reactions to the present hostile intrusion of Databank.

Two weeks later Ms. A stated she was still "pretty relaxed." She was still on vacation, thinking of her return to work and the possibility of being transferred to an out-of-state office. She wondered how she could live without her job, whether she could ever support herself with her art. She reported she was talking to her friend G and asking herself and G whether art was "just a hobby. I'm so obsessed with it."

I was telling her I'm attracted to my painting teacher. It's like I want to sleep with my painting—I'm so into it . . . it's all the art. He's a nice man and everything. He's a nice man, but that's what does it . . . I've decided to put up some rules in my studio . . . if you want to paint the model you're committed to four sessions . . . if you can't make it you're still committed to it. Let's say I couldn't make a Wednesday night; I still owe $9, my share . . . *I* can decide what *I* want in my painting.

She continued:

> Simple rules to resolve ambiguity. . . . Pay your bills when
> they come in. Then there's never a problem . . . there's such
> a tendency to forget . . . this definitely came from my work
> with Jerry and Eric. I set up the company and Eric would
> come in and muddy the waters. I created it and he'd come in,
> at a higher salary, and say we need to do this. The noncreative
> person, the editor, and that made me nuts.

Ms. A, usually easy going with friends, seemed here to
be obsessed with establishing rules. She was trying very hard
to remain in control of what was important to her and to
reestablish a feeling of security. The language she used to
explain the rules, commitment to four sessions, payment for
missed sessions, the wish to determine "what *I* want in my
painting" established the link to the treatment situation.

Unaware that Ms. A was responding to the "editorship"
of Databank, I wondered about the possibility of some transference communication (myself as editor). Thus I invited
her associations to "editor." She said:

> Some friends say "my therapist says I ought to do this or
> that." I don't experience that here. That's why it works for
> me. Yet the approval—the acceptance of my feelings for Pe-
> ter—is very important for me. It enables me not to block
> things I may not want to block.

I inquired further. Ms. A's associations led to her father
and a recent discussion about a gallery opening. Ms. A said,
"I'm on notice about him taking over my art."

In the next sessions Ms. A began with a statement that
she felt her art "is more original" than it was. She asked me
if I would see Ms. W, a younger colleague who was deeply
involved in an emotionally abusive relationship. "I know you

could help her." She commented on her comfort with her art teacher, her realization that her attachment to him was "very self-centered; as long as you help me with my art the better I like you." She liked him because he "doesn't play mind games, is nice."

The next session began: "Before I forget, the test claims came back from Z (the insurance company). I had bad PMS last week . . . I was in a pretty foul mood." She reported that she got mad at Pam who criticized a painting. She then alluded to Pam's "vulnerability with men" and compared it "with the female stupidity I experience in my mother, can see in myself and in my mother." "What further infuriated me was her shrink. This 80-year-old woman advised her 'half a loaf is better than nothing at all.' " She added that her friend Pam is smart, "has done a lot of work in the securities business." Associations led to the birth of her first brother, then to Jerry's hiring Eric, and to the medication prescribed by her male medical doctor. With mounting anger she said: "I was running the company for him day to day, and all the systems were under my control. . . . " Referring to her father's remarriage and a stepmother she despises: "She cut off the money; felt I was spoiled. Big deal, she [Ms. A] is going to graduate school. *Out of left field a third party is introduced and it completely undermines my comfortable situation.*"

As has been reported, during this six-week period discussion of the activity related to the review was kept to a minimum. Ms. A had indicated on one occasion that "it doesn't matter that much"; on another that "it's the principle of the thing." Ms. A, generally quick to anger, had been enjoying a period of calm, even of satisfaction in her life. She was deeply gratified by her involvement in her art. She was thoughtful about her relationship with Peter, recognizing that she was "using him" to develop herself. There had been an important shift in her identification with her father. After a beginning treatment phase where subtle, paranoid transference elements were present she was enjoying a feeling of safety and security in her relationship with me. She saw me as helpful, nonintrusive, and like Peter interested in helping her "to develop my art"/self. This thoughtful, relatively peaceful mood where Ms. A was consolidating a great many gains, was palpable. Neither one of us wanted to disturb her work to discuss issues related to insurance reimbursement. Moreover, there appeared to be no therapeutic value in doing so. Ms. A attempted to keep the impingements of Databank out of the room and instructed me to do the same. This was her conscious choice. The unconscious impact of the review, and of the threatened loss of benefits could not, however, be avoided. The communications from Databank and the anticipated loss of benefits affected her. She experienced bouts of irritation outside of treatment, and within the treatment situation associated to prior situations in which her security was threatened. These included the birth of her first sibling, father's leaving the family and marrying a woman who was not sympathetic to Ms. A, the loss of her favored position with her boss, and the actual loss of her job.

Six weeks later benefits were reinstated. Neither Ms. A nor I knew why. I think it most likely that it was Ms. A's memo to her employer that was effective. Three months later Ms. A increased her sessions to twice weekly. The case was never again reviewed and treatment ended successfully three years later.

DISCUSSION

Periodic case review by an insurer, which has traditionally raised concerns about patient confidentiality, and may be experienced as an administrative nuisance by the therapist, is accepted by most practitioners as part of the normal course of business. Review that is conducted where there is no real intent to reimburse, where "medical necessity" is determined by economic policy, presents particular dilemmas for the psychotherapist. Specifically, what is the therapist's obligation to the patient? To himself? Professional associations have been forced to develop guidelines which address this problem. Paul Appelbaum, member of the Department of Law and Psychiatry at the University of Massachusetts, states that "if an emergency exists . . . there is an obligation to continue with treatment until the emergent (sic) state resolves or until an alternative provider of care can be found" (Appelbaum, 1993, p. 254). The National Association of Social Workers maintains the same position: "the social worker has an obligation to assure that appropriate services are made available to the client. The options include acceptance of private payment at a regular or reduced fee, pro bono services, referral to alternative treatment sources, or termination of treatment" (NASW, National Council on the Practice of Clinical Social Work, 1993).

In the case reported, the patient was neither destitute nor in crisis. I was guided in my decision to "fight" for Ms. A's treatment, responding immediately to the persistent and unreasonable demands made by Databank, with an instinctive sense of protectiveness toward the treatment—a kind of kneejerk reaction to Databank's pressured and threatening behavior. Once a negative determination was made, I made a decision, more carefully considered, based on my understanding of Ms. A's transference needs and in response to my needs as a professional, to address a malignant practice situation. Hence my letter of complaint to the New York State Insurance Department.

But was this activity necessary or even appropriate? Ms. A perceived her mother as weak and ineffectual, the opposite of the tough-minded businesswoman that Ms. A is. Ms. A's remarks to Pam, about the stupidity (vulnerability) of women, and her irritation with the 80-year-old [fashioned] shrink who says, "be happy with half a loaf" reflect this position. I felt that to not pursue actively the denial of benefits would negatively reinforce the female gender related aspect of the transference. The main work up to this point had been on the analysis of Ms. A's tie to her father, a more idealizable, but paranoid, controlling and narcissistic man. Money and financial security were extremely important to Mr. A and to the patient. Reviewing the case retrospectively I can better appreciate how much of a shift in Ms. A's identifications had taken place. When Ms. A says that the money doesn't matter, she means it. She really has come to understand that it symbolically represents her need for security and for a secure attachment to her father. At the same time, Ms. A readily signed release forms, and seemed pleased that I planned to pursue the denial. It is possible that my joining her in this battle, both as her therapist, and in tandem out of my own sense of professional conviction, helped to strengthen this bond. A very strong sense of our working together as a pair developed and continued undiminished until the end of treatment. Ms. A had by then established this "pairship" relationship with her husband.

Still there is the question of analytic neutrality. While advocating for Ms. A may have helped rather than harmed the treatment, it can be argued that not to act would have allowed for the emergence of equally valuable material. As a practical matter, clinicians cannot be expected to advocate for the insurance rights of every patient. For analysts repeated involvement of this kind must invade the neutral inner space required for them to work.

The Case of S: Trying to Create a "Comfortable Situation"

S is one of the very few patients referred to me by a managed care company. Her case illustrates the obstacles to establishing a viable treatment frame and stable therapeutic alliance when the duration of benefits is unknown and ready access to necessary treatment facilities is blocked. In this case it is not clear whether the impersonal structure of the managed care company matched the needs of this patient, or how it shaped the transference.

BACKGROUND

S is a striking, 35-year-old woman who evidenced no awareness of her attractiveness. She is the second of five children. The first three are girls who are close in age; the last two are boys. S reported an early memory of getting up at night to help her mother fold clothes. She reported this information without affect and with no associated ideas. S's father is a successful architect who provided well for the family but whose business was the main focus of his attention. S's parents divorced when she was 21. Following the divorce S's mother became seriously depressed and was hospitalized. S sought treatment for herself at this time and continued in treatment for one year. As an adolescent S wanted to pursue a career in medicine, but decided in her second year of college that the demands of such a career were too rigorous for her. She completed a liberal arts degree and obtained work in the entertainment industry. S describes herself as a serious student who only tried drugs at the urging of friends. She first used heroin when she became involved with her boyfriend, J. Her use escalated during the relationship with her current boyfriend, N. She sought help at the point where she realized that her drug use was out of control.

THE CASE: S & PC CARE

PC Care contacted me directly to find out whether I could do a substance abuse assessment; the clinician to whom S was first referred could not. Initial assessment determined that S needed detoxification from heroin. I was not able to arrange for a referral directly, as I normally would; this had to be done through the case manager, Mr. C. There was a several day delay as Mr. C, based in California, checked which area hospitals had contracts with PC Care. I managed the delay, a major problem for an addict who must continue to use drugs until detoxification is available, by providing S with a second appointment. It was clear from the beginning that I was not in authority.

At the outset Mr. C and I agreed that following inpatient detoxification S should be referred to a structured aftercare program. The aftercare program with which PC Care had a contract is one of the best in New York. I was pleased to support this plan and spoke convincingly with S about it prior to her inpatient admission. S, truly shaken by the situation she found herself in and suffering from symptoms of acute withdrawal, agreed to attend the program. I was in contact with Mr. C and the inpatient coordinator while S was in the hospital. My goal was to facilitate implementation of this plan, and to remain available should S want to be in contact. Predictably, the inpatient coordinator had difficulty reaching Mr. C. S was discharged and was given an intake appointment for the structured program. She kept the appointment, but told me that she was refused admission, and that it had something to do with the contract between PC Care and the program. I never learned exactly why this referral didn't work out. Mr. C neither denied the problem nor explained it. He subsequently authorized twice weekly sessions for the period immediately following S's detoxification, a far cheaper alternative for PC Care. S, shaky after a brief detoxification, kept her appointments but used heroin intermittently during the next several weeks. She tried to get readmitted, feeling that she needed more time in the hospital, but was unable to reach the doctor. She subsequently arranged for long weekends at her family home away from

the city, and this, plus her therapy sessions and strong motivation, helped her to stop using. She did not want to attend
a self-help group, stating that she had felt uncomfortable in
the 12-step hospital meetings.

After the first round of certified sessions, activity related
to insuring continued care for S resumed. Sessions were certified at three at a time. Though forms were mailed in prior
to each certification date Mr. C never read them. Thus, after
repeated attempts to reach him on the phone, when we did
make contact a lengthy conversation about the case ensued.
Mr. C required that S attend a self-help group. In every conversation we had I would assure him of my concurrence with
this goal; at the same time I tried to convey that the patient
couldn't be forced to comply. Part of my dilemma as S's
therapist was to try to create the therapeutic milieu necessary
for good analytic psychotherapy to take place while staving
off the pressure from the managed care company to dic-
tate treatment.

Establishing a treatment contract with S was not easy. S
did unusual and specialized work that required some travel,
and she assumed that there would be accommodation to
the demands of her job. Since I could not count on the
continuance of treatment certifications the point became
moot; there was no way to establish a reliable treatment
frame. Given the precariousness of the insurance situation,
and wishing to establish a therapeutic alliance that did not
depend on this support, I suggested to S early in the process
that we think of her treatment needs apart from the determinations of the insurance company. S could not consider her
treatment needs apart from the concrete involvement of
PC Care.

After six months S's case was transferred from Mr. C to
Dr. F. During the period of transition I learned from an
unwitting assistant who checked the policy that S had thousands of dollars available for treatment. This contradicted

Mr. C's report that S's union's policy provided for very little mental health coverage. Dr. F certified sessions at 10, returned calls more promptly, and seemed to have a greater appreciation of the clinical issues described.

S was in treatment for two years, for a total of 48 sessions. In the initial weeks treatment focused on helping S to control her drug use and on our beginning to understand its determinants. S reported feelings of boredom which she attributed to the lack of structured activity between jobs. She liked her work, which paid well, but felt she must prepare for a longer and more "grown-up" career. She experienced herself as without direction. It was important to S to feel productive in therapy as well as in her day-to-day life. Thus much session time was spent exploring career directions, and developing strategies for their pursuit.

In the seventh month of treatment S began to talk about her relationship with N, revealing her wish for a family and her frustration that N did not share this goal.

After ten months of treatment and following a month-long break which included two weeks of my vacation, S raised the question of stopping treatment. "I just feel I'm not utilizing it." When I asked her to elaborate she said: "Certainly at the beginning when I was in the throes of withdrawing I felt it was keeping me on track and keeping me thinking about it. Felt I was actually doing something to fix that. Then I felt I needed it to keep myself level, on a plateau."

I asked S how she had experienced the recent break. "The first week it was a little weird. Then I felt it was okay. You can't just put your thought processes on hold 'til you have another session. My thought processes went along okay. It was mostly the fact that I'm used to doing something on Monday night."

S then commented that she had five sessions left before the next recertification. In the next session we explored what S felt her treatment needs to be. S said, "Ideally, I'd like to

come in whenever I felt like coming in." I asked S how she
would identify a need to come in. She said she would come
in "if I were depressed and confused. If everything was going
great I wouldn't." I encouraged her to elaborate:

P.   If I was slipping into drugs—heroin, or becoming very
      depressed because of my family or N. If my career
      fell to pieces—I couldn't get anything going. I'd want
      someone to talk to, some objective person to lay my
      shit on."
Th.   Lay your shit on?
P.   I'm here to talk about the things that are dis-
      turbing—that I can't come to grips with on my own.
Th.   But the phrase, "lay your shit on" seems to have a
      particular connotation.
P.   I don't think that's the way therapy should be. . . . Ide-
      ally it should be pure exploration; not necessarily good
      or bad . . . also in the pure sense, it [lay your shit on]
      seems less involved with a person. Sometimes I feel
      like the process we have going is very personal, but all
      about me—but not very deep—superficial.
Th.   You seem to have an idea of something different.
P.   Not clear—but something deeper, and more . . . less
      about how can I make myself go to the gym every day
      and more about why I think the way I think.

      S acknowledged that the feeling of something missing
in her relationships was an experience she had with others.
She also said that it was important for her to make a decision
about therapy that felt like it was hers, that "doesn't ignore
myself or my voice." S decided that she would like to come
in "every few weeks." Every few weeks seemed naturally to
become every month. Recognizing S's need for structure as
well as autonomy, I offered her a regular monthly appointment.

Subsequently, when a new recertification was due, I asked S what she would like to do. She said that she would like to continue to come in once a month. There was some anxiety evident in her question to me about whether I thought that PC Care would continue to recertify monthly sessions.

Six monthly sessions were recertified, this time by "Ann," the third case manager. S discontinued treatment after this certification. She had not returned to drugs and felt that her life situation was stable.

DISCUSSION

S was a managed care company's dream. She had a substance abuse problem; she used treatment appropriately to deal with the problem. If PC Care had denied benefits after six months the patient, herself motivated to achieve concrete results, would have concurred with this plan. The two year span gave her more recovery time. There was some movement, demonstrated by S's awareness that there was something "missing" in our relationship. My own experience of S was that there was no real engagement with me; that what had developed is some engagement with the structure of the treatment relationship, structure that was codetermined by PC Care. It is difficult to know how much of S's apparent reliance on PC Care was determined by the fact that PC Care had from the beginning controlled and shaped her treatment. It is possible that PC Care, a corporation, combined elements of the concrete, impersonal, and powerful that made it, rather than the analyst a more ready and perhaps safer target of transference needs. It is possible that it represented the needed, but distant or unreliable authority of S's father. It is possible that both S's and my relation to PC Care—the struggle to keep the company involved, the

feeling that without PC Care's involvement things (the treatment) would fall apart—constituted a repetition in the treatment situation of important elements of S's early
relationship to her father and mother. The latter might well
have been emotionally unavailable to S (due to depression)
following S's birth or following the birth of S's sibling when
S was one year old. This would account for the lack of connection I felt between S and myself as well as the dependence, on both our parts, on a third party.

The impact of PC Care, its role in shaping the transference, can never be fully known; it is woven into the fabric
of the treatment relationship. In the countertransference I
experienced myself as without authority in matters related
to major treatment decisions; continuance of the treatment,
especially in the early critical months, was never assured. A
great deal of activity in relation to PC Care was required
while the patient's personal needs remained difficult to engage. Unfortunately all of PC Care's routine administrative
practices also worked against the establishment of a therapeutic alliance. Recertification activity required therapist
participation and advocacy furthering the therapist-case
manager alliance rather than the patient-therapist alliance.
Fee setting by PC Care and the therapist's responsibility for
filing claims further supported S's lack of involvement. Her
10 percent copayment seemed to reinforce the sense that
her participation was insignificant.

Unfortunately all of PC Care's administrative practices
worked against the establishment of a therapeutic alliance.
Recertification activity required therapist participation and
advocacy furthering the therapist–case manager alliance
rather than the patient–therapist alliance. Fee setting by PC
Care and the therapist's responsibility for filing claims further supported S's lack of involvement. Her 10 percent copayment seemed to reinforce the sense that her
participation was insignificant. We finally agreed that S

would pay the copayment at the beginning of each appointment, reinforcing her participation in her care.

Summary

Managed mental health benefits do not provide the relatively silent, unobtrusive support of the traditional indemnity insurance plan. An active third party, the managed care company can nonetheless never be the self-conscious participant that the analyst strives to be. Forced to conform to the requirements of such corporations, the analyst who agrees to work within the system must expend a great deal of energy both to assure that benefits continue and to maintain the integrity of the treatment situation. He must manage his own reactions to the intrusions, demands, and subtle undermining of his professional role while remaining available to understand and respond to the needs of his patients. While the skilled and committed analyst may negotiate successfully with "case managers" for once a week treatment, he cannot be expected to sustain this level of constant extraanalytic involvement; nor can he succeed fully in protecting the internal "analytic space" necessary for him to do his work.

References

Appelbaum, P. (1993), Legal liability and managed care. *Amer. Psychologist*, 48:251–257.

Austad, C. S., & Hoyt, M. F. (1992), The managed care movement and the future of psychotherapy. *Psychotherapy*, 29:109–117.

Bennett, M. (1988), The greening of the HMO: Implications for prepaid psychiatry. *Amer. J. Psychiatry*, 145:1544–1549.

Chodoff, P. (1972), The effect of third-party payment on the practice of psychotherapy. In: *The Last Taboo: Money as Symbol and Reality in Psychotherapy and Psychoanalysis*, ed. D. Krueger. New York: Brunner/Mazel, pp. 111–119, 1986.

_____ (1985), The effect of third-party payment on the practice of psychotherapy. In: *The Last Taboo: Money as Symbol and Reality in Psychotherapy and Psychoanalysis*, ed. D. Krueger. New York: Brunner/Mazel, 1986, pp. 119–120.

Cummings, N. A. (1991), The somatizing patient. In: *Psychotherapy in Managed Health Care: The Optimal Use of Resources*, ed. C. S. Austad & W. H. Berman. Washington, DC: American Psychological Association.

Freud, S. (1913), On beginning the treatment. *Standard Edition*, 12:121–144. London: Hogarth Press, 1958.

Gaeta, E., Lynn, R., & Grey, L. (1982), AT&T looks at program evaluation. *Employee Assistance Digest*, May–June:22–31.

Goldensohn, S. (1986), Transference, countertransference, and other therapeutic issues in a health maintenance organization (HMO). In: *The Last Taboo: Money as Symbol and Reality in Psychotherapy and Psychoanalysis*, ed. D. Krueger. New York: Brunner/Mazel, pp. 158–168.

Haak, N. (1957), Comments on the analytic situation. *Internat. J. Psycho-Anal.*, 38:183–194.

Halpert, E. (1972), The effect of insurance on psychoanalytic treatment. *J. Amer. Psychoanal. Assn.*, 20:122–133.

_____ (1986), The meanings and effects of insurance in psychotherapy and psychoanalysis. In: *The Last Taboo: Money as Symbol and Reality in Psychotherapy and Psychoanalysis*, ed. D. Krueger. New York: Brunner/Mazel, pp. 169–174.

Kennecott Cooper Corporation, Utah Copper Division (1970), *A Program for Troubled People*. Salt Lake City, Utah: Kennecott Cooper.

Langs, R. (1979), *The Therapeutic Environment*. New York: Jason Aronson.

Manuso, J. (1980), Corporate mental health programs and policies. In: *Strategies for Public Health*, ed. L. K. Ng & D. Davis. New York: Van Nostrand Reinhold, pp. 368–378.

National Association of Social Workers, National Council on the Practice of Clinical Social Work (1993), *The Social Work Perspective on Managed Care for Mental Health and Substance Abuse Treatment*. Washington, DC: NASW.

Paris, J. (1983), Frame disturbances in no-fee psychotherapy. *Internat. J. Psychoanal. Psychother.*, 9:135–146.

Raney, J. O. (1983), The payment of fees for psychotherapy. *Internat. J. Psychoanal. Psychother.*, 9:147–181.

Sjödin, C. (1991), The impact of the social welfare system on the psychoanalytic process. *Amer. J. Psychoanal.*, 51:55–60.

Stern, S. (1993), Managed care, brief therapy, and therapeutic integrity. *Psychother.*, 30:162–175.

Thakur, N., & Jacobson, J. (1992), *The Effectiveness of Psychological Services in Improving Employee Productivity and Attendance.* Washington, DC: American Psychological Association, Practice Directorate.

VandenBos, G. R., & DeLeon, P. H. (1988), The use of psychotherapy to improve physical health. *Psychother.*, 25:335–343.

Weissberg, J. H. (1992), The psychoanalytic envelope. *J. Amer. Acad. Psychoanal.*, 20:497–508.

Winegar, N. (1992), *The Clinician's Guide to Managed Mental Health Care.* New York: Haworth Press.

Treatment of Psychotic and Borderline Patients

6

The Survival of Psychoanalytic Psychotherapy in Managed Care: "Reports of My Death Are Greatly Exaggerated"

William S. Pollack, Ph.D.

Mark Twain once opened a newspaper and was shocked to read his own obituary. Regaining his composure, he wired the Associated Press: 'The reports of my death are greatly exaggerated!'' The same, I believe, may be said of the empathic or long-term psychoanalytic psychotherapies within the context of managed mental health care and national health care reform.

A decade of biological discoveries, economic constraints, and the management of medical care has revolutionized the treatment of mental illness. Such a paradigm shift has, however, tended to eclipse both the psychological salience and the therapeutic efficacy of our *most potent psychosocial treatment* tool: scientifically prescribed, psychoanalytically derived, *intensive psychotherapy*, provided by well-trained, highly skilled, empathic clinicians.

Research will be reviewed to support the hypothesis that long-term, psychoanalytically oriented, dynamic psychotherapy is not only an empirically verified mode of cure for serious emotional disturbance; but is also a cost-efficient, consumer driven, treatment alternative. The historically insidious (now acute) prejudices against such intensive curative treatment will be tied to the stigmatization of mental illness itself, now deftly and dangerously projected onto a significant scapegoat subgroup of its most skilled treating clinicians. Recommendations will be made for reinvigorating the cause of psychoanalysis and psychoanalytic psychotherapy within the context of managed care and national health care reform.

I will argue that an empathically attuned, psychoanalytically oriented, and developmentally informed individual psychotherapy has a central role in any well-planned, integrated, biopsychosocial treatment model for serious mental illness, and, therefore, in any meaningful reform of our national health care system (Dion and Pollack, 1992). To support my hypothesis, I will show evidence of psychoanalytic psychotherapy's *efficacy* and *cost-efficiency* in the treatment and care of even the most prevalent and serious of mental disorders. I will outline my theory as to how a belief in the opposite—that long-term dynamic treatment is unnecessary, unsuccessful, and too "costly"—is promulgated against the scientific evidence; and how this "big lie" must be addressed.

What then has tended to block our acceptance of a more scientific–objective understanding of the cost-efficient therapeutics of intensive long-term psychotherapy in the alleviation of severe psychological suffering and emotional distress? I will outline a series of *five* negative, unproven assumptions—dangerous myths or misconceptions—some due to ignorance or prejudice and others promulgated directly by vested interests bent on perpetuating unfairly gained profits from the overmanagement of outpatient mental health benefits (at the expense of employers, to the emotional harm of employees and patients), that must be forcefully debunked prior to the promulgation of national health care reform.

Five Myths: Dangerous Misconceptions

The first myth says that most serious mental illness is biologically based and therefore will not significantly respond to psychosocial or psychotherapeutic treatments. This assumption suggests an unproven certainty and reflects a confusion between etiology and praxis recommendations for mutative change.

The NIMH Epidemiological Catchment Area (ECA) study—the most extensive scientific undertaking thus far to unearth the real extent of mental disorder in the United States—showed evidence of a lifetime prevalence for serious mental disorders at the rate of approximately 29 to 35 percent of the population (Robins, Helzer, Weissman, Orvaschel, Gruenberg, Burke, and Reiger, 1984). Affective disorders, anxiety disorders, and substance abuse/dependency made up the lion's share of the illnesses estimated. In all three of these major mental illnesses there are continua of severity rates and treatment response that still generate debate as to the relative loading of environmental or developmental (interpersonal) causality versus genetic predisposition. And, in fact, even where biological markers or predisposing hereditary factors have been more securely identified, psychodynamic therapies have had significant impact on the triggers of interpersonal distress or stress which are often implicated in the symptomatic expression of the underlying disease. Put simply: biology alone can neither sufficiently explain etiology nor define treatment response.

There is also no reason that psychological intervention cannot be of use, even in an illness that may have a complete biological cause. Indeed, in modern medicine it has become more and more common to utilize "behavioral medicine" techniques. These are not "medical" or "behavioral" at all. They are sophisticated psychological interventions designed to bring about change in physical illnesses through impact upon the unconscious. Although it is not the major focus of this article, I believe we are at a point of what noted scientist and author Thomas Kuhn (in his innovative book *The Structure of Scientific Revolutions*) called a *paradigm shift* (Kuhn, 1970). The long-standing heuristic attempt to separate mind from body is being deconstructed, particularly in the biomedical sciences, so as to utilize higher order conceptual models of integration between mind and brain to the curative benefit of patients. How ironic it is that at a time when general medicine recognizes the unconscious effects of stress, affect, and emotional attitude on such diseases as arthritis, diabetes, hypertension, and cancer, that we in psychiatry/psychology continue obsessionally to isolate biological, genetic, and environmental factors. The "decade of the brain" will have its greatest benefit on minds that can be open to therapeutic flexibility.

In addition, the remediating effects of biological or somatic interventions, particularly medications, are somewhat limited. For example, in schizophrenia the use of antipsychotic medication and its effects on the positive symptoms of schizophrenia are well established. However, in the area of negative symptoms (particularly apathy and difficulties in interpersonal and social role functioning), neuroleptic medications appear to have limited effect, and may indeed, at times, exacerbate such conditions through side effects (Fenton and McGlashan, 1994).

A second dangerous conception is the belief that psychotherapy has no proven efficacy in the treatment of serious mental illness and has clearly been replaced by more "modern" technologies. This I refer to as the dinosaur assumption, the belief that psychotherapy is outmoded, unscientific, and no longer state-of-the-art. I believe this

erroneous assumption comes about by blaming only psychotherapy for the still somewhat limited success in the results
of all of our present-day treatments for the ravages of many
serious mental illnesses. Indeed, I will argue that intensive
dynamic psychotherapy has been shown by empirical means
to be useful in the treatment of serious mental illness. The
data actually provide robust support for this therapeutic intervention as a major contributor to the treatment of both
schizophrenia and affective disorder, with likelihood of potent results in anxiety states, character disorder, and post-
traumatic states.

The earliest empirical studies testing the psychological
effects of dynamic psychotherapy in schizophrenia were
equivocal. Indeed, some yielded very negative results (Fairweather, Simon, Gebhard, Weingarten, and Reahl, 1960;
Rogers, Gendlin, Keisler, and Truax, 1967; May, 1968;
Grinspoon, Ewalt, and Shader, 1972), although a study by
Karon and colleagues began to suggest more positive outcomes (Karon and VandenBos, 1972, 1981). Most of these
studies could be criticized on methodological grounds. To
address the limitations of prior studies, the NIMH-supported
interhospital study, referred to as the Boston Psychotherapy
Study, was structured in order to create a rigorous empirical
test of dynamically based psychotherapy with nonchronic
schizophrenic patients. Based upon the knowledge and theories of the time, patients were randomly assigned to one
of what were meant to be two distinct treatments: (1) an
exploratory intensive insight-oriented (EIO) psychotherapy
(a therapeutic derivative of psychoanalysis); and (2) a reality-
oriented adaptive supportive treatment (RAS) (Stanton,
Gunderson, Knapp, Frank, Vanicelli, Schnitzer, and Rosenthal, 1984).

What was most striking about the outcome of this study
was that both RAS and EIO patients improved in almost
every area evaluated, throughout! In retrospective analyses

of the nature of the differences between the two therapy groups, it was found that RAS and EIO therapists provided very similar levels of support, including suggestions, reality testing, encouragement, and warmth. So, what was striking was that "supportive activity" must also be an integral aspect of depth, empathically oriented psychoanalytic psychotherapy with psychotic patients, if it is to be successful (Gunderson and Frank, 1985; Frank, Gunderson, and Gomes-Schwartz, 1987).

The maintenance of a treatment alliance, that is, continuity of treatment with psychotic patients (which historically has been seen as one of the most difficult challenges), differentiated those patients who did well with more exploratory dynamic treatment. Put most simply, patients with more active positive symptoms of schizophrenia appear to feel better understood and "held" by supportive therapists, while patients with more classic negative signs of schizophrenia (those most resistant to medication treatment), anhedonia and affective impoverishment, tend to stay longer and do better with long-term dynamic treatment (Glass, Katz, Schnitzer, Knapp, Frank, and Gunderson, 1989; Frank and Gunderson, 1990).

So the dilemma really becomes a more sophisticated one. No longer is it a question of whether intensive therapy helps patients with serious mental illness, but which particular therapy helps which particular type of patient. And, in addition, what therapist factors make for a difference in treating and improving the patients' problems?

When more sophisticated in-depth analyses were carried out on the results of therapists in the insight-oriented intensive treatment program, three central technical aspects of their style were found to account for the differences in outcome. These were described as: the therapists' capacities for dynamic exploration, directiveness, and support. The most significant relationship uncovered was the connection between the capacity for skillfully conducted psychodynamic exploration—which was described as the "extent to which the therapist was judged to show a *sound psychodynamic understanding* and accurate attunement to the patients' underlying concerns and motives" (Katz and Gunderson, 1990, p. 84)—and the greatest improvement in negative symptom areas of schizophrenia. I believe this finding is an important one. In the area of severe psychotic illnesses, which have historically been least amenable to other forms of biological treatment, and often are the stumbling blocks over which patients and therapists fail, it is found that a more empathically attuned, psychoanalytically oriented therapeutic approach, carried out by a highly skilled practitioner, is a most efficacious treatment (Pollack, 1989).

What else do these results show us? First and foremost they argue for the efficacy of intensive psychoanalytic psychotherapy. They also show that the therapists providing the therapy must be skilled in the activity (i.e., well trained) and must have a personal belief in and commitment to the work so as to facilitate patient change in such a severely disturbed group. Neophytes, ambivalent practitioners, and "case managers" will not be up to the task, or will fail at it, giving therapy a bad name. Perhaps one other point worth underscoring is the fact that, in this case, psychotherapy affected the capacity for change in the biological sphere as well.

In studying the therapeutic alliance with these severely disturbed patients, Frank and Gunderson (1990) showed "that patients who formed good alliances with their therapists within the first six months of treatment were significantly more likely to remain in psychotherapy, comply with their prescribed medication regimes and achieve better outcomes after two years, with less medication than patients who did not" (1990, p. 228; emphasis added). So, compliance with biological interventions, long a major issue in the treatment of serious mental illness, is also enhanced with psychoanalytic psychotherapy through the capacity to create a holding environment with a therapeutic alliance!

When one moves into the area of affective disorders, the therapeutic efficacy of psychotherapy is even more apparent. In the NIMH collaborative study of treatment of depression (Elkin, Shea, Watkins, Imber, Sotsky, Collins, Glass, Pilkonis, Leber, Docherty, Fiester, and Parloff, 1989), a highly sophisticated, "manualized," empirically verifiable set of psychotherapies were integrated into a sophisticated outcome study for the treatment of depression. The two psychotherapies studied were cognitive behavior therapy and interpersonal psychotherapy—a specifically modified, psychoanalytically oriented treatment, practiced by well-trained dynamic practitioners (Klerman, Weissman, Rounsaville, and Chevron, 1984). The findings, at first striking to the psychiatric community, should no longer surprise us. It was found that the flag-bearer biological treatment—Imipramine with clinical management—was no more effective in general than either of the two psychotherapies! Interpersonal psychotherapy appeared to be a superior intervention, and in the statistical analyses of the most severely depressed and functionally impaired patients, interpersonal psychotherapy was still particularly effective—even when compared with Imipramine. Given the structure of their particular outcome study, there was no treatment condition which combined pharmacotherapy with specific forms of psychotherapy, but the authors suggested: "It is possible that effects of such a combination would have been superior to that of any of the individual treatments . . ." (Elkin et al., 1989, p. 981).

In a long-term follow-up of patients with recurrent depression who were treated with Imipramine and/or interpersonal psychotherapy over time, it was not only found that the medication had the predicted prophylactic effect, but that monthly interpersonal psychotherapy served to lengthen the time between episodes in patients not receiving active medication (Frank, Kupfer, Perel, Cornes, Jarrett, Mallinger, Thase, McEachran, and Grochocinski, 1990). A recent comprehensive review article exploring all controlled research outcome studies on the psychotherapy of depression and utilizing state-of-the-art statistical techniques, concluded that: "depressed clients benefit substantially from psychotherapy" and that, "the gains appear comparable to those observed with pharmacotherapy" (Robinson, Berman, and Neimeyer, 1990, p. 30). So much for the assumption that psychotherapy is ineffective with patients suffering from serious mental illness!

The third assumption, usually made as a resistance to the utilization of psychodynamic psychotherapy, is that patients with serious mental illness are "too sick" to benefit from "talking" therapy. And if indeed they do benefit, then they must be "too well" and, therefore, not really suffer from serious mental illness. I call this the "stigma" false assumption. There is a confusion here between the *person* suffering from the disease process and the disease process itself. As previously shown, it is clear that even the most regressed schizophrenic patient with many negative symptoms can benefit from psychotherapy. They certainly are not "too well," but are more likely on a road, a long road, to recovery. In addition, many patients with severely paralyzing personality disorders who require long-term intensive dynamic therapy have a very high morbidity risk. John Gunderson and I have argued elsewhere, that there is a continuing misunderstanding that erroneously links the distinctions between DSM-IV (1994) Axis I and Axis II disorders (APA, 1994) with levels of severity and dysfunction (Gunderson and Pollack, 1985). Today, the growing ranks of patients with legitimate posttraumatic disorders adds to the number of people who require long-term intensive psychotherapy as the treatment of choice. People who benefit from therapy are neither "too well" to be suffering from serious mental illness, nor "too sick" to benefit from the psychotherapeutic process. It is the potency of the dynamic treatment that makes the difference.

The fourth point, on which we meet resistance for the use of psychotherapy in the treatment of serious mental illness, is the belief that psychoanalytic psychotherapy is too "regressive" and may hurt sicker patients through its unstructured activity. This, I believe, involves a long-standing antipsychoanalytic bias and the erroneous belief that psychodynamic treatments cannot be tailored to the nature of the illness process itself. In addition, it represents a confusion between the skill of the practitioner and the illness severity. In the Boston psychotherapy study, it was clear that the therapists, utilizing more depth oriented dynamically inspired treatments, recognized the need to limit severe regression and to actively intervene to support the patient's functioning in daily life. Empathically attuned therapists, however, were also interested in helping the patient to understand what really went on inside themselves, in a manner that was equally facilitating of personal growth as well as of control over psychotic symptomatology. I do not argue that unmodified classical psychoanalysis will be the treatment of choice for patients with serious mental illness. However, this does not mean that treatments based on an empathic understanding of human development and a connection with a patient's deepest, unconscious sense of self cannot facilitate personal change or, for that matter, ameliorate symptoms. Indeed, the development of interpersonal psychotherapy by Weisman and Klerman is distinct evidence that an empirically based, scientifically replicable, and reliable treatment can be created and implemented for patients with serious mental disturbance, all the while maintaining fidelity to basic psychodynamic–psychoanalytic principles.

The fifth, most recent, and perhaps most dangerous of all the misconceptions concerning intensive psychotherapy and serious mental illness is that psychotherapy is too costly a treatment, or at least not sufficiently cost effective. Here I believe the supporters of this argument are blaming the treatment and the patient (i.e., the victim), rather than the illness. In addition, there is a confusion between time and money. It is true that intensive psychotherapy, in general, takes a substantial period of time to have its effects; and it certainly is not without costs. But against what benchmark are we measuring it? Certainly, the outcome studies in depression show dynamic therapy to be as much or even more use than medication or support. In addition, even maintenance interpersonal therapy seems to forestall the emotionally costly and economically devastating recrudescence of depressive symptoms. So, are we measuring cost efficiency against how *few* human and person hours we can provide to the patient? Or, are we taking as our normative base the cost of the illness itself?

An epidemiological study on depression, conducted by Regier, Boyd, Burke, Rae, Myers, Kramer, Robins, George, Karno, and Locke (1988), found that in any one month almost 8 million people experience depression at an annual cost of $16 billion, $10 billion of which is attributable to absenteeism and dysfunction in the workplace. More recent estimates by MIT economists suggest a combined cost of $43.7 billion a year in the United States due to depressive illness, of which less than one-third is for direct care, and the remainder is due to lost incomes and missed work days. A staggering figure! (Miller, 1993). Could psychoanalytic psychotherapy of an empathic or supportive sort really cost more than this? No, indeed it provides a cost savings when work-loss costs are factored in.

In fact, there is every reason to suspect that one of the largest hidden costs in the treatment of depression belongs—not to long-term therapy, which is consistently cost effective, but rather—to mis- and underdiagnosis of affective illness by prepaid health plans who regularly and inappropriately under report and mistreat early stages of depression: leading to more costly, severe and untreatable illness for the patients under their care (Potts, Burnham, and Wells, 1991; Tarlov, Ware, Greenfield, Nelson, Perrin, and Zubkoff, 1989; Verbrugge, 1985; Wells, Hays, Burnam, Rogers, Greenfield, and Ware, 1989; Wells, Stewart, Hays, Burnam, Rogers, Daniels, Berry, Greenfield, and Ware, 1989).

In addition, there is the long-standing data on "cost offset." The classic studies by Cummings and colleagues showed that over 60 percent of all health care visits to general practitioners and internists are made by people with no physical problem; rather, that they are suffering from emotional stress, or the prodromal signs of more serious mental illness. The provision of psychotherapy significantly reduced medical utilization and cost (Cummings and Follette, 1992; Cummings, Dorken, and Pallak, 1990). When Medicaid patients who were hospitalized for physical disturbances were provided with mental health interventions, a cumulative savings of $1500 per patient over $2^1/2$ years ensued (Fiedler and Wight, 1989). In a longitudinal outcome study of a large private insurer, Aetna, a dramatic cost offset effect was noted after mental health treatments were provided with greater access (Holder and Blose, 1987).

So, psychotherapeutic treatments for serious mental illness are cost efficient when placed side by side with the devastating emotional and fiscal costs caused by workplace dysfunction, the personal, emotional toll in depression and schizophrenia; and the cost offsets for medical utilization which ensue. If we add to this data the recognition that appropriately prescribed empathic psychotherapy (carried out by well-trained clinicians) leads to enhanced patient medication and medical compliance (Frank and Gunderson, 1990), the salience and potency of intensive dynamic long-term psychotherapy stand out above all other treatment alternatives.

Perhaps the most insidious and successful campaign waged against long-term dynamic therapy has come from some within the mental health managed care industry. As a group, these economic entities too often have sold their *costly* services to large corporations and small businesses alike by targeting what they describe as the "out of control" nature of mental health and substance abuse treatment costs. Like any Madison Avenue strategy or "big lie" there is an important kernel of truth here. When utilization review programs, staffed by competent clinical personnel, are aimed at reducing inpatient hospital stays (specifically for adolescents and substance abuse treatment), substantial savings accrue. Yet many of these same managed care companies continue to tar intensive psychoanalytic psychotherapy with the same brush of inappropriate utilization when, indeed, it is this very outpatient therapy alternative that provides the reasonable cost-offset solution to overutilized, inpatient care. In fact, appropriately prescribed psychodynamic outpatient psychotherapy is and continues to be one of the most cost efficient treatment alternatives in medical care today, in part due to its self-regulating utilization, based upon patients' legitimate needs. The facts: First, fully 70 percent to 80 percent of the cost of all psychological/psychiatric care is for inpatient treatment alone (Stanton, 1989; Lewin/ICF, 1990). The substitution of a full range of outpatient services leads to a 25 to 75 percent savings in total mental health costs—often with improvement in quality (U.S. House of Representatives Select Committee on Children, Youth and Families, 1987; Dickstein, Hanig, and Grosskopf, 1988).

Further studies have shown that the introduction of a broad range of mental health services (with choice of outpatient care) has little increase over time in "psychiatric" service utilization (Sharfstein, Muszynski, and Arnett, 1984). A large sample study conducted by the Rand Corporation found that the utilization of mental health services was directly related to genuine distress (not to coverage, per se) and that enrollees—even without close management—were unlikely to use mental health services inappropriately, no matter how plentiful the coverage (Ware, Manning, and Duan, 1984).

In fact, the vast majority of patients, regardless of their insurance benefits, enter psychotherapy for brief periods to solve important problems. The median length of therapy treatment in the United States is six to ten sessions, with evidence that between 75 and 90 percent of patients terminate by the twenty-fifth session—all this primarily without costly and intrusive outpatient utilization review (Garfield, 1986; Pollak, Mordecai, and Gumpert, 1992; Ackley, 1993). So why then are we investing so much energy and money in micromanaging and attempting artificially to limit an outpatient psychotherapy which is naturally limiting, cost efficient, and "self-rationed" by appropriate clinical diagnosis and patient autonomous decision?

Here, the "big lie" goes into full swing. I believe that the stigma once reserved for serious mental illness is now projected onto a subgroup of treating clinicians—psychoanalytically informed and long-term psychotherapy experts. We are being told directly or indirectly that patients are being made too dependent upon treatment; and that psychologists and psychiatrists are encouraging this hurtful regression through their own greed, misguided philosophy, or outdated treatment methods.

Indeed, the historical roots of the most common and successful short-term treatment techniques lie within the psychoanalytic and psychodynamic treatment camps. Numerous creative, innovative, modified (and shorter-time span) treatments were devised for patients seeking more limited interventions; and for patients likely to benefit from such modifications (e.g., the work of Sifneos, Malin, Budman, Mann et al.). Yet when well-trained clinicians prescribe and utilize longer-term intensive techniques, it is not (usually) due to greed or ignorance, but rather a realistic treatment plan based upon scientific outcome knowledge of specific illness entities, clinical impressions of the patients' needs, and upon patient historical response or lack of response to prior interventions.

In clinical medicine, for example, most patients with elevated cholesterol can be treated with a regime of education and diet. If this fails and/or there is a strong hereditary risk, then medication will be utilized. Concurrently, closer observation and more frequent testing will ensue. With certain clinical signs and additional testing, and evidence of severe atherosclerotic process, surgery may be indicated. That 90 percent of patients may be best helped by simpler, cheaper, shorter interventions is not a reason for denying more intensive, costly care to the 10 percent for whom it is medically necessary. Yet this is precisely what many managed mental health care companies attempt to do! The 10 to 20 percent of all patients who need more than twenty-four sessions of outpatient therapy, require intensive psychodynamic treatment not because short-term techniques or medications have not been tried, not because therapists "just don't get it," and not because of misdiagnosis or excessive "dependency." Instead, given our present state of knowledge, the range of our therapeutic armamentarium, and the severity of many emotional disorders, intensive psychoanalytic psychotherapy (often in conjunction with other treatments like medication) is the most efficacious, cost-efficient, and reasonable treatment of choice. To "save" money here is not only to squander resources better spent on treatment than on needless management and UR, but essentially to stigmatize serious emotional disorders as unworthy of equally effective care as medical conditions. Moving this stigma from the prejudice against the depressed, "immoral," "weak," and "morally bankrupt" patient, to castigating the "greedy" and "ignorant" dynamic therapist is a victory for intolerance, short-sightedness, and genuine ignorance of scientifically proven long-term treatment modalities. True savings are garnered by diverting dollars from unnecessary, and, at times, wasteful inpatient care to more intensive psychotherapy. The overreview of outpatient therapy is based on half-truths and distortions meant to make management of care look more complex than it really is, in order to justify its too costly price to industry and consumer alike.

Brief Vignette

Mrs. R was a 35-year-old married professional woman with three children. Her husband was a career civil servant. Although both Mr. and Mrs. R had overcome great adversity in their earlier years in order to achieve economic security and family stability, the pain of childhood abuse and abandonment weighed heavily upon Mrs. R.

When she first came to my attention she had already undergone more than ten brief psychiatric hospitalizations (15–45 days each) and numerous short-term therapies meant to address her chronic depression and suicidal ideation, which often flared up acutely in frightening self-destructive actions.

Her recurrent self-destructive enactments, repeated hospitalizations, and apparent nonresponsiveness to outpatient treatments had led her treaters and insurance companies alike to add the diagnosis of borderline personality disorder to the already extant difficulties of depression and PTSD. Once so diagnosed, both prior treaters and the insurance companies managed care reviewers felt that it was no longer wise to invest economically in therapeutic care, as the patient was seen as "self-defeating" and likely to be continually rehospitalized.

After meeting briefly with the patient for an evaluation, I was convinced that the opposite was true. I informed the insurance company that they were indeed correct that Mrs. R suffered from a severe psychological disturbance, and that there were characterological elements which made it difficult for her to achieve any sense of well-being or personal safety. I told them that I differed, however, with their diagnosis of why prior treatment had failed. I explained that far from being too intensive, that the prior treatment was indeed too costly but also too brief, too unsupportive, and too limited in scope to be likely to effect any change in Mrs. R's condition. I explained, further, that Mrs. R required the creation of a safe "holding environment" within an outpatient psychotherapy with a skilled clinician capable of dealing with her severe distress while helping her to achieve personal growth and change. Such treatment, I added, would be long term in nature and require intensive frequency (3–4 sessions weekly) in order to have any chance of success. I suggested that, although costly, such outpatient treatment would be much less expensive than the continued rehospitalizations which appeared to have no therapeutic affect whatsoever; and suggested that a trial period of intensive therapy ensue.

The insurance company and Mrs. R agreed to the treatment, with a review monthly. Over the course of the last three years the patient has been hospitalized for a total of only five days, during one acute crisis. Although major characterological changes have been slow, Mrs. R has shown a growing sense of self-awareness and safety, diminished suicidal thinking, major improvement in her symptomatic picture, and is better able to function with family and friends. The net cost to the insurance company has diminished significantly, and review has been relaxed to every six months.

Conclusion

The data supporting the efficacy of in-depth long-term psychodynamic psychotherapy and other psychoanalytically derived treatments are not awaiting further scientific investigation, as many managed care entities would suggest, but are already available. Although there are even more and better designed studies under way, those already published substantiate our clinical experience: long-term therapy is a cost-effective treatment of choice for a large range of psychological/psychiatric disturbance, either as a solo treatment intervention or in conjunction with other outpatient psychosocial and biological modalities.[1]

As dynamic clinicians we have to move from a more comfortable position of passivity or neutrality into a more proactive set of political activities. We should, indeed, gather and present our data to the larger managed care entities, making logical and scientific argument for the efficacy of long-term dynamic psychotherapy versus more costly inpatient and physical health care.

Most especially, we must direct our energies toward repositioning psychoanalytic psychotherapy as a treatment of choice, a cost effective, efficacious intervention—not as the managed care entities would have it for the "worried well" —for the most seriously disturbed, psychologically. Indeed, I

---

[1]The recent survey research conducted by *Consumer Reports* substantiates this argument, finding indeed that psychotherapy is an effective, successful treatment; and the longer the therapy, the greater the improvement! (Does therapy help?, 1995).

believe that it is the deconstruction of the "big lie"—that psychotherapy is not effective in the treatment of serious mental illness—that represents our greatest hope for the future. The outcome data on the treatment of serious depression and anxiety, for example, go a long way toward refuting the misconceptions promulgated in the media that serious emotional disturbance is best or only treated by somatic or pharmacological means.

Although the reports of the death of intensive psychotherapy are so far still exaggerated, the forces of mechanization, bureaucratization of health care, restigmatization of mental illness, and biological reductionism are powerful. So we must redouble our efforts to keep alive both the science and art of one of the most innovative, creative, and therapeutically efficacious components of our treatment armarmentarium—long-term intensive, dynamic psychoanalytic psychotherapy.

References

Ackley, D. C. (1993), Employee health insurance benefits. A comparison of managed care with traditional mental health care: Costs and results. *Independ. Practit.*, 13:159–164.

American Psychiatric Association (1994), *Diagnostic and Statistical Manual of Mental Disorders*, 4th ed. (DSM-IV). Washington, DC: American Psychiatric Press.

Cummings, N. A., Dorken, H., & Pallak, M. S. (1990), The impact of psychological intervention on health care utilization and costs. *Biodyne Inst.*, April.

—— Follette, W. T. (1992), Psychiatric services and medical utilization in a prepaid health plan setting. *Med. Care*, 6:31–41.

Dickstein, D., Hanig, D., & Grosskopf, B. (1988), Reducing treatment costs in a community support program. *Hosp. & Community Psychiatry*, 39:1033–1035.

Dion, G., & Pollack, W. (1992), A rehabilitation model for persons with bipolar disorder. *Compreh. Ment. Health Care*, 2:87–102.

Does therapy help? (1995, November), *Consumer Reports*, 60:734–739.

Elkin, I., Shea, M. T., Watkins, J. T., Imber, S. D., Sotsky, S. M., Collins, J. F., Glass, D. R., Pilkonis, P. A., Leber, W. R., Docherty, J. P., Fiester, S. J., & Parloff, M. B. (1989), National Institute of Mental Health treatment of depression collaborative research program. General effectiveness of treatments. *Arch. Gen. Psychiatry*, 46:971–982.

Fairweather, G. W., Simon, R., Gebhard, M. E., Weingarten, E., & Reahl, J. E. (1960), Relative effectiveness of psychotherapeutic programs: A multicriteria comparison of four programs for three different patient groups. *Psychology Monographs*, 74:1.

Fenton, W. S., & McGlashan, T. H. (1994), Antecedents, symptom progression, and long-term outcome of the deficit syndrome in schizophrenia. *Amer. J. Psychiatry*, 151:351–356.

Fiedler, J. L., & Wight, J. B. (1989), *The Medical Offset Effect and Public Health Policy: Mental Health Industry in Transition*. New York: Praeger.

Frank, A. F., & Gunderson, J. G. (1984), Matching therapists and milieus: Effects on engagement and continuance in psychotherapy. *Psychiatry*, 107:201–210.

———— ———— (1990), The role of the therapeutic alliance in the treatment of schizophrenia: Effects on course and outcome. *Arch. Gen. Psychiatry*, 47:228–236.

———— ———— Gomes-Schwartz, B. (1987), The psychotherapy of schizophrenia: Patient and therapist factors related to continuance. *Psychotherapy*, 24:392–403.

Frank, E., Kupfer, D. J., Perel, J. M., Cornes, C., Jarrett, D. B., Mallinger, A. G., Thase, M. E., McEachran, A. B., & Grochocinski, V. J. (1990), Three-year outcomes for maintenance therapies in recurrent depression. *Arch. Gen. Psychiatry*, 47:1093–1094.

Garfield, S. L. (1986), Research on client variables in psychotherapy. In: *Handbook of Psychotherapy and Behavior Change*, 3rd ed. ed. S. L. Garfield & A. E. Bergin. New York: John Wiley.

Glass, L. L., Katz, H. M., Schnitzer, R. D., Knapp, P. H., Frank, A. F., & Gunderson, J. G. (1989), Psychotherapy of schizophrenia: An empirical investigation of the relationship of process to outcome. *Amer. J. Psychiatry*, 147:603–608.

Grinspoon, L., Ewalt, J. R., & Shader, R. I. (1972), *Schizophrenia: Pharmacotherapy and Psychotherapy*. Baltimore, MD: Williams & Wilkins.

Gunderson, J., & Frank, A. (1985), Effects of psychotherapy in schizophrenia. *Yale J. Biol. & Med.*, 58:373–381.

_____ Pollack, W. S. (1985), Conceptual risks of the axis I–II division. In: *Biologic Response Styles: Clinical Implications*, ed. H. Klar & L. J. Siever. Washington, DC: APA Press, pp. 81–95.

Holder, H. D., & Blose, J. O. (1987), Changes in health care costs and utilization associated with mental health treatment. *Hosp. & Commun. Psychiatry*, 38:1070–1075.

Karon, B. P., & VandenBos, G. R. (1972), The consequences of psychotherapy for schizophrenic patients. *Psychother.: Theory, Res. & Pract.*, 9:111.

_____ _____ (1981), *Psychotherapy of Schizophrenia: The Treatment of Choice*. New York: Jason Aronson.

Katz, H. (1989), A new agenda for psychotherapy of schizophrenia. *Schizophr. Bull.*, 15:355–359.

_____ Gunderson, J. G. (1990), Individual psychodynamically oriented psychotherapy for schizophrenic patients. In: *Handbook of Schizophrenia*, Vol. 4, ed. M. I. Herz, S. J. Keith & J. P. Docherty. New York: Elsevier, pp. 69–90.

Klerman, G., Weissman, M., Rounsaville, B., & Chevron, E. (1984), *Interpersonal Psychotherapy of Depression*. New York: Basic Books.

Kuhn, T. S. (1970), *The Structure of Scientific Revolutions*. Chicago: University of Chicago Press.

Lewin/ICF (1990), *Analysis of CHAMPUS Mental Health Policies*. Final report submitted to the Department of Defense, Health Affairs Health Program management.

May, P. R. A. (1968), *Treatment of Schizophrenia: A Comparative Study of Five Treatment Models*. New York: Science House.

Miller, (1993), Dark days: The staggering cost of depression. *Wall Street J.*, December 2:B1, 8.

Pollack, W. S. (1989), Schizophrenia and the self: Contributions of psychoanalytic self-psychology. *Schizophr. Bull.*, 15:311–322.

Pollak, J., Mordecai, E., & Gumpert, P. (1992), Discontinuation from long-term individual psychodynamic psychotherapy. *Psychother. Res.*, 2:224–233.

Potts, M. K., Burnham, M. A., & Wells, K. B. (1991), Gender differences in depression detection: A comparison of clinical diagnosis and standardized assessment. *Psycholog. Assess.*, 3:609–615.

Regier, D. A., Boyd, J. H., Burke, J. D., Jr., Rae, D. S., Myers, J. K., Kramer, M., Robins, L. N., George, L. K., Karno, M., & Locke, B. Z. (1988), One-month prevalence of mental disorders in the United States. *Arch. Gen. Psychiatry*, 45:977–986.

Robins, L. N., Helzer, J. E., Weissman, M. M., Orvaschel, H., Gruenberg, E., Burke, J. D., & Regier, D. A. (1984), Lifetime prevalence of specific psychiatric disorders in three sites. *Arch. Gen. Psychiatry*, 47:949–958.

Robinson, L. A., Berman, J. S., & Neimeyer, R. A. (1990), Psychotherapy for the treatment of depression: A comprehensive review of controlled outcome research. *Psycholog. Bull.*, 108:30–49.

Rogers, C. W., Gendlin, E. G., Kiesler, D. J., & Truax, C. B. (1967), *The Therapeutic Relationship and Its Impact: Study of Psychotherapy with Schizophrenics.* Madison: University of Wisconsin Press.

Sharfstein, S. S., Muszynski, S., & Arnett, G. M. (1984), Dispelling myths about mental health benefits. *Business & Health*, 7–11.

Stanton, A. H., Gunderson, J. G., Knapp, P. H., Frank, A. F., Vanicelli, M. L., Schnitzer, R., & Rosenthal, R. (1984), Effects of psychotherapy; in schizophrenia, I. Design and implementation of a controlled study. *Schizophr. Bull.*, 10:520.

Stanton, D. (1989), Mental health care economics and the future of psychiatric practice. *Psychiatric Annals*, 19:421–427.

Tarlov, A. R., Ware, J. E., Greenfield, S., Nelson, E. C., Perrin, E., & Zubkoff, M. (1989), Medical outcomes study. *JAMA*, 262:925–930.

U.S. House of Representatives Select Committee on Children, Youth, and Families (1987), *Children's Mental Health: Promising Responses to Neglected Problems—A Fact Sheet.* Washington, DC: U.S. Government Printing Office.

Verbrugge, L. M. (1985), Gender and health: An update on hypotheses and evidence. *J. Health & Soc. Behav.*, 26:156–182.

Ware, J. E., Manning, W. G., & Duan, N. (1984), Health status and the use of outpatient mental health services. *Amer. Psychologist*, 39:1090–1100.

Wells, K. B., Hays, R. D., Burnam, M. A., Rogers, W., Greenfield, S., & Ware, J. (1989), Detection of depressive disorders for patients receiving prepaid or fee-for service care: Results from the medical outcomes study. *JAMA*, 262:3298–3302.

———— Stewart, A., Hays, R. D., Burnam, M. A., Rogers, W., Daniels, M., Berry, S., Greenfield, S., & Ware, J. (1989), The functioning and well-being of depressed patients. *JAMA*, 262:914–919.

7

Managed Care and the Borderline Patient: Where Treatment Was, There Management Will Be

Paul M. Lerner, Ed.D.

A 28-year-old, single female was referred for long-term, intensive psychotherapy following the latest of a series of hospitalizations. The patient presented a long, involved psychiatric history including alcohol abuse, sexual promiscuity, self-mutilating behavior, and an inability to fully and successfully separate from her family.

After a stormy, turbulent, and precarious beginning, treatment went well and the patient showed much evidence of benefit and growth. After two-and-one-half years in treatment she was maintaining sobriety, had stopped her promiscuity, had secured and was holding a full-time job which afforded economic self-sufficiency, and was gradually separating from her family.

Her employer changed insurance companies, and not long afterwards her therapist was contacted by a managed care company. Impressed with the significant behavioral

I thank Charles S. Jones, Ph.D., for supplying several of the case examples.

changes and having judged that treatment was no longer necessary, the reviewer authorized only five more sessions. In response to the therapist's protests, the reviewer, in a haughty and supervisory manner, instructed the therapist to use the reality of the intrusion as a "lesson in life," that sudden changes do occur and that this was part of the patient's learning to face the adult world.

The recommendation was offered in reference to a patient, who, as a child, had been thoughtlessly shifted from caregiver to caregiver, had been abandoned by her father as an adolescent when he suicided, and who had been jilted by a boyfriend just before she had been hospitalized.

Unfortunately, this case is not special nor the exception. As several authors (Cord, 1993; Jones, 1993; Barron, 1994; Shore, 1994) have noted, managed care with its narrowly symptom-focused emphasis, accent on brevity, and devaluation of the patient–therapist relationship, is increasingly intruding into and affecting the sanctity of treatment and the treatment relationship.

While much has been written of the impact, overall, of managed care on the nature of psychoanalytically informed treatment, little has appeared regarding the particulars of how managed care may affect specific aspects of treatment.

The treatment of the borderline patient presents a unique opportunity for studying up close ways in which managed care can impact upon specific elements of the treatment process. In contrast with our work with less disturbed individuals, treatment with the borderline patient tends to be longer, is more intense and dramatic, and is usually more complicated and demanding. We are all familiar from our work with these individuals of their assaults on the therapeutic alliance, their proclivity for action, and the turbulent nature of the transference–countertransference struggles. More so than others, these patients test our capacity to tolerate chaos, hate, and despair.

The Borderline Concept

The borderline concept, including its delineation as a pathological entity, arose from the convergence of two streams of conceptual development within psychiatry descriptive psychiatry, with its emphases on discrete and observable phenomena and exclusive nosological categories, and psychoanalysis with its view of attempting to establish the structural, dynamic, and developmental roots of the disorder.

Major contemporary contributions to the descriptive line come from three major areas: empirical research and reviews (Grinker, Werble, and Drye, 1968; Gunderson and Singer, 1975), genetic and adoption studies (Rosenthal, 1975; Wender, 1977), and psychopharmacological studies (Klein, 1977). These studies have demonstrated consistently that borderline patients are psychologically similar to but distinguishable from both schizophrenics and neurotics, and that borderline patients are characterized by: (1) intense affects (anger and depression); (2) consistent lapses in impulse control; (3) social adaptiveness; (4) transient, circumscribed psychotic episodes; and (5) erratic interpersonal relationships.

The value of this approach depends upon accurate clinical description and the reliability and validity of the diagnostic concept. It emphasizes conceptual clarity and precise diagnostic criteria (Perry and Klerman, 1978), and is based on a careful observation of signs and symptoms clustered into well-defined categories and syndromes.

The origins of the psychoanalytic stream are found in the work of Reich and his systematic application of psychoanalytic concepts to the study of pathological character types. In his 1925 book *The Impulsive Character*, he used the term *borderline* and described the pregenital conflicts, ego and superego defects, immature defenses, and narcissistic orientation of the impulsive personality in a way that Sugarman and

Lerner (1980) refer to as having a "remarkably contemporary cast" (p. 13).

Following Reich, several investigators have contributed to the psychoanalytic literature on borderline pathology. Alexander (1930) coined the term *neurotic character* to describe a group of patients who presented with "an irrational style of life" as contrasted with discrete symptoms, and Stern (1938) extended Alexander's concept of the neurotic character to the "borderline group." Deutsch (1942) wrote of the "as if" personality, an individual who manifested impoverished object relations, feelings of inner emptiness, intact reality testing, fleeting feelings of depersonalization, and narcissistic identifications. Schmideberg (1959) used the evocative phrase "stable in their instability" to characterize a group of patients who were unreliable, intolerant of rules, unmotivated for treatment, unable to make use of insight, and lacking in a capacity to establish meaningful emotional contact with others.

Beginning in 1966 with a reexamination of the borderline concept and the spectrum of disorders of character from the perspective of structural derivatives, the writings of Kernberg (1975, 1976) have had a remarkable impact. By integrating the British school of object relations with the structural theories of ego psychology, he has been able to develop a unitary process conceptualization of psychopathology and demonstrate that a descriptive clarification of borderline disturbances contains only "presumptive diagnostic elements." He asserts that a structural analysis revealing nonspecific manifestations of ego weaknesses, shifts toward primary process thinking, a reliance on primitive defensive operations, and a pathology of internalized object relations, differentiates the syndrome as a stable entity (as a personality organization), between neurotic and psychotic organizations.

Although the descriptive and psychoanalytic approaches tend to be complementary, there are significant differences. One difference, which is methodological, may be likened to the disagreements surrounding idiographic and nomothetic approaches to the study of personality. A second difference is more substantive. Whereas the descriptive view places exclusive emphasis on symptoms and overt behavioral expressions, the psychoanalytic perspective, while subsuming symptomatic expression, also pays close attention to the underlying personality structure including manifestations of ego weaknesses, the level of the defenses, the quality of internalized object relations, and the nature of superego development and integration.

Third, unlike the psychoanalytic approach, the descriptive approach is not wedded to any one broader theory of personality. Because the psychoanalytic approach is embedded in a comprehensive theory of personality and psychopathology, it permits one to account for observations and findings which appear contradictory and to explore matters of development and etiology.

Managed care, given its value structure and assumed perogatives, poses a major danger here. More specifically, the language of managed care—the language of diagnosis, behavioral description, and target symptoms—and the underlying view of psychopathology it reflects, are compatible with the descriptive approach but incompatible with the psychoanalytic one. What this means is that managed care and its proponents, beyond impinging upon the nature of practice, threaten to influence and shape our conceptions of psychopathology; that is, the theories and principles that inform and help guide our clinical work.

Our theories of psychopathology and specific clinical entities cannot be based upon or influenced by forces outside of our profession, including factors occurring in the marketplace. Historically, our understanding of psychopathology has come from careful clinical observation and empirical research based upon those observations. To do otherwise would destroy the scientific foundations upon which our work as psychoanalysts is based.

Structural Frame

Various terms have been coined such as the *analytic situation* (Greenson, 1967), the *contract* (Menninger and Holtzman, 1973), and the *psychoanalytic frame* (Bleger, 1967) to describe those structural conditions that provide the framework for treatment to occur. There is general agreement (Chasseguet-Smirgel, 1992) that the treatment process cannot proceed until the frame has been established. Likening the therapist to the artist, Chasseguet-Smirgel (1992) characterized the importance of the frame this way:

> In studying works of art, where the term "frame" is used, one understands that the basic condition for creation is the possibility of finding a place—a frame, a wall, a stage. . . , to serve as a container for the artist's psychic productions, his projective identification, in the shape of a painting, a drawing, a fresco, a play. . . , for want of which there could only be hallucination. It follows that in addition to giving precise form to his projective identifications, the artist must also contain these within defined limits. There must be a space between the artist and his work, for without this he would be psychotic [p. 22].

The structural frame of treatment includes the place where sessions will be held, the duration and frequency of sessions, the agreed upon fee, the way in which missed appointments and vacations will be handled, and in analysis, the fundamental rule and the patient lying on the couch. Apart from practical considerations, these conditions allow the appearance of certain psychic phenomena and their investigation. The stability and permanence of the frame distinguishes, spatially and temporally, the inside from the outside, regulates the physical and psychical attitudes of the two participants, and permits the emergence and observation of transference reactions.

Each of these conditions impacts upon the treatment process and has meaning in its own right. Frequency of sessions, for example, often affects the level of regression and intensity of transference reactions. According to Freud (1913), that sessions are paid for maintains a link with reality. Monetary transactions have other meanings too such as sacrifice and exchange. Because sacrifice is at the heart of most religions and exchange is basic to human interactions, attitudes toward the fee extend to these areas as well.

For the individual organized at a borderline level, the structural frame has special importance. Modell (1978), for instance, has suggested that the stability of the frame, especially for more disturbed patients and during the initial phase of treatment, provides a holding function and affords the individual feelings of safety and security and a sense of being psychologically held. Along similar lines, other authors (Adler, 1985; Epstein, 1979; Cohen and Sherwood, 1991), mindful of the borderline patient's difficulty regulating affects, and reliance on projective identification, highlight the containing function provided by the frame.

Because of the nature of borderline pathology—proneness to rapid regressions, failures in achieving object constancy, vulnerability to feelings of abandonment, and difficulties regulating aggression—in establishing the frame, specific aspects require careful attention. For example, in deciding upon frequency of sessions one needs to consider the patient's regressive tendencies and capacity to conceive of the therapist as a constant object. In addition, given the borderline patient's struggle with feelings of abandonment, interruptions in treatment, such as vacations, can be particularly disruptive. Therefore, in setting the frame the therapist has to consider how separations will be handled.

The impact of managed care on the establishment of the treatment frame with a borderline patient is nothing short of devastating. Decisions which should be based on the unique needs of the patient and the requirements for treatment to take place are taken out of the hands of the treater and placed in those of a third party. Typically, that individual responsible for deciding such weighty matters is external to and distant from the treatment, is less well trained and experienced than the therapist, and has a different agenda and holds a different set of values.

In consultation, a therapist saw a 32-year-old woman who had taken a nonlethal overdose following her husband's announcement that he intended to end the marriage. The patient reported a chaotic and painful past including severe verbal abuse from a puritanical stepfather, a series of failed heterosexual relationships including two earlier unsuccessful marriages, and an out-of-wedlock pregnancy in which she carried to term and gave the baby up for adoption. Other losses figured prominently in the patient's history. Apart from her history, the consultant was impressed with the patient's grit and determination, capacity to experience genuine loss, and unsophisticated reflectiveness.

In typical fashion, the managed care reviewer focused on the suicide attempt, immediate crisis, and break-up of the marriage, and little else. She authorized eight sessions for crisis intervention, insisted that the patient see a psychiatrist to assess the need for antidepressants, and recommended divorce mediation.

The frame established by the reviewer, unfortunately, had little to do with the patient's needs or personhood. The suggestion of crisis intervention ignored the consideration that creating and then attempting to resolve crises had become the patient's way of life. Entertaining the possible use of medication for her depressiveness flew in the face of the recent overdose and failed to consider the patient's history of and vulnerability to loss. Capacities the patient presented which favored a more long-term, insight-oriented approach, went unnoticed.

As illustrated in the example, such externally based frames inevitably reflect little interest in or awareness of the dynamics or characteristic features of the borderline patient. A treatment frame suited to a crisis intervention model misses the point that for these individuals crises are not isolated experiences, but rather, are a way of being and feeling in the world. The limited number of sessions and usual prescription that treatment be on a once-per-week basis do not recognize borderline patients' struggles with trust, conflicts around attachment, and need for containment. The emphasis on medication undermines the need for these individuals to feel and assume responsibility for regulating their own feelings and actions. The omnipresent threat that treatment may be terminated at any time and with minimal warning fuels their sense of helplessness and fears of separation and abandonment.

Efforts by the therapist to establish his or her own frame usually involve negotiations and place the therapist in the role of advocate, diplomat, defense attorney, or labor negotiator. Such roles necessarily impinge upon the treatment, including threats posed to the matter of confidentiality. Negotiated frames are compromise frames. They are better than externally imposed frames but they are not ideal, and to paraphrase Chasseguet-Smirgel (1992), they can impede the treatment process (which is movement) from establishing itself.

Countertransference

Andre Green (1975) has suggested that the term *borderline states* could be profitably amended to "borderline states of analyzability." His suggestion, which we all resonate with, comes from the recognition that these patients often test the limits of the clinician's skill and empathic sensibility.

The role of countertransference reactions in both assessing and treating the borderline patient is well recognized. Gunderson (1977) has noted that the eventuation of intense transference–countertransference dilemmas during treatment can be used as a salient diagnostic criterion. Green (1977) goes even further in contending that the ultimate criterion for diagnosing borderline pathology is the intense variability of "the affective quality of the patient's communications and the analyst's own inner response" (p. 3).

Several authors (Green, 1975; Boyer, 1977; Gorney and Weinstock, 1980) have pointed to the therapist's vulnerability to malignant forms of countertransference including confusion, despair, massive anxiety, or intense rage as constituting the major therapeutic problem in treating the borderline patient. Indeed, work with borderline patients has prompted a reexamination of the concept of countertransference and of its role in treatment.

Two strands, each rooted in the writings of Freud, have intertwined throughout the historical development of psychoanalytic conceptions of countertransference. In his 1910 paper, "The Future Prospects of Psycho-Analytic Therapy," Freud speaks of countertransference as a hindrance or interference to treatment. Yet, barely two years later he writes that the analyst "must turn his own unconscious like a receptive organ towards the transmitting unconscious of the patient. . . . so the doctor's unconscious is able . . . to reconstruct [the patient's] unconscious . . ." (Freud, 1912, pp. 115–116). Here, then, countertransference is not regarded as a hindrance but rather as a source of understanding the patient.

While these two divergent attitudes toward countertransference have pervaded the psychoanalytic literature on the theory of technique, treatment experiences with the borderline patient have resulted in a third position. This position holds that such reactions are neither a hindrance nor a help, but instead, are intrinsic and inevitable components of the treatment, and that the understanding and working through of both countertransference reactions and the patient's transference reactions that induced them is at the heart of treating borderline individuals.

Representative of this line of theorizing is the work of Epstein (1979) and Gorney and Weinstock (1980). Epstein (1979) contends that in treatment the therapist quickly becomes the object for the borderline patient's transference projections. In response, equally intense and powerful reactions, both conscious and unconscious, are stirred in the therapist. Such counterreactions in the therapist are not considered idiosyncratic, but rather as representative of the types of reactions the patient's projective processes provoke in others. The patient's transference projections and the therapist's counterreactions are thought to be based upon and expressions of pathological internalized object relations. Treatment, for Epstein, consists of the activation and externalization of these pathological object relations in the transference–countertransference relationship. The therapist's task is "to learn how to function with the patient in such a way as to structurally correct this persistent internal pathological self and object relationship" (p. 377).

Gorney and Weinstock (1980) take up the issue of therapeutic impasse, suggesting that the transference–countertransference stalemate is a necessary and inevitable development in the treatment of the borderline patient. Accordingly, "It is within stalemate that the original interactional pathology in object relating comes to be fully revealed and the seeds of its possible resolution germinated" (p. 169). Based upon the developmental distinction Winnicott (1969) drew between "object relating" and "object usage," the authors regard impasse as a necessary intermediate phase of object relating in which the object (therapist) is recurrently destroyed and recreated. The therapist's capacity to survive the patient's efforts at destruction eventuate in the dissolution of omnipotent control and lead to resolution of stalemate through the gradual establishment of object usage.

If the arousal of malignant forms of countertransference and the resolution of transference–countertransference struggles lie at the core of one's work with borderline patients, then managed care renders this type of treatment impossible. The limit placed on number of sessions, the relative infrequency of sessions, the liberal use of medication, and the recurring need to secure additional sessions counteract the conditions necessary for patiently and carefully dealing with transference–countertransference dilemmas. From a managed care perspective, countertransference is a meaningless concept and therapeutic impasse is translated into a lack of progress and signals that treatment should be severely altered if not discontinued. Surviving the patient's destructive urges becomes secondary to warding off the assaults of the case reviewer.

Managed care affects the countertransference in work with borderline patients in another way too. This involves what Racker (1968) has referred to as "indirect countertransference." Racker distinguishes between direct and indirect countertransference. Direct countertransference consists of the therapist's reactions to the patient. Indirect countertransference, by comparison, is the therapist's response to a significant other who is external to the therapeutic setting. For example, a highly valued referrer, someone the therapist would like to impress with his or her skill, is apt to stir in the treater a pressuring desire to succeed with the patient.

With managed care, the case reviewer, or whomever the therapist has contact with, quickly becomes an inducer of and target for a range of indirect countertransference reactions. Typically, the therapist is required to formulate a treatment plan. That plan is scrutinized and judged, and then approved or disapproved. Most therapists experience the review process as degrading and devaluing. Feelings of hostility, ranging from annoyance to rage, frustration, helplessness, and bewilderment are experienced in relation to the reviewer.

Equally degrading and infuriating is the process of negotiating for additional sessions. To secure more sessions, a therapist presented to the reviewer evidence of progress the patient had made in treatment. The patient sought treatment because of powerful dissociative experiences. Whereas these events had been disruptive to his life, increasingly, they were being confined to the treatment sessions. Upon hearing this, the reviewer commented, "They are only occurring in the sessions. Good! Then, if you end the sessions soon, the episodes should stop completely." The therapist was understandably stunned and flabbergasted by the reviewer's remarks.

Although these indirect countertransference reactions are provoked by someone outside the treatment, they can and do affect the therapist's feelings and behavior within the treatment. For instance, such external experiences can intensify the therapist's feelings of anger and impotence with the patient. Or, especially with the borderline patient, the therapist may find himself or herself less tolerant of the patient's manipulativeness, impulsiveness, or need to spoil.

When treated unjustly by a reviewer, the therapist must resist the powerful pull to identify with the patient and the patient's sense of victimization and entitlement. One is tempted, at these times, to suspend objectivity and neutrality and to collude with the patient in the service of retaliation. Borderline patients are particularly attuned to vulnerabilities in their caretakers, and sensing a split between the therapist and the reviewer, they often step right in and attempt to widen the gulf (Main, 1957).

Faced with an unsympathetic, often hostile reviewer, having to fend off pressures to refer the patient to a biologically oriented psychiatrist, and feeling demoralized by a process one has little control over, the therapist may consider entering into a special arrangement with the patient that bypasses managed care. While allowing the therapist to reclaim a lost sense of control, such a step also has countertransference implications. If, for example, the arrangement calls for the therapist lowering his or her customary fee, it may arouse feelings of resentment toward the patient. With certain borderline patients, such practices run the risk of confirming the individual's overriding need to be regarded and treated as special. That is, an arrangement authored by the therapist to allow treatment to progress may inadvertently fuel the patient's omnipotence which, in turn, will likely arouse strong counterreactions in the therapist.

To briefly recapitulate, the intrusion of managed care into the therapeutic arena seriously impacts the therapist's direct and indirect countertransference reactions. The time needed to work through transference–countertransference struggles, a process critical to psychoanalytic treatment with borderline patients, is not available. Reactions provoked in the therapist by the managed care reviewer are in themselves burdensome, and inevitably enter into the treatment.

Standing Still and Time

In their book *Becoming a Constant Object* (1991), Cohen and Sherwood take seriously and build upon the proposition that at the core of borderline pathology is the individual's not having attained object constancy. As a consequence of this failure, subsequent developmental achievements including the capacity for mature attachments, the ability to tolerate aloneness, and a sense of continuity of self over time are all faulty or amiss.

Following from their basic proposition, the authors suggest a general framework for treating borderlines that takes into account the patient's struggle in forming attachments, ongoing fear of abandonment, difficulty in modulating affects, and most importantly, distorted sense of time.

The authors pay careful attention to the beginning phase of treatment or to what they refer to as the preconstancy stage. They suggest that the therapist needs to recognize that before the patient can make use of treatment in a more conventional sense, he or she needs the therapist to become a constant object. Toward this end, the therapist's task during this phase is to create a context in which an object tie can be experienced.

To assist the therapist in becoming a constant object, in providing such a context, Cohen and Sherwood offer two general guidelines. The first involves the therapist "standing still." By this they mean the therapist's maintaining an empathic presence without being intrusive, problem solving, or interpretive. Such restraint, they argue, provides a model of steady continuity in the face of powerful affects such as rage, despair, or elation. Standing still also addresses the patient's inability to experience gradations of feeling and continuing fears of separation.

The second guideline involves the reminder that in treating borderline patients, "time is the therapist's best ally and a sense of urgency the therapist's worst enemy." This guideline recognizes that borderline patients experience time in a distorted way and that time itself is a vehicle for change.

The borderline's overly narrow time sense and related sense of urgency is well reflected in their experience of affects and difficulty with affect tolerance and regulation. These individuals lack a perspective to place affects in; hence, they experience an urgency to rid themselves of painful feelings. As Cohen and Sherwood (1991) note, their "experience of affects is perpetually frozen in the present. There is no readily accessible, broader context of a remembered past and anticipated future against which to weigh current feelings. These patients consequently have trouble imagining that they will ever feel differently than at the moment" (p. 19).

The technical suggestions outlined by Cohen and Sherwood, that the therapist not act but maintain an empathic presence in response to affective storms and pleas for relief, recognize and begin treatment where the patient is at, understand that time is an ally, and time is a means of change, while especially suited for borderline patients, are also part of good analytic technique.

Managed care, in emphasizing activity, ready prescriptions, and responding to overt overtures rather than underlying structures and meanings, clearly promotes a treatment approach totally opposite from that of Cohen and Sherwood. That approach, interestingly but unfortunately, supports, encourages, and legitimizes what, from a psychoanalytic perspective, are basic difficulties and defects in the borderline patient. For instance, demands for immediate relief from tension or some other discomforting affect are quickly responded to with medication or introduction of an anxiety reducing behavioral regime. Insistence that ready solutions be found for seemingly pressing problems prompts suggestions or outside referral to divorce mediators, learning disability specialists, or a self-help group. More than an exclusive focus on symptoms, the treatment approach promoted by managed care regards certain psychological experiences such as need satisfaction, affect regulation, time, and urgency in a way similar to that of the borderline patient.

Cohen and Sherwood (1991) also found a parallel to the borderline patient's time distortions; however, rather than with managed care, it was with Western society more broadly. They suggest that such individuals seem to caricature the fluidity, flux, and reactivity of contemporary life. Like the borderline patient, the instability and intensity of Western life prompts the expectation that problems be addressed immediately and solutions found instantaneously.

Conclusion

A consideration of three important aspects of psychotherapy—establishing a structural frame, the role of countertransference, and the importance of standing still and one's time perspective—indicates that the tenets and practices of managed care and a psychoanalytically informed treatment of borderline patients are incompatible.

Borderline patients and their treaters require a treatment frame that addresses the patient's core pathology and unique needs. In terms of basic ingredients such as setting, number and frequency of sessions, and fee arrangement, the structure must take into account the patient's struggles with attachment, fears of abandonment, and poor affect control, and also, allow for psychological holding and containment. An externally imposed frame or even a negotiated one cannot do this. These frames, noninternal to the treatment, are based upon a view of psychopathology, an attitude toward treatment, and a system of values strikingly divergent from those of the treater.

Increasingly, psychoanalytic clinicians are recognizing that transference–countertransference dilemmas and the arousal of intense countertransference reactions are at the heart of the treatment of the borderline patient. It is within these struggles that the patient reenacts earlier interactional pathology, reveals associated structural and developmental defects, and provides the opportunity for growth and change. The structural frame, as designed by managed care, prohibits all this from occurring. The limits set on time, the direct response to the patient's complaints and symptoms, and the uncertainty as to if and when treatment will be precipitously terminated, all obviate the possibility of such a process unfolding.

Within managed care, the process and the reviewer become inducers of and targets for intense indirect countertransference reactions. Being forced to advocate, negotiate, justify, and submit typically leaves a therapist feeling demeaned, frustrated, angry, misunderstood, and controlled. Such reactions, wittingly or unwittingly, inevitably seep into the treatment.

Analytic techniques, basic ones such as not acting but being steady and present in the midst of affective storms, viewing time as a vehicle for change, and understanding rather than gratifying a sense of urgency, while helpful in working with borderline patients, are unerringly out of sync with a managed care perspective. Indeed, one senses that proponents of managed care share with borderline patients the fantasy that meaningful change is magical, quick, effortless, and painless.

In essence, managed care, rather than offering a different approach to the treatment of the borderline patient, in effect, replaces treatment with management. Psychoanalytic models of treatment emphasize insight and self-understanding, with therapy seen as a unique type of self-education, and the therapeutic relationship as a context for experiencing, exploring, and working through dynamic patterns as they emerge in the transference. By contrast, managed care models emphasize relief and control, see therapy as a series of short-ranged problem-solving activities, and assign little meaning to the therapeutic relationship. The patient, with managed care, is managed not treated and the therapist's role is one of a manager rather than a treater.

It is ironic that managed care, as a force in the psychotherapy field, comes at a time when researchers are beginning to empirically demonstrate the efficacy of long-term, intensive psychoanalytic psychotherapy in effecting structural change in borderline patients. Blatt and his colleagues (Blatt, Ford, Berman, Cook, and Meyer, 1988; Diamond, Kaslow, Coonerty, and Blatt, 1990; Gruen and Blatt, 1990) have found that in a sample of adolescent and young adult borderline patients long-term treatment modified pathological representations of self and other. Measures obtained at the end of treatment when compared to those obtained pretreatment indicated that self and object representations showed a clearer sense of boundaries and separateness and a greater sense of empathic relatedness. These structural changes in representations paralleled changes taking place in the transference relationship as reported by the therapist.

The evidence of structural changes reported by these researchers confirms what therapists have observed in their practices and described in their clinical reports. Such internal change cannot and will not be achieved in a climate that seeks quick fixes and conceives of treatment in terms of management.

References

Adler, G. (1985), *Borderline Psychopathology and Its Treatment.* New York: Jason Aronson.

Alexander, F. (1930), The neurotic character. *Internat. J. Psycho-Anal.*, 2:292–311.

Barron, J. (1994), Incompatibility of managed care and psychodynamic psychotherapy. *Psychologist Psychoanalyst*, 14:1–2.

Blatt, S., Ford, R., Berman, W., Cook, B., & Meyer, R. (1988), The assessment of change during the intensive psychotherapy of borderline and schizophrenic young adults. *Psychoanal. Psychol.*, 5:127–158.

Bleger, J. (1967), Psychoanalysis of the psychoanalytic frame. *Internat. J. Psycho-Anal.*, 48:511–519.

Boyer, B. (1977), The treatment of a borderline patient. *Psychoanal. Quart.*, 46:386–424.

Chasseguet-Smirgel, J. (1992), Some thoughts on the psychoanalytic situation. *J. Amer. Psychoanal. Assn.*, 40:3–26.

Cohen, C., & Sherwood, V. (1991), *Becoming a Constant Object: In Psychotherapy with the Borderline Patient.* New York: Jason Aronson.

Cord, E. (1993), How does managed care impact on the practice of psychoanalytic psychotherapy. *Newsletter of the Appalachian Psychoanal. Soc.*, 4:2.

Deutsch, H. (1942), Some forms of emotional disturbance and their relationship to schizophrenia. *Psychoanal. Quart.*, 11:301–321.

Diamond, D., Kaslow, N., Coonerty, S., & Blatt, S. (1990), Changes in separation-individuation and intersubjectivity in long-term treatment. *Psychoanal. Psychol.*, 7:363–398.

Epstein, L. (1979), Countertransference with borderline patients. In: *Countertransference*, ed. L. Epstein & A. Feiner. New York: Jason Aronson, pp. 375–406.

Freud, S. (1910), The future prospects of psycho-analytic therapy. *Standard Edition*, 11:139–152. London: Hogarth Press, 1957.

——— (1912), Recommendations for physicians practicing psychoanalysis. *Standard Edition*, 12:109–120. London: Hogarth Press, 1958.

——— (1913), On beginning the treatment. *Standard Edition*, 12:121–144. London: Hogarth Press, 1958.

Gorney, J., & Weinstock, S. (1980), Borderline object relations, therapeutic impasse, and the Rorschach. In: *Borderline Phenomena and the Rorschach Test*, ed. J. Kwawer, H. Lerner, P. Lerner, & A. Sugarman. New York: International Universities Press, pp. 167–188.

Green, A. (1975), The analyst, symbolization and absence in the analytic setting. *Internat. J. Psycho-Anal.*, 56:1–22.

———— (1977), The borderline concept. In: *Borderline Personality Disorders: The Concept, the Syndrome, the Patient*, ed. P. Hartocollis. New York: International Universities Press, pp. 15–44.

Greenson, R. (1967), *The Technique and Practice of Psychoanalysis.* New York: International Universities Press.

Grinker, R., Werble, B., & Drye, R. (1968), *The Borderline Syndrome: A Behavioral Study of Ego Functions.* New York: Basic Books.

Gruen, R., & Blatt, S. (1990), Changes in self and object representation during long-term dynamically oriented treatment. *Psychoanal. Psychol.*, 7:399–423.

Gunderson, J. (1977), Characteristics of borderlines. In: *Borderline Personality Disorders: The Concept, the Syndrome, the Patient*, ed. P. Hartocollis. New York: International Universities Press, pp. 173–192.

———— Singer, M. (1975), Defining borderline patients: An overview. *Amer. J. Psychiatry*, 132:1–10.

Jones, C. (1993), Why are we working with managed care? *Newsletter of the Appalachian Psychoanal. Soc.*, 4:4–8.

Kernberg, O. (1966), Structural derivatives of object relations. *Internat. J. Psycho-Anal.*, 47:236–253.

———— (1975), *Borderline Conditions and Pathological Narcissism.* New York: Jason Aronson.

———— (1976), *Object Relations Theory and Clinical Psychoanalysis.* New York: Jason Aronson.

Klein, D. (1977), Psychopharmacological treatment and delineation of borderline disorders. In: *Borderline Personality Disorder: The Concept, the Syndrome, the Patient*, ed. P. Hartocollis. New York: International Universities Press, pp. 365–383.

Main, T. (1957), The ailment. *Brit. J. Med. Psychology*, 30:129–145.

Menninger, K., & Holtzman, P. (1973), *Theory of Psychoanalytic Technique.* New York: Basic Books.

Modell, A. (1978), The conceptualization of the therapeutic action of psychoanalysis. The action of the holding environment. *Bull. Menninger Clinic*, 42:493–504.

Perry, J., & Klerman, G. (1978), The borderline patient. *Arch. Gen. Psychiatry*, 35:141–150.

Racker, H. (1968), *Transference and Countertransference*. New York: International Universities Press.

Reich, W. (1925), The Impulsive Character. In: *The Impulsive Character and Other Writings*. New York: New American Library, 1974.

Rosenthal, D. (1975), The concept of subschizophrenia disorders. In: *Genetic Research in Psychiatry*, ed. R. Fieve, D. Rosenthal, & H. Brill. Baltimore: Johns Hopkins University Press, pp. 199–215.

Schmideberg, M. (1959), The borderline patient. In: *American Handbook of Psychiatry*, Vol. 1, ed. S. Arieti. New York: Basic Books, pp. 398–416.

Shore, K. (1994), To stand up and say "no." *Psychologist Psychoanalyst*, 14:4–5.

Stern, A. (1938), Psychoanalytic investigation of therapy in the borderline neuroses. *Psychoanal. Quart.*, 7:467–489.

Sugarman, A., & Lerner, H. (1980), Reflections on the current state of the borderline concept. In: *Borderline Phenomena and the Rorschach Test*, ed. J. Kwawer, H. Lerner, P. Lerner, & A. Sugarman. New York: International Universities Press, pp. 11–37.

Wender, P. (1977), The contribution of the adoption studies to an understanding of the phenomenology and etiology of borderline schizophrenias. In: *Borderline Personality Disorders: The Concept, the Syndrome, the Patient*, ed. P. Hartocollis. New York: International Universities Press.

Winnicott, D. (1969), The use of an object. *Internat. J. Psycho-Anal.*, 50:711–716.

Treatment of Children, Adolescents, and Families

8

The Analyst Versus the "Gate-Keeper": Psychodynamic Treatment of Children

Thomas F. Barrett, Ph.D.

There is little disagreement among mental health practitioners that the past decade has been a period of frustration and confusion resulting from encounters with the ever increasing and constantly changing cadre of health maintenance organizations (HMOs) and managed care firms. This has been especially true in the experience of psychoanalytically oriented psychotherapists and analysts who, by virtue of their training and experience, can appreciate the value of intensive, long-term psychotherapy or psychoanalysis. All too often, the recommendation for such treatment, following the completion of a careful and thorough evaluation, founders on the cursory rejection by an insurance company's gatekeeper whose preapproval looms as a foreboding prerequisite.

This process would not be nearly so frustrating if it occurred in the context of a system of peer review. Unfortunately, however, this is not the case. When an intensive psychotherapy or psychoanalytic treatment plan is presented to and rejected by a third-party payer it is not possible to request that an analyst review the material and reconsider the rejection. Managed care firms and HMOs typically do not have psychoanalysts as consultants on their staffs. At best, and sometimes with reluctance, a gatekeeper might consent to asking for a review by a psychiatrist serving as a consultant to the company. This may result in a reversal of the rejection or, as more often occurs, a modification that allows for a brief period of intensive intervention. I would argue that this is still not a process of peer review and, instead, constitutes a situation wherein an insurance company with no direct access to the patient in need of treatment determines and dictates the course of clinical care.

Another source of frustration that must often be experienced by practitioners occurs when treatment that has long been underway and supported by a patient's insurance company, suddenly becomes threatened and compromised when that carrier is replaced by a different company or managed care plan. The previously completed review and approval process is suddenly abandoned as no longer acceptable and the process must begin again. If, as often occurs, there has been sufficient improvement in the patient as a result of the treatment that has been underway, the apparent symptoms at the time of this second review process are determined not to be of a sufficiently severe quality to warrant such intensive intervention. This kind of thinking, of course, fails entirely to take into account the need to complete a working through process to enable the therapeutic gains to become solidified and autonomous.

Since 1990 I have served as the Director of the Cleveland Center for Research in Child Development. For more than twenty-five years our facility has made five times per week psychoanalytic treatment available to children in need of such treatment, regardless of their ability to pay. Primarily we have been able to do this work because the child analysts working in our clinic have all done so part-time, carrying cases there for a rate of reimbursement that is less than one-third of what they otherwise earn in their private practices. We have also been fortunate to have the support of a devoted Board of Trustees that has worked hard to establish an endowment fund to provide additional financial support for our efforts.

Nevertheless, we do remain dependent upon whatever third-party reimbursement we are able to procure. Typically this has been limited to the minimal amount of coverage available for such treatments through a family's health insurance plan.

Increasingly, my work as Director has required me to communicate with the managed care companies who have assumed responsibility for determining whether or not psychiatric benefits will be paid. I do feel that there has been some improvement, over time, in the extent to which they have responded with an appreciation of what we are trying to accomplish. It still often occurs though that our arduous attempts to explain and justify our work are not understood, and at times, not even respected.

In this article I would like to briefly describe two such experiences to illustrate something of the frustration but also something of what can sometimes be achieved through such efforts.

The first example is of a child who entered analysis in our clinic following enrollment and a period of treatment in the therapeutic nursery school with which we are affiliated, the Hanna Perkins School. All of the children at Hanna Perkins are assigned a child analyst/therapist who meets on a weekly basis with their parents. The model is one of "treatment via the parent" resulting from a team approach wherein the analyst, parents, and classroom teachers all share observations and discuss how the child might best be helped. During the weekly sessions with the parents the therapist might offer developmental guidance, might discuss environmental influences that might be amended or altered, and might offer suggestions of issues that might be discussed with the child by his parents. The school setting provides the opportunity for an extended period of close and careful evaluation so that, should a recommendation for analysis be forthcoming, it is based on an extensive preliminary period of consideration.

When Mary (the name is fictitious) came to our school, she was 4¹/₂ years old. She had virtually no language and spent most of her day rocking back and forth from foot to foot, drooling and making unusual facial expressions. At times she would erupt into episodes of screaming that could literally last for hours and be heard throughout the building. Her gait was so unusual that a pediatric consultant had recommended an evaluation for cerebral palsy. In her previous nursery school she had bitten other children, and at home she had become so fearful and phobic she would not leave her house without her parents, and would especially not go into her yard unattended. During her tenure in the school it quickly became evident that a more extensive, child analytic intervention would be required.

A therapist began to meet with Mary in five times a week psychoanalysis, patiently listening and trying to understand. Soon, Mary began to talk but her verbalizations consisted of repetitions of television commercials. Gradually, the therapist could come to recognize and appreciate how these commercials always revolved around thoughts of food or things to be eaten or put into a mouth. Eventually, Mary was able to verbalize how she had been molested orally in the bushes beside her yard by a neighborhood assailant. She had been unable to tell her parents because it had occurred when Mary was still at an age when she did not have sufficient language. As a result of this trauma, she had become the regressed and overwhelmed girl who had entered the school.

Mary remained in the school for two years in the Nursery and one year in Kindergarten. Her analysis began at the end of her first year in the Nursery and the analytic work continued through third grade. At the start of her second grade year Mary's father's company switched insurance providers. During the first part of the work Mary's analysis had been supported to the limits of the policy benefits ($2500 per year). In addition, the parents paid what they could afford, and the remainder of the fee was made up via a scholarship.

From the outset, the managed care firm that assumed third-party reimbursement responsibility was skeptical about the need for such intensive intervention. The analyst carefully and patiently responded to all of their inquiries, providing extensive documentation about presenting symptomatology, and what by then had become significant progress made during the course of the analysis.

In this instance the gatekeeper was a nurse who elected to focus on a small part of the report that eluded to a period during which Mary evidenced ticlike symptoms. The analyst explained how each of these disappeared through the analysis as they were gradually understood as partial bodily responses to or reenactments of what had occurred during the actual traumatic fellatio experience.

Despite this evidence, the nurse insisted that the insurance company would only consider continuing to support the analysis if the family and the analyst consented to having the child evaluated by a pediatric neurologist (someone completely unknown to the child and the family). The stated objective was to rule out Tourette's Syndrome. The family balked at this intrusion, as did the analyst. The family's pediatrician issued a letter clarifying that, in his opinion, there was no need for such an evaluation and no evidence of Tourette's. Regardless, the managed care firm elected to discontinue all support of the analysis, refused any opportunity for appeal, and even refused to allow further review by an independent consultant.

Mary's analysis continued for two more years. While this total, five-year duration may seem to some to be excessive, it is important to appreciate how completely overwhelmed and devastated this young girl's personality was by the trauma she had endured before the age of 3. Furthermore, it is worth considering that when such traumatized children go untreated at such an early age, and when their pathological personalities have an opportunity to crystalize, they typically become candidates for life-long intervention or treatment efforts. These interventions can cost hundreds of thousands of dollars over the course of a lifetime, and such children are never able to become productive, working, contributing citizens.

The happy ending to Mary's story is that she is now well into middle school, functions as an honor roll student, and reads at a level more than two years beyond her grade level. She enjoys many appropriate friendships and participates in a variety of clubs and sports.

With another child, Gerald (again, not his actual name), our experience with managed care was, at the outset, challenging and difficult but there was a more positive ending. Like Mary, Gerald had first been referred to the Hanna Perkins School. He was an awkward youth who was essentially unable to participate in relationships, and his interactions with others were limited to emitting nonsense language and animal sounds that had no apparent rational basis. He spent much of his time talking to himself in an animated, agitated, and indecipherable way and moved about the room in a jerky, bizarre fashion. There is little question that during another era he might have been diagnosed as "psychotic," "childhood schizophrenic," or "autistic." In compliance with DSM-III-R nomenclature, we had diagnosed him as evidencing signs of an "atypical pervasive developmental disorder" (APA, 1987). Like Mary, it quickly became evident that Gerald would need more extensive, in-depth treatment, and following the above mentioned evaluation process in the school a decision was made to enter Gerald into an analysis.

When the claim went to the insurance company I received a call from the gatekeeper who specifically wanted to question the diagnosis and ask if it really was the diagnosis I had intended. When I said it was he said, "Well, we can't pay for that." When I asked why not, he said, "That diagnosis is not treatable." I said, "I beg your pardon?" And he said, "You can't use any therapy in such cases. That diagnosis is only eligible for medication."

Having, by then, weathered other similar encounters, I responded calmly by explaining that I could understand that he might have had that impression. I described for him, however, how, since the early 1950s, analysts at our center had been working with such severely disturbed children in our therapeutic school and in analysis with some reasonable success. I went on to explain that some of our therapists had published professional articles (E. Furman, 1956, 1988; R. Furman and Katan, 1969) about such work, and I respectfully asked to be able to speak with the HMO's psychiatric consultant. This was allowed, and it was agreed that I could send a more extensive write-up about the case in question as well as copies of the above mentioned articles.

The favorable outcome was that the psychiatrist concurred with the treatment planned and agreed that the managed care company would pay to support the treatment, to the limited extent allowed by the policy ($1,000 per year). The experience helped me realize how important it is to try and gain access to someone other than a gatekeeper in situations where there are unusual or extenuating circumstances. This is perhaps almost always the case when a determination has been made that a child or any person is in need of intensive, long-term psychodynamic or psychoanalytic intervention. While the case examples in this article involve treatment of children, therapists working with adults encounter similar difficulties and might anticipate the need to respond to insurance carriers in like fashion.

It perhaps goes without saying that interference in the treatment process on the part of an insurance company or managed care firm constitutes a parameter that cannot help but influence both transference and countertransference issues. It is the kind of intrusion into the therapy process that is anathema to the ideal. Short of refusing to accept patients with insurance coverage, however, which some therapists do, it becomes necessary to deal with these kinds of intrusions, ultimately, in the context of the therapy.

With adults, courses of resistance might be explored, and there may evolve an opportunity to consider what can feel like a repetition of similar forms of intrusion or interference from earlier or childhood situations.

In work with children, the issues are often more centered in the analyst's or therapist's interactions with the parents. In particular, any ambivalence about the therapy process, felt by the parents, may be expressed or acted out via concerns or issues revolving around the insurance company's willingness to pay or their opinion regarding the need for or efficacy of the therapy.

Countertransference factors must also be monitored. Burdened by frustrations incumbent upon dealing with insurance companies or managed care firms, a therapist will need to be aware of the extent to which these frustrations influence his feelings about the patient and the course of the work.

As I stated at the outset, the process of interacting with a representative from an HMO or a managed care firm can be an exasperating one. I suspect, however, and I think many would agree, that the process of insurance company oversight of clinical work is not going to go away. It has been my impression that the situation has improved, somewhat, over time, and this is perhaps the joint result of clinicians becoming more amenable and patient with the process while, at the same time, gatekeepers and insurance adjustors have become more knowledgeable, appreciative, and perhaps even respectful of some of the long-term benefits that can be realized by intensive, psychoanalytically oriented therapy. I suspect that it is important that this educational process continue with clinicians remaining steadfastly committed to maintaining such long-term, intensive treatment efforts when they seem indicated, despite whatever obstacles might be put in the way and even if it means having to carry more low fee cases. A possible benefit is that, as successful outcomes from those cases can be compiled, this becomes an additional point of reference that can be used in illustrating the effectiveness and appropriateness of such treatment efforts.

References

American Psychiatric Association (1987), *Diagnostic and Statistical Manual of Mental Disorders*, 3rd ed. rev. (DSM-III-R). Washington, DC: American Psychiatric Press.

Furman, E. (1956), An ego disturbance in a young child. *The Psychoanalytic Study of the Child*, 11:312–335. New York: International Universities Press.

_____ (1988), L'Emperiene due travail avec des enfants atypiques. (Experiences in working with atypical children). *J. Psychoanalyse de l'Enfant*, 5:14–32.

Furman, R., & Katan, A., Eds. (1969), *The Therapeutic Nursery School*. New York: International Universities Press.

9

A Holding Environment for Children in the Era of Managed Care

Joshua Williams, Ph.D.

Psychodynamic Treatment in the Hospital Setting

East Tennessee Children's Hospital Integrated Psychiatric Services (CHIPS) is ten years old. It offers adult education, multidisciplinary diagnostic evaluations, and emergency assessment. CHIPS treats latency aged children and young adolescents in both an inpatient and partial hospitalization program. The medical hospital location is optimal in that it allows clinicians to treat children's emotional and developmental problems, armed with a wider range of medical and psychological interventions and assessment technologies than might be found in the more familiar free-standing psychiatric facilities.

Inpatient treatment is a highly assertive therapeutic and diagnostic intervention used to enter the patient's object relations field: the internal world. Each activity within the milieu has a specific therapeutic design. Stringent environmental controls, applied over time, make it possible for patients to integrate higher order defenses, to explore

165

alternative relationships, and to seek adaptive modes for the expression of affect. The vigorous control of interpersonal and physical events within the treatment unit is an extension of Winnicott's holding environment (Winnicott, 1960). Here, the holding environment as a metaphor suggests not only safety from external peril, but also protection from dangers within. "For the holding implies a restraint, a capacity to hold the child having a temper tantrum so that his aggressive impulses do not prove destructive to either himself or the caretakers" (Modell, 1976).

The advent and evolution of managed care have dramatically affected the nature of treatment in the CHIPS program. In 1985 the average length of stay for youngsters at CHIPS was sixty to ninety days. A ninety-day admission was an acute or short-term treatment by 1985 standards of care. Ninety days allowed for vigorous treatment efforts in the confrontation and remediation of the children's globally maladaptive behaviors. For many children, the sheer novelty of the setting and isolation from exacerbating home circumstances contributed to three- and four-week "honeymoon" periods of quiescent behavior. After a period of settling-in, most children would begin to act out. The patient's oppositional responses to basic behavioral constraints demonstrated an engagement in the therapeutic process. Using standard behavioral interventions (e.g., time out, loss of privileges) the clinical team helped patients to contain aggressive and unreflected impulses and to discover more adaptive modes for expressing underlying conflict and their associated affects.

During a ninety-day admission, therapeutic relationships would develop between therapists and patients, and also among patients. Transferential sibling relationships would emerge, permitting therapeutic interpretation and modification. On occasion, parents, acting out their resistance to treatment and change, would precipitously remove their child from the program against the advice of the treatment team. This event was traumatic to the discharged child, the staff, and the children remaining behind. Patients would resonate to the issue of abandonment and the loss of security in the holding environment; the place that previously held great promise was now less powerful, secure, and less able to meet the child's needs. The patient's premature discharge provided powerful material for the exploration of traumatic themes in expressive therapies (group, art, music therapies, and individual psychotherapy) by the remaining patients. With the passage of time, patients would be able to process the event within a therapeutic context and gain from the experience.

It is the view of most practitioners that the family is the wellspring of character pathology in children. The physical separation caused by an inpatient admission creates a coerced physical individuation between the child and those objects that have repetitively, and often unwittingly, reenacted intrapsychic traumas. Through the compression of treatment time within the therapeutic milieu, characterological acting out emerges readily. Nonpunitive, nonjudgmental, and constant hospital staff members quickly evolve as transference objects. Patients are able to repeat dysfunctional familial interactions for reconstructive treatment.

During a ninety-day hospital admission, parents participated in dynamic group psychotherapy. With sufficient time therapeutic groups gain cohesiveness, and character pathologies emerge. Characterological parental acting out is also part of the therapeutic process. Through the establishment of therapeutic alliances, parent–child and parental relationships open themselves to interpretation, insight, and change. Parental investment in the overall program also serves to deepen the child's idealized transference and the child's view of the program as trustworthy.

Time is a critical factor in the fostering of both working and therapeutic relationships within the holding environment. Time is necessary to allow patients to gain better impulse control and negotiate conflict and depression.

Internal issues and dynamics emerge with greater speed and intensity than in an outpatient setting. This is the result of the assertive ego support provided by therapeutic structure. Immediate, predictable, and benign behavioral consequences directly challenge maladaptive defense mechanisms. Patients come into more immediate confrontations with their underlying conflicts. The inpatient structure shortens the time required for critical events to emerge within the patient's psychodynamic treatment.

Transferential expressions are far more likely to appear when the milieu therapists (i.e., "front-line" staff) take on parental roles. The studied neutrality and nurturing posture of the hospital staff raise issues of object constancy, abandonment, deprivation, and narcissistic entitlement in patients.

Abandonment is a central concern of hospital patients. Consequently, a focus of early treatment includes the patient's eventual discharge and departure from the hospital. The seemingly fleeting nature of a ninety-day admission brings into focus the issue of object constancy and the need to facilitate the development of evocative memory. The mechanics and associated affects of arrival, departure, and rituals for loss directly address these concerns. This component of a patient's treatment underscores the need for deliberate planning and attention to discharge and termination.

Managed Care and Hospital Practice

The effort of managed care organizations to arrest the flow of capital toward health *care* has cast a wide net. Caught in this net are all forms of psychological practice linked to insurance reimbursement. The language of business does not readily lend itself to the dialects of affect, cognition, and motivation. Affect, cognition, and motivation are at times less than tangible and likewise do not readily correlate to concrete cost and effect. Thus the culture of business and the identified culture of professional psychology have skirmished and ultimately found themselves in full conflict.

In the mid-1980s hospital-based clinicians experienced utilization review and heard the term *medical necessity* applied to treatment formulations. In auditing psychological care, case reviewers express a strong preference for quantifiable symptom-based behaviors as opposed to descriptive psychodynamic formulations of behavioral and defensive constellations. The reviewer tends to focus on primary or presenting complaints that can often be resolved by short-term, behaviorally focused interventions. As a business tool, utilization review conflates fiscal concern with the consideration of patient need. Lost in the exchange is the vital consideration of etiology and of efforts to enact lasting change. The clinician has lost authority over the patient's treatment. Clinicians now find their patients' resistance to change and treatment joined in a perverse alliance with auditors of care who maintain a narrow symptom-based focus (Williams and Wahler, 1994).

Reviewing agencies often keep as proprietary information the criteria for establishing the length of a patient's stay (U.S. General Accounting Office, 1993, p. 31; Shueman, Troy, and Mayhugh, 1994). Practitioners working in hospital settings report instances of denied benefits, interrupted treatment, and treatment recommendations that contradict psychodynamic and developmental considerations. It is not uncommon for managed care reviewers to insist that drugs be used as a first line of treatment intervention. The benefit of psychotherapy receives little regard. Thus, the impact of managed care upon the inpatient holding environment has been profound.

Two aspects of managed care appear to work most powerfully upon the treatment of children in the inpatient setting: the clinician's loss of control over length of stay and the supplanting of clinical judgment by fiscal considerations. For patients, families, hospital staff, and clinicians, the result may be a barrier to achieving a successful outcome to treatment—a very costly result for the individual and society.

EFFECT UPON THE PATIENT

The present length of stay in most inpatient treatment programs for children ranges between seven and twenty-eight days. The short length of stay leaves children with insufficient time to pass beyond a settling in or honeymoon following admission. Children who are not clearly out of control, threatening to themselves or others, are apt to lose insurance coverage for their continued inpatient treatment. A subtle yet discernible pressure exists for patients to misbehave to justify continued admission.

Interpersonal bonding among patients and others within the therapeutic milieu is thwarted by truncated admissions. Opportunities to explore the limits of object constancy, trust, and reality itself are also hindered.

Patient turnover destroys cohesiveness and continuity in group therapy. Patients have inadequate time for the expression and therapeutic redress of internal dynamics. Recidivism becomes more of a problem as the length of stay in the hospital is reduced. Short admissions may offer patients a brief respite from the circumstances that have reinforced their maladaptive coping mechanisms; however, premature return to the circumstances that prompted their admission may induce greater and more aggressive expressions of disappointment and rage.

EFFECT UPON THE FAMILY

Through the child, as well as in their own right, the patient's parents and families experience the impact of managed care. The shortened length of stay severely limits opportunities for therapeutic relationships to develop, particularly in the group setting. Analytic group therapy becomes a futile endeavor. Group membership is constantly shifting. Weekly instruction on fundamental group conventions consumes valuable treatment time.

Parents sense that their involvement in the program may be fleeting, so they seek direct instructions instead of interpersonal or intrapsychic exploration. A withholding culture masks the parent's internal conflicts. As a result, maladaptive coping skills remain undetected and outside clinical intervention. Paradoxically, group and milieu events remain low key and civil, while internal and intrafamily conflicts erupt.

EFFECT UPON THE STAFF

Managed care exacts a toll from the nurses, aides, and ancillary therapists on the hospital unit. They choose to work in the inpatient setting because they want to know and help children. With the succession of interrupted relationships, staff begin to unconsciously titrate their availability and willingness to relate to patients. Veteran staff remember the time of longer admissions and begin to miss their sense of purpose and identity. Any prior regard for clinical leadership changes to one of cynicism and helplessness.

Staff begin to lose faith that clinical acumen is meaningful in the world beyond the hospital. Psychoanalytic formulations, while interesting, become irrelevant to their work. Curiosity and desire to learn fall victim to disappointment and emotional fatigue. Manifest pathology, that has in the past justified a longer length of stay, can no longer shield their charges or themselves from the incursion of managed care. They experience the locus of control for treatment as external, unpredictable, intangible, and punitive. Less experienced staff may fail to understand the developmental perspective of psychopathology in children and may become more focused on purely behavioral considerations. Supervisors who previously could devote time for training and staff consultation find their time and energy sapped by litigious reviews and paperwork.

The staff as a whole loses the assurance that there is a plan, a method, or a reason for their actions with patients. As they attempt to maintain the overall structure of the therapeutic milieu, the constant disappointments, and worry for the well-being of their patients, subvert staff confidence that the program is complete, coherent, and hopeful.

EFFECT UPON THE CLINICIAN

The practitioner's frustration and desperation are well articulated in professional journals and publications. The clinician's loss of time with his or her patient within the hospital impedes the treatment of psychopathology. Clinicians accustomed to working in a less restrictive frame find few recognizable points of reference. Some clinicians resort to highly directive forms of treatment with little or no open inquiry into patient dynamics. Others use what little time they have to try to convey their neutrality to their patient. Now, the therapist's goal is to rapidly forge a working relationship to build upon in the outpatient setting. Practitioners express little hope of effecting characterological reorganization within their patients. The effort has shifted toward hasty repair in lieu of lasting change.

There are legal ramifications for the clinician as well. Regardless of whether a hospital-based treatment team supports the discharge recommended by an insurance company, both the team and the hospital share liability with the insurance company for any untoward results of discharge. Clinicians, working within the ethical code of their discipline, may elect to continue treatment despite the threatened withdrawal of funding. In some cases, clinicians must continue treatment in spite of contracts that allow a managed care organization to remove them from their provider panel. These conditions create endogenous conflicts among treatment teams, the individual clinicians comprising these treatment teams, and the institutional interest in avoiding noncompensated services. Most managed care contracts indemnify patients from costs exceeding their contracted co-payments. Similarly, contracts indemnify managed care organizations from costs for services rendered beyond those authorized through their review process. When clinicians prescribe continued hospitalization in defiance of the utilization review edict, clinicians commit their institution to providing these services without reimbursement. This situation in turn creates pressure, even within the most progressive not-for-profit facilities, to limit the scope of treatment and length of stay. The therapist is often a nominal factor in the decision-making process within the hospital.

Psychoanalytic/psychodynamic treatment for severe character pathology in hospitalized children is a highly effective and worthwhile endeavor. However, the erosion of clinical control over critical aspects of care directly threatens the use of traditional psychoanalytic methods. The trend that precludes the use of analytic modes of assessment and treatment in the inpatient setting is growing and may become calcified in business-directed health reform.

A MEDIATING VIEW

The holding environment of years past—the deliberate, nurturing setting of ego coverage and developmental support—will be no more. However, there are ways in which analytically oriented programs can create responsive or dynamic holding environments despite the challenges posed by this state of affairs. Treatment programs can work to create a flexible and responsive milieu: a *fostering environment.*

A fostering environment is one in which strategic planning for patient care incorporates actions designed to maintain positive object seeking in patients. The goal is to foster the possibility of continued treatment for each patient: to inculcate a psychological work ethic within the patient, the family, and community. With this response the therapeutic milieu, however threatened, can provide direction, structure, and hope for patients and staff alike. These suggestions are reasoned approaches to the harsh buffeting of psychoanalytically informed and guided inpatient treatment at the hands of managed care.

The creation of a fostering environment demands an altered focus, a different emphasis in each component of the inpatient program. Shorter admissions to inpatient facilities slash the amount of therapeutic control (i.e., ego support) that the patient can receive. At most, the program exerts influence let alone control. Enhanced structure and frequency will maximize the therapeutic outcome of each activity. Now, the goal is to help the patient discover holding environments outside the hospital.

Group therapy should be conducted no less than five times per week. Morning and evening sessions would double the number of group sessions. A ritualized and regular review of group conventions will help to orient newcomers.

More frequent individual therapy sessions are also highly beneficial. Here therapists should work to address directly the unconscious dynamic processes as they unfold within the milieu. It is natural for emotionally needy children to forge emotional bonds with the psychiatric treatment unit. Because this nurturing environment will be so short-lived, the therapist must anticipate the possible recapitulation of prior experiences of neglect, abandonment, and rejection.

Transitional contacts must be built into the treatment planning process. Patients must be allowed to withdraw from hospital-based treatment incrementally. For example, a patient nearing the end of an admission in the partial hospitalization program may attend her own school during school hours and attend therapeutic activities in the hospital after school. Or patients may alternate daily attendance in school and the hospital. Other patients may benefit from attendance in the hospital based school with after-school hours spent in a community or home-based activity. Enrollment in partial hospitalization for a five-day week does not suffice. A six- or seven-day partial hospitalization program is far more potent. With each additional day there is more opportunity to involve families in classes and therapeutic activities.

Treatment staff must quickly explore the patient's demographics to ascertain community-based facilitating objects and environments. Thorough social histories at the time of admission, as well as a full knowledge of community resources are essential.

The program must seize upon each event of the inpatient's daily life and explore ways to make them therapeutic. Events such as waking up, personal grooming, cooking, eating, going to school, playing, and working provide opportunities for the imposition of therapeutic predictability, constancy, and routine, in stark contrast to the inner chaos each child brings to the hospital.

Diagnosis is critical in the fostering environment. Comprehensive psychological testing and behavioral observation

are vital in anticipating postdischarge environmental shifts
such as changes in parents, parenting style, and school place-
ment. Accurate diagnostic work helps to structure strategi-
cally focused interventions. Clear diagnostic formulation
also assists the program in representing itself to reviewers
and ancillary treatment programs.

Documentation takes on expanded meaning in the effort to maximize the impact of the hospital based program.
Documentation will validate the clinical rationale for continued inpatient and subsequent outpatient treatment. Symptoms that are undocumented do not exist. Treatment that
is undocumented did not happen. Protecting the confidentiality of the treatment is becoming increasingly problematic.
To satisfy the needs of utilization reviewers, notes must include specific behavioral observations and psychodynamic
formulations. Reviewing agencies will discount notes mired
in psychoanalytic minutiae in favor of their own price index.

There must be great care to provide front-line staff with
ongoing education and support. Frequent meetings, consultation, and supervision for those individuals in the therapeutic milieu will help stave off staff disillusionment and
depletion. Staff members deserve frequent reminders that
they serve as positive introjects for patients. Both inspiration
and consolation come from knowing that they are planting
seeds for developmentally appropriate growth. Staff may
need frequent reminders that sowing these seeds is a critical
aspect of their work.

The clinician's loss of control over length of admission
and clinical interventions has compromised the nature of
treatment and treatment planning. From here on, decisions
about hospitalized patients must take into account the program's limitations. Careful treatment planning is essential
to create a fostering environment. Within the fostering environment patients will develop an intrapsychic awareness of
object possibility. The hope is that they will then seek more

benign parenting figures and other help-providers in their lives.

With these therapeutic maneuvers the unit will survive—a place of constancy that meets dependency needs on an emergent and transient basis. For the patient the experience is both palliative and frustrating. It is the palliative aspect of the experience that will foster constructive object seeking in the patient's post discharge life.

THE HOSPITAL

Not all treatment programs are fortunate enough to exist in well-informed, well-funded, and supportive hospitals. Hospitals do have fiscal realities, and treatment programs must deal with these. The medical community, as a business community, has maintained an uneasy alliance with mental health programs for many years. Psychopathology is not as tangible as physical complaints. A trauma unit may lose money, but this does not negate its necessity. Medical facilities contemplating flattened revenue may see their mental health services as expendable. They may look at the inpatient program, with its decreased patient admissions, shortened length of stay, and lowered reimbursement, as a costly white elephant. It behooves clinicians to educate hospital administrators as to the benefits of inpatient care. Clinicians must assist the policy makers and management in maintaining inpatient psychological care as a part of the hospital's corporate identity.

The hospital itself serves as an institutional holding environment. It is the safekeeping within the hospital that allows the unit to continue its struggle with the internal emotional events and external fiscal constraints. It warrants our full attention. It is imperative that analytically informed clinicians obtain hospital admitting privileges and recognition as bona fide health care providers. Only through the clinician's full participation in hospital governance systems will analytically guided care and treatment find representation.

The tempestuous world of fiscal management has engulfed the field of psychoanalytic treatment with a vengeance. How can analytic inquiry, guided by the patient's internal needs, conflicts, and capacities, be maintained within this context? The answer may be that it cannot; to yield to these management forces may defy the basic canons of analytic practice and theory.

Analytically oriented practitioners must not rest with less than optimal circumstances. It is necessary for clinicians to attend to the institutional environment in which their treatment programs exist. To maintain psychoanalytic inquiry and inpatient treatment as part of a medical center's identity requires concrete educational efforts. The political considerations that exert influence upon mental health practice should also not escape the practitioner's attention.

Psychologists should look to themselves as progenitors of the analytic field of inquiry in all possible treatment venues. No avenue of analytic inquiry is expendable. There will always be individuals with basic ego injuries and developmental arrests that require intensive psychotherapeutic attention and ancillary environmental control. Thus, there is a continuing need for inpatient treatment programs, just as there is for medical trauma units. The support of analytic practitioners for inpatient venues will go a long way to reviving the sanctity of hospital-based analytic treatment programs.

References

Modell, A. H. (1976), "The holding environment" and the therapeutic action of psychoanalysis. *J. Amer. Psychoanal. Assn.*, 24:285–308.

Shueman, S. A., Troy, W. G., & Mayhugh, S. L. (1994), Some questions and answers about managed behavioral health care. *Register Report: The Newsletter for Health Service Providers in Psychology*, 20:1–28. Washington, DC: Council for the National Register.

U.S. General Accounting Office (1993), Managed health care: Effect on employers' costs difficult to measure. *Report to the Chairman, Subcommittee on Health, Committee on Ways and Means, House of Representatives.* Washington, DC: GAO/HRD-94-3.

Williams, J., & Wahler, R. (1994), The perverse triangle comprising parents, providers and health care managers: Can anybody help this child? (In progress.)

Winnicott, D. W. (1960), The theory of the parent–infant relationship. *Internat. J. Psycho-Anal.*, 41:585–595.

10

The Blind Oppressing the Recalcitrant: Psychoanalysis, Managed Care, and Family Systems

Gerald Stechler, Ph.D.

Three doctors have died and are waiting at the pearly gates to enter heaven. The first is asked what he did on earth, and replies that he was an oncologist and was able to help many cancer patients. The archangel says, "Fine, you may come into heaven." The second is asked the same question, and replies that she was a cardiologist and helped many patients with heart disease. "Fine, please come into heaven." In response to the same question, the third replies that he left clinical practice and worked for a managed care company evaluating requests for treatment. The archangel says, "Fine, you may come into heaven, for three days."

Managed care, as we now experience it from the vantage point of psychoanalytic psychotherapy, is an onerous, objectionable system. But we would be wrong to isolate it as the source of our problems. It is but one manifestation of much larger market issues that are sweeping the country's health care system. These market forces are transforming health care in ways that are difficult to predict, much less control in any direct manner. The current system is defective because it is too expensive, and because far too many people either lack coverage or are in danger of losing it. Managed care is one response to the problem of expense, focused on the issue of overutilization of benefits. The idea is that without managed care, no one in the health system loop (patient, payer, or practitioner) is adequately concerned with costs or efficiency. Of course, the managed care system itself works by taking money away from practitioners and hospitals, while feeding its own coffers. It is very difficult to calculate the overall value of this system, how much it costs to run, how it impacts on quality of care, and how much it reduces health care expenditures. My own personal experience with managed care is highly negative. Some actions strike me as deceptive, while others are burlesques of bureaucratic bungling. One deception occurred when I applied to a system that had never previously been in my state of Massachusetts. It was taking over the management responsibility for an insurance company that had been insuring four of my patients. I wanted to be able to provide continuing therapy for these people, so I applied to be one of their providers as soon as the announcement of the shift was made. The reply I received a couple of months later was a printed form letter stating that they had no need of further providers in my area. I called to say that their response made no sense since they had just opened in this area. I was told that my application would be reconsidered, and a few weeks later received another copy of the same letter. Whatever their reasons for rejecting me, it could not have been the one they stated. Most of the psychologists and psychiatrists I know have been rejected from all of the managed care plans, and the few who have been accepted have been accepted by many plans. While I don't have any hard data to back up my impression, it appears that the most experienced therapists are the least likely to be accepted.

If we imagine the system without any insurance at all, as it was in the old days, we may have a better appreciation of the task that is before us as therapists. Let us say that I am a very knowledgeable patient, paying out of pocket for my own psychotherapy. What considerations will be uppermost in my mind? Roughly speaking it will be a complex multivariate function called *value*, an entity made up of many components. What is my state of need? What are my resources (i.e., what will I have to sacrifice to get this treatment)? Will the treatment I seek best address my needs? Is it the cheapest way of getting the help I need? What are the trade-offs between cost and effectiveness? If we can satisfy a hypothetical individual client that good value will be received, then we should have demand for our services. It is likely that under any health care delivery system there will always be a demand for psychotherapy by people willing and able to pay out of pocket. It will, of course, be a small fraction of those who would come if they had substantial insurance coverage.

The addition of the insurance policy into the loop does not alter the salience of these questions of value. It does, however, alter another important variable, the allocation of resources in a situation in which the demand for services exceeds the available resources. As soon as resources are pooled, the question becomes how to distribute them. In social psychology this is referred to as the problem of the commons. How many cows can each household graze on the town commons without depleting the grass, and how is the equitable distribution of the resource managed? The premium cost for coverage of outpatient psychotherapy is kept within reasonable limits by the fact that only a small percentage of the policyholders avail themselves of this benefit. If each policyholder feels that there would be a personal gain from psychotherapy, and, at the same time, believes that he or she does not have to reckon with the question of cost, there will be overutilization of that resource. In the absence of self-monitoring by client or practitioner, it becomes the task of the insurer or their agent, the managed care company, to ration the benefit.

Thus with the addition of the concept of health insurance, we as therapists have a twofold task. The first part remains the same as it would be in a self-pay system. How do we establish our value? How do we demonstrate our value? How do we increase the value of our services over time, so as to remain competitive with other services? How do we answer the informed consumer who asks us why he or she should choose our form of treatment? If we can give a satisfactory answer to that consumer, then we can give a satisfactory answer to the managed care company regarding the issue of value.

The insurance company tries to address the second question, that of utilization, by requiring a determination of medical necessity, and by husbanding the resources, as, for example, doling out payment approval, hour by hour. Another powerful way in which they attempt to contain costs is by limiting the number of approved providers. This then limits the field from which their subscribers may choose a therapist, and gives the company a chance to select and maintain a small number of providers who will conform to company policy.

We as practitioners are examined, licensed, monitored, reeducated, and held accountable to our professional associations and state licensing boards for meeting professional and ethical standards. Not so these companies who decide how we should practice. They belong to the business world, operate without uniform standards, and fundamentally are accountable only with respect to their profit margins.

A bill now before the Pennsylvania legislature (1994) seeks to regulate the managed care companies by requiring them to ensure that reviewers are qualified, of the same profession as the provider, respectful of patient confidentiality, and obligated to submit a written evaluation to provider and patient. While this may answer some of our complaints, it adds yet another layer of bureaucracy and eats further into the premium dollar.

The public needs to know the costs of this elaborate management apparatus. Some day, soon I hope, the insurance companies and the managed care companies will be called to account for their own inefficiencies, their clogging of the system, and their soaking up of the health care dollar. Estimates I have seen indicate that over one-third of the health care dollar is used for this administrative overhead. It is a sterling example of the new golden rule, "Those with the gold, rule." One of the major reasons that a single payer system, with much lower overhead, is viewed negatively in this country, is that the insurance companies have been able to use their financial and political power to promote that negative view. It did seem that the Clinton plan, and some of the proposed alternatives then circulating in Congress, recognized the problems created by the insurance industry, and sought to remedy them.

Sadly, the affective attitude that seems best to capture the overall picture is one of cynicism. It is very hard to find a player in this game who is not trying to maximize his own gain with little regard to the effect on the entire system. Insurers, practitioners, hospitals, employers, as well as the public, all display the expected excesses of self-interest. Furthermore, they disguise their self-interest through disdain for the other and by the expected projections of stupidity and cupidity. The stakes are very high. Some will become very rich and some will perish. The annual health bill for the country has just passed the $1 trillion mark. A headline in *The New York Times* on March 13, 1994, reads, "Gold Rush

Fever Grips Capital as Health Care Struggle Begins: Everyone Sees a Stake, and It's Usually Money." Nevertheless, this
is the way in which our democratic capitalistic process has
always worked, and perhaps out of this chaotic array some
reasonable problem solving will occur. The debate that is
taking place in public is serving the purpose of educating
all of us. Ultimately the power of that knowledge will overcome the power of any particular group.

While it is not the purpose of this paper to suggest possible variations within a managed care system, I do believe
that with respect to psychotherapy the best insurance plan
would consist of full coverage for the first few hours, with a
moderate (perhaps 20%) copayment for the next fifteen or
so hours, and then a steeper 35 percent copayment for subsequent hours. Some income-related reduction in the copayment would be a very useful adjunct. It could be simply
administered by having the policies for low-income families
written with a reduced copayment clause. One substantial
advantage with the copayment concept is that it places some
responsibility for value assessment and utilization review
back in the patient's hands, where it belongs. For those of
us who believe the dual issue of client autonomy and responsibility is a key aspect of treatment, full insurance coverage
for psychotherapy is not an unmixed blessing.

Another major advantage of such a copayment system
is that it might get the insurance companies out of places
where they do not belong, that is, in the micromanagement
of outpatient psychotherapy. Nowhere is the system more
ludicrous than in the companies' expenditure of substantial
amounts of the premium dollars paid to them by subscribers,
in order to expand their own staff, so as to be able to get us
to expend our own unpaid time trying to justify hour-by-
hour utilization of what may be a $500 annual benefit. One
expert in this field has estimated that a group practice in
psychotherapy, wishing to contract with a managed care

company, should be prepared to spend 30 to 40 percent of gross revenue on the time and office systems that will be necessary to meet the reporting requirements of the company (Harris, 1993). The insurance company pays itself to gather all this information, while we are expected to absorb the expense. It is added to our costs, but not to our charges. If the insurance industry uses up about one-third of the total health budget for their administrative costs, and then covertly forces us to use another third for our administrative costs, there isn't much left for the patient. One is reminded of those fraudulent charities that keep the bulk of the money they collect to feather their own nests and give only a pittance to the legitimate recipients.

Professional Responsibility

It has already been implied that the therapist should share in the overall responsibility of regulating the utilization of resources, even if that may be an unfamiliar role for us. We like to think of ourselves as distinct individuals, each engaged in a personal and unique relationship with each of our patients, and not as elements in some larger system. The paradox of our position is that both statements are true. Our work makes sense and is effective only in the context of a highly personal and unique encounter, and yet, in toto, we influence and are part of much larger systems.

How can we, as practitioners, take on some of the responsibility for value assessment and utilization review? How can we go even further, and seize some of the initiative for the planning and implementation of the health care system? The history of attempts at having professionals monitor their own performance and utilization has not been encouraging. Nor has the public-spirited leadership among health care professionals been notable. The AMA and other professional organizations have had over half a century in which to address the health care delivery system, but through narrow self-interest and a disregard of the public interest, they have become largely disenfranchised. This is a new era, however, and the stark realities of our unemployment, or loss of professional autonomy, could lead to a different process. The chaos and threat that now pervade the scene must be viewed as an opportunity to be proactive and to provide leadership, rather than to adapt to someone else's agenda. Whatever form our concerted efforts may take, they will be effective only if we adhere to certain principles.

1. We must unite with other health professionals, or at least with all other mental health professionals, so that the public, the Congress, and the health care industry know we are united and that we have a unified agenda. Conflict among professional groups defeats all of them. The essence of that agenda should be that mental health is an indispensable component of health, that we have effective methods for restoring mental health, and that the cost of treating dysfunction and mental illness is much less than the cost of not treating them.

2. Our agenda must reflect the needs of the community first, and our own parochial professional interests only secondarily. If we wish to argue that there are many clinical situations in which long-term psychotherapy or psychoanalysis should be the treatment of choice, we must be prepared to do so with clinical examples and with outcome data.

3. We must demonstrate our capacity to be self-regulating, and to be as concerned about costs and effectiveness as any other group. In our own subdiscipline of psychoanalytic psychotherapy, we have the particular obligation of demonstrating that the quality of the outcome justifies the duration of treatment.

4. We must be ready to create and explore new modalities of treatment, ones that are consistent with our basic

understanding of psychodynamics, but which are open with respect to form and structure; for example, short-term models, consultative models, multiperson models, and models which integrate different modalities of treatment.

5. We must tackle some of the most pervasive mental health problems of our time, such as family violence, overt and covert. Throughout our society it affects children and adults, males and females, and leads to intergenerational patterns of profound disturbance. The technical knowledge needed to deal effectively with these complex problems is far from complete, but there is much that is presently available to interested psychoanalysts, and much more that they could help to develop.

6. We must revamp the disease model so that we are not forced into the arbitrary straitjacket of locating pathology within an individual. This will be one step in enhancing our ability to deal directly with systemic problems. Right now we recognize the fundamental truth of systemic disorder, while we remain obliged to use the old-fashioned language of individual symptom configuration to describe these problems in medically acceptable terms.

Psychoanalytic Systemic Approaches

Psychoanalysis gives us a comprehensive, content-rich model of the functioning of the inner being. General systems theory gives us a broad scientific framework within which psychoanalysis can be examined, expanded, and transported to new domains. Psychoanalysis is too powerful a theory to remain limited to a narrow range of techniques. By adopting a systemic approach to psychoanalysis, we can keep the essence of what is important to us, while at the same time become very free about where we go with the theory and practice.

To move from individual to couples or family therapy we must adapt a few principles that are inherent in psychoanalytic theory but have not yet become standards of practice.

1. Triadic relationships are held as a more complex and mature form of social existence than are dyadic relationships. Yet the treatment model is exclusively dyadic. We need not speculate about how psychoanalysis came to limit itself to a dyadic treatment situation (or how for so long the analyst was viewed purely as a transference object, thereby creating a monadic treatment situation, congruent with a one-person psychology). We need to demonstrate that a triadic treatment model is not only possible within psychoanalysis but, in many circumstances, advantageous.

2. Unconscious processes are as valid and as useful in couples and family work as in individual treatment. They may become accessible by an important route in addition to the more familiar routes of fantasy material and transference toward the therapist. That is, the observable, often affect-laden, interactions among family members can reveal the operation of unconscious processes quickly, and with drama and clarity. The double messages, expressing both sides of ambivalent affective states, can be seen from the first moment of treatment. The repressed sides of ambivalent polarities become enacted, so that interpersonal conflicts can be reframed as manifestations of each party's own inner conflicts. Another higher-order concept, namely the shared unconscious of the couple or family, can also be inferred from the material, and employed with great advantage to help the family understand its chronic problems. The unspoken rules which regulate the functioning of each family member become illuminated to the therapist, who may then reflect them directly back to the family. One can imagine how long this might take working with a single individual. The rules governing family relationships are not easily or quickly revealed in the material from one person.

3. The empathic process can be extended to the group, albeit with an interesting and valuable twist. Imagine a couples therapy in which the two spouses are strongly antagonistic toward each other, and the therapist starts with an

empathic connection to one of them. The irritation in the other is likely to be quite obvious, and he or she may even try to break in, out of a feeling of being neglected or treated unfairly. In due time the therapist turns to the second and regards him or her with the same empathic stance accorded to the first. The irritation of the second will change, but the first will now feel astonished and perhaps betrayed. How can the person who appeared to be so caring and approving of me now lavish the same care and approval on my "enemy"? This is another powerful demonstration of the exigencies of triadic relationships, and depending on the psychological maturity of the couple, perhaps the beginning of the assimilation of the metamessage that it is possible to be "on the side of" two conflicting people at the same time, without betraying either. One can sense the liberation that comes along with the experiencing of this paradigm shift. The projections onto the other spouse can become ameliorated when one sees that spouse winning the affirmation of a valued person. The dynamics of the couple may then shift to a competition for first place in the alliance with the therapist, but that developmentally more advanced position may then itself become the field for further exploration of dyadic and triadic dynamics. Along with this, a shift in the organization of the self may be perceived and commented on. Thus the extension of the therapist's empathic stance is not only possible within a triad, but when implemented can result in a whole set of dynamic reconfigurations that are not immediately possible in a dyadic setting. Again, we can work within the familiar principles of psychoanalytic psychodynamics, but raise the application of these principles to a systemic level.

4. Structural change, the sine qua non of psychoanalytic work, is not only achievable through the use of systemic interventions, but is facilitated. Systems theory, with a modern view of structure, does not confuse durability with mutability.

Some patterns that seem very ingrained can be altered fairly rapidly under the right conditions. Sometimes we see a client suddenly feel much better very early in the treatment. When that happens, we are likely to denigrate this quick turn-around with a label such as "flight into health," or "transference cure." As psychoanalysts we predict that it will be transitory, and sure enough we are right, thereby reinforcing our view that structural change must be slow. What if we valued (rather than disparaged) such change, and in fact did everything we could to promote it? What if, when we witnessed such a sudden shift, we set ourselves the task of nourishing and consolidating it, rather than predicting its demise? Systems theory, with its strong biological bias, would predict that newly developed functions are fragile and need support, but not that they are inherently ephemeral. It would also acknowledge that in complex systems many nonlinear, that is, sudden and dramatic, shifts in organization are to be expected. It does not hold to the heavy leaden view of structure that characterizes classical psychoanalysis.

Furthermore, our common sense tells us that changes which become part of a culture are more likely to endure than isolated shifts that run against the current. Thus, if we want a new pattern to persist, that is, become self-sustaining, we need to create a hospitable environment for it. This would imply trying to grapple with as much of the overall system as possible, rather than focusing on a single element or individual within the system, and leaving it to hope and chance that the beneficial changes will suffuse throughout the system (Koman and Stechler, 1985; Stechler, 1990).

The Clinical Process

What are some of the processes by which changes occur with some rapidity in therapy, and what are the processes by which those changes can become self-sustaining? This is a very large and complicated question, and can be touched on here in only the briefest way. At the foundation of all change in psychotherapy is the relationship. This assumption tends to favor a slow process because of the belief that the client–therapist relationship is itself built only slowly and carefully. While this may be true in a general way, we also know that transference is instantaneous, and may even occur prior to and in anticipation of the first meeting. In addition to the power of the transference itself, there are other processes, ones that are more under the control of the therapist, and that can be used to alter immediately the client's perspective of and adherence to the presenting problem. One of these is reframing the presenting problem while at the same time validating the client's beliefs and affective states. This can be very subtle. For example if a client presents a bleak depressing picture of his life, and concludes that things look very dark and hopeless, the therapist can agree and yet change the frame ever so slightly by saying something like, "Yes, things do look very dark and hopeless now." The addition of the word *now*, while not invalidating anything the client has said, can transform the perspective from an eternity to a moment in time. Another shift in perspective may result from the therapist suggesting a paradoxical intervention to the client. For example, in a similar presentation, the client may enumerate all of the failures and losses in his life as the basis for his depression. The therapist, instead of trying to reassure the man that there are some bright spots, a technique which we all know to be the unempathic, misguided, counterproductive stance often taken by family members, friends, and ill-trained therapists, might say, "It's amazing that you are not more depressed than you seem to be, given all the terrible things that have happened to you." This can help the person both to feel understood and, by reversing the field, to have him become the one to see the bright side. The reason that the dynamic is so open and susceptible to reversals of direction in the twinkling of an eye, is not foreign to psychoanalysis, but is rather based on one of the foundation stones laid by Freud, namely, the propositions concerning ambivalence. Strongly held positions may appear to be monolithic, but we know that they are but the manifest side of an affective polarity, the other side of which may live in repression. As such, they are open to sudden and dramatic shifts if there is a good way of addressing the repressed side, while not invalidating the manifest side.

A brief case vignette may help to illustrate this point. On the recommendation of his preschool teachers, a bright, healthy looking 5-year-old boy was brought to see me by his mother. The teachers said that he was so painfully shy that he never asserted himself in class, never spoke up, and never asked for help. The other children either ignored him or scapegoated him. When they were asked to form a line, the children invariably shunted him to the rear. As his mother was presenting this story to me, and embellishing it with a litany of her own complaints, poor Joey was sinking lower and lower into the chair. It was as if each statement by his mother was a hammer blow that was driving him deeper and deeper into a hole. When she finally subsided after about twenty minutes, I did not respond to her, but rather turned to the boy and said, "Joey, it's all right to be shy, as long as you get what you want." At first he looked at me with a rather puzzled expression because of the inherent contradiction within my statement. But then, something clicked in his mind, and he started to sit up straight, puff out his chest, and smile broadly, almost triumphantly, at me. We can only speculate about what might have happened in that brief instant, but whatever it was, there was a total reversal of affective state. We spent the remainder of that first session virtually ignoring the mother, while Joey and I talked about things he could do in class to get what he wanted without having to become not shy. In the session he became wonderfully lighthearted as he seemed to grasp the essence of the paradox, which is that it was all right for him to retain his own essential identity, while using me as a coach to learn the specific things he could do in order to assert himself. At the next appointment, some three weeks later, his mother said that the teachers had reported a major shift in Joey's behavior. He was speaking up and asserting himself with the other children. They were astounded at the change but were concerned that it would not last. Joey may have seemed happier at class, but he did not look very happy in my office. I asked him if something was bothering him after his mother had had such good things to say about him. He responded by turning to his mother and launching into a series of complaints about her, about how she did not support him, how she favored his siblings, and how she did not think he could do anything well. She started to get angry and was about to argue with him and shut him down. I told her that I knew it was difficult to listen to this criticism, but it was important that Joey had a chance to say what was on his mind. Could she please just sit and listen to him, which she did. The third and last session was again some three weeks later. The two of them were happy, and were kind and loving toward each other. The behavior in the classroom had continued to improve. We all decided that no further meetings were necessary unless some trouble reappeared.

Are such rapid changes comprehensible within our normal understanding of psychoanalysis? I would maintain that they are, and furthermore, they should become a focus of clinical and theoretical inquiry. In addition to already noted fluidity and transformability of affective states, there is another factor derived from Freud's thinking that facilitates our endeavor. Some of the current thinking about resilience dates back to Freud's idea about active mastery of the passively experienced trauma. In "Beyond the Pleasure Principle" (1920) he noted this mechanism and suggested that it was the most ubiquitous of all psychological mechanisms. His further inquiry, however, was not about how this mechanism worked, but rather how it failed, as exemplified by the repetition compulsion. Nevertheless, we are aware that natural restorative forces exist in human beings and are involved in the therapeutic process. Our task is to learn more about these forces, and how to tune in to them, so that they can become a central element in the therapeutic encounter. We now know that other natural mechanisms, such as seeking of positive ambience, and catalytically making use of affirming experiences, can also serve to support the transformational process. Further exploration is necessary, but clearly we should recognize that just as there are ingrained intrapsychic and systemic forces that are working to hold the dysfunctional patterns in place, there are also intrapsychic and systemic forces that are working in the direction of promoting healthy change. Our job is to understand these forces and to engage the clients and families around them.

There are many clinical situations in which the multiperson setting might be superior for creating and maintaining change. In all cases in which a key presenting problem is about interpersonal conflict with a family member or members, it is wise to think about some variation of couples or family treatment as the most expeditious way of addressing the issue. Even in cases in which conflict with others is not so obvious, as for example when the major complaint is depression or anxiety, it would be well to investigate the systemic aspects of the symptom presentation, and to think about how a systemic intervention could lead to the desired structural change.

One of the clear ways in which a change can be maintained is if it becomes a change for all parties. In that way we avoid the common situation in which one person's growth is sabotaged and eroded by the unwillingness of the other family members to endorse that growth. It is better not to try to swim upstream against the current. This can be stated as a theoretical proposition, namely that the only enduring change is a systemic change. Individual change can lead to systemic change in a couple or family by virtue of the fact that when one part of a system changes, it forces a change throughout the system. This is known as the first law of complex organizations, that is, "You cannot change one thing." But it is very risky to bet on the likelihood that the growth of one party will lead to the growth of the system. We have seen too many examples to the contrary. The reactive stance of the system to the growth of one member may well be a strong conservative push to restore the pretreatment equilibrium.

This was beautifully illustrated in the John Cassavetes film, *Woman Under the Influence* (1974). In that story a married woman, with two young children, slashes her wrists for somewhat obscure reasons. We see only her sense of being taken for granted, and being overwhelmed by family responsibilities. Following the suicide attempt, she is sent to a mental hospital for a number of months (obviously, premanaged care). The pivotal dramatic action takes place after her discharge and return home. She has a budding new sense of herself, but it is delicate, fragile, and uncertain. As she tries to exercise her barely unfolded wings, her husband, parents, and in-laws, all portrayed as benign well-meaning folks, are clearly uneasy with this new persona. Ever so subtly and insidiously they ease her back into her old, familiar, and pathological way of being.

Managed Care Revisited

If we adopt a psychoanalytic systems perspective, I believe we are in a much better position to face the challenges of the new market era, whether or not the current specific configuration of managed care survives. With a broad array of treatment modalities at our disposal, with short-term as well as long-term models, with a willingness to tackle the difficult family problems of our times, we would not have to be on the defensive with respect to the insurers. We could be the ones calling them to task for the narrowness and rigidity of their models, for their blindness to the real mental health needs of the public, and for their misrepresentation of themselves as the benefactors of the people. The other day, on the radio, I heard a preferred provider organization soliciting subscribers by advertising that they are "tough on doctors." They define and split the triad by saying that you (the client), and I (the PPO), can defeat the enemy (the doctors), in your own best health interests. I didn't know whether to laugh or cry. A health system can be run without insurance companies. It is more difficult to do it without doctors. Nevertheless their message does not fall on deaf ears. The public is, and always has been, ambivalent about doctors, and it is all too easy to prey upon that ambivalence, particularly in times of high frustration and uncertainty. To counteract this, we must seize the high ground as professionals, doing everything we can to meet the legitimate mental health needs of the country. This means broadening our knowledge and skills, and the flexibility of our treatment models.

Support for effective psychotherapy can emerge from several sources. If insurance buyers become more knowledgeable and become smart shoppers, they will seek better coverage for their dollar. The increase in social, school, and marital/family problems will keep up pressure for solutions, including psychological solutions. If we do our jobs well, as innovators, as researchers, and as spokespersons for the public interest, we too will influence the system. The insurers seem all powerful and monolithic, but they are in competition and are seeking subscribers, who in turn will be shopping for value.

Many planners are also proposing a return of the family doctor for primary physical health care. We should propose an equivalent concept of a comprehensive therapist, who is brought into service when the need exists. The comprehensive therapist would become the primary mental health provider. He or she might provide all of the treatment and case management that is required, and/or refer to other professionals as necessary. The salient point is that the responsibility for the coordination of treatment would rest with the comprehensive therapist. One of the worst scenarios I have encountered is that of multiple individual therapists treating various members of a single family with little or no coordination, generating a sense of chaos or competition in the overall treatment picture.

Under our existing system provisions for payment for family or couples therapy are not at all uniform from one insurer to another. Some even go so far as to bar it, and would consider the submission of a family therapy bill through one or another member under their individual coverage to be a fraud. The disease model under which health insurance is written is itself not systemic, always defining the individual as the bearer of the illness. The needed revolution in thinking will have to cover not only such mundane matters as how to bill, but will also have to recognize and systematize the concept of family dysfunction, providing a diagnostic nomenclature for it. At the very least there should be a uniform policy in which all insurance companies recognize and allow for billing under the appropriate category of therapy. Benefits for family treatment should be greater than those for a single individual, but not as much as would be gained by simply totaling the individual benefits of all family members. There would also have to be some provision for those cases in which both family and individual treatment was needed.

We as professionals find our cottage industry crumbling around us as we are either sucked up or extruded by the controlling corporate structures. Our own fear and uncertainty is quite palpable and is more and more the center of attention at formal or informal professional gatherings. Whatever we do as individuals in trying to achieve short-term adaptation to an essentially hostile system, our group goals will be achieved through political action, public information, and development of better models. We should support and lobby for plans that have outpatient psychotherapy benefits that are reasonable and justifiable. We should also support proposals that provide for conversion of inpatient days to other modalities such as day, residential, and outpatient treatment.

Someday we may be able to look back at this era for what it is, the blind oppressing the recalcitrant. Meanwhile, whether or not the health plans allow us to adopt a systems perspective, we can gain our own emotional and intellectual satisfaction in expanding the horizons of psychoanalysis.

References

Cassavetes, J. (1974), *Woman Under the Influence.*

Freud, S. (1920), Beyond the pleasure principle. *Standard Edition,* 18:3–64. London: Hogarth Press, 1955.

Harris, E. (1993), *Mass. Psychologist,* March:3.

Koman, S. L., & Stechler, G. (1985), Making the jump to systems. In: *Handbook of Adolescents and Family Therapy,* ed. M. P. Mirkin & S. L. Koman. New York: Gardner Press.

Pennsylvania, Senate bill 903 (1994).

Stechler, G. (1990), The integration of psychoanalysis and family systems. In: *Tradition and Innovation in Psychoanalytic Education: Clark Conference on Psychoanalytic Training for Psychologists,* ed. M. Meisels & E. R. Shapiro. Hillsdale, NJ: Erlbaum.

Historical, Ethical, and Legal Dimensions of Managed Care

11

The History of Managed Care and Its Impact on Psychodynamic Treatment

Jerry A. Morris, Jr., Psy.D.

The Establishment of the Managed Care Movement

Primitive managed care systems of the late 1970s and early 1980s were *managed costs systems* which relied principally on decreasing access and utilization (Bengen, 1993). The very purposes of early health maintenance organizations (HMOs) during the formative years were to establish cost savings through prepaid health plans with guaranteed limits on total costs (a kind of health underwriting), and group practice service delivery designed to minimize overhead and maximize the uniformity of service delivery (Bittker, 1992).

In the early HMOs or independent practice organizations (IPOs) mental health services were peripheral to nonexistent. They were considered too costly to incorporate in the mainstream of controlled health care programs. In fact, even the federal government took this approach when it made laws and subsequent rules and regulations concerning managed care in the Medicaid system. The Medicaid statute (Code of Federal Regulations, 1992, pp. 469–470) does not include *mental health services* in required basic services, but rather makes these services optional in qualified health maintenance organizations.

In the Health Maintenance Organization Act of 1973, and subsequent revisions, details of how HMOs could become federally qualified were established (Health Maintenance Organization Act of 1973, 1976, 1981). This act set the general form and foundation of HMOs throughout the United States. These laws focused on primary care delivery, but did require crisis intervention mental health services, alcohol and drug detoxification, and referral services for alcohol and drug abuse treatment. The HMO movement was set on a course which attempted to control costs through limiting access to services, discouraging utilization of health services, and ignoring or providing cursory crisis services in the important area of the mental and behavioral health needs of the population.

By 1981 the opportunity for abuses inherent in managed care and similar corporate health systems had led to widespread problems in California. Problems ranging from poor quality, restricted access, selective enrollment, refusal to allow patients to opt out of the system, and financial abuses, led Congress to effect the regulatory amendments of 1976 and 1981 (Congressional Research Services, 1993). A qualified HMO was defined by broad overarching principles with a list of required general primary care services. Some lip service was paid to crisis mental health intervention, and referral requirements for substance abuse services. By the late 1970s these primary care oriented HMOs could receive federal aid to encourage their development and maintenance.

To qualify for a subsidy an HMO had to adopt community rating as opposed to the traditional experience rating method of setting premiums. Employers approached by a federally qualified HMO were required to offer the managed care plan as an alternative to traditional insurance. Standards were weak and global.

Therefore, the United States Government has a long-standing commitment to managed care dating to 1973. This juggernaut took place without serious supervision or comprehensive controls. The monitoring of HMOs in general, and in particular, federally qualified HMOs, has never been required nor undertaken. Recently, some states have developed HMO laws to control the quality of care and practice style in these businesses, but by and large there is weak to nonexistent monitoring of managed care entities.

Managed Care as a Business

By 1983, when subsidies were discontinued, for-profit HMOs and IPOs entered the marketplace. Within a short time 20 percent of psychiatric hospitals owned managed care organizations (Dorwart and Epstein, 1992), and by the late 1980s 53 percent of HMOs surveyed in a large study were for-profit organizations (Levin and Glasser, 1992). Taking profits by restricting services had evolved as one of the primary motives of the HMO movement.

As the profit motive became one of the dominant forces in the managed care industry, cost control devices such as restriction of access to care, and policy prohibitions on extended care gained a central role in managed care delivery systems. Nowhere was this more apparent than in the case of intensive or psychoanalytic psychotherapy. In many managed care corporations policies encouraging short-term behavioral therapies and defining therapeutic goals in terms of acute symptom amelioration were developed and enforced. Gatekeepers and case managers began to resist treatment plans which focused on maturational development, long-term improvement, increased creativity and quality of life,

and structural change. Intermediate and long-term psychotherapists were discriminated against and refused admission
or readmission to doctor panels.

The psychodynamic frame and the managed care frame
were set on a collision course. Psychodynamic and intensive
psychotherapy practitioners were antithetical to the need to
limit access to services, and to shift patients to symptom oriented palliative interventions. The shifting of health care
resources from change and cure to crisis intervention and
symptom relief occurred without careful analysis of the long-
term cost and potential human consequences.

Adoption of magical thinking about "biological imbal-
ances," "genetic control of decision bases and styles," and
ritualized interventions focused on "symptom relief, palliative, and prophylactic remedies" were offered to an unsus-
pecting, and often unsophisticated public under the
symbolic rubric of "best science and cost effectiveness." The
shift to symptom eradication as opposed to structural personality change occurred as an artifact of corporate and governmental rather than patient needs. This shift occurred
hypnotically, and without significant call for scientific valida-
tion and in-depth study of the underlying tenets and their
long-term effect. Certainly, the associated developmental
level of these magical constructions, the impulsive rush to
implementation, rather than science based conclusions,
were never thoroughly examined.

The Cost Shell Game

The problem of cost shifting emerged as a major market
force in health care delivery systems in the 1980s. As managed care organizations took over increasing numbers of
patients, health care prescription left the hands of doctors
and became the province of business managers. Often, managed care corporations strictly limited reimbursement for

mental health services to referral to public resources, short-term interventions with physical medicine follow-up, and denial of payment to uncontracted systems forced to provide for HMO patients who were uncovered. Costs were shifted to the government under Medicare and Medicaid, and to traditional private indemnity plans resulting in claims of managed care savings. The government retaliated by setting capitations on Medicaid hospital day rates at around $277 per day, by severely limiting diagnosis-specific length of stay, and by embarking on a program of aggressive exclusions of items on Medicare audited cost reports (Commission on Professional and Hospital Activities Staff, 1988). By 1991, thirty-one states were operating some type of managed care Medicaid project and shifting costs to private insurance (Congressional Research Services, 1993).

Costs were shifted to medical services by treating mental illness as a medical disorder. This further militated against psychoanalytic and long-term structurally oriented psychotherapies by trivializing personality development and organization; focusing on psychotropic interventions which limited or accentuated perception, cognition, impulse thresholds, and initiative; or writing the patient off as a genetic anomaly. While prevalence studies indicate that as much as 18.7 percent of the adult population, and 11.8 percent of children in the United States suffer from mental illness (Muszynski, Brady, and Sharfstein, 1987), managed care companies spend only 3 to 4 percent of their health care budgets on mental health services (Kessler, 1984). In fact, national expenditures for mental health services as a portion of all health care expenditures are at 14.2 percent, far below the prevalence rates in the general population (Muszynski et al., 1987). Mental health expenditures are not out of line with the problem at hand.

Another health care utilization problem fueling the rush to managed care approaches is hospital cost overruns.

Approximately 55 percent of national health care expenditures are for hospital stays and drugs. The utilization of outpatient mental health services has remained reasonably stable, but there has been an 11 percent rise in inpatient days from 1982 to 1986 (Levin and Glasser, 1992). Approximately 70 percent of all mental health treatment costs are for inpatient treatment (Stanton, 1989). The prevailing managed care practice of having a general physician perform the screening and referral for mental disorders predisposed treatment recommendations toward biomedical approaches and hospitalization.

In this approach, first echelon efforts often involve reassurance and pharmacological or expensive medicodiagnostic interventions. Significant or intensive outpatient psychotherapy interventions are avoided and conceptualized as "expensive, unnecessary, or unscientific." In some cases this approach results in temporary or palliative relief and subsequent serious regression or relapse, thereby increasing the need for inpatient services. The result is a system which vacillates between the extremes of overly simplified and overly complex settings, philosophies, and approaches to the treatment of mental illness.

Very little control of practices, policies, and effects of the managed care system has been established by the government or by unifying forces in the industry itself. Practices involving assessment, referral, treatment outcome, and comparative models lack uniformity and a body of research which would validate the procedures as optimally configured.

Pyramid Versus Multidisciplinary Approaches

The cornerstone of many modern managed care service models involves the use of the primary care physician as the entry level diagnostician and treatment planner. This case management or gatekeeper approach to patient care was most prominently first developed in Massachusetts in 1979 under the Section 1115(a) demonstration waiver through the Medicaid program (Congressional Research Services, 1993). In this approach a beneficiary would have health care services controlled by a single primary care physician. The physician would manage overall care in an attempt to reduce unnecessary referral services or hospital admissions.

A body of evidence is available which indicates that primary care physicians and nurses have low recognition of mental disorders ranging from 10 to 50 percent (Muszynski et al., 1987). Managed care programs and national health care agendas which rely on primary care physicians and nurse specialists to identify and plan for the mentally ill are, by design, restricting access and cutting off the opportunity for cost effective early identification and intervention.

This shift of the gatekeeper functions to general medical personnel had been tried and had failed prior to the 1980s when medical referral was often a required procedure prior to initiating third-party funding of mental health services. The procedure was discontinued when issues of quality of care, freedom of choice, early identification and treatment, and overutilization of chemotherapy emerged. National managed care approaches which use general physicians as gatekeepers for mental health services seek to return to models which had previously proven ineffective and had been discarded.

Even though the Massachusetts project was not successful and encountered significant problems, the pyramid approach to case management has been adopted in most managed care agencies. The Omnibus Budget Reconciliation Act (OBRA) 1981 gave states the option of forcing managed care companies to require this case management approach. In the case of the diagnosis and treatment of mental illness, this method has been a quality and cost nightmare. Specific evidence is mounting that most mental illness is not caused by an underlying biochemical or physical problem. The practice of assuming this mechanistic position and treating the mentally ill with drugs alone is scientifically inappropriate, cost ineffective over the long haul, and results in significant overuse of medical services (Seligman, 1993). Psychology as an organized science has been an all-but-muffled whimper against the onslaught of publicity for the biochemical and pharmacological approaches.

The pyramid approach to diagnoses and treatment should be replaced by a multidisciplinary primary care model which recognizes the high prevalence of mental illness and the frequent cost effectiveness of intensive and long-term psychotherapy. The traditions of the medical pyramid, topped by the physician, should be exchanged for reasonable planning, model testing, and encouragement of constructive competition among practitioners of all the health disciplines.

The Government-Induced Health Care Crisis

The results of these forms of price controls and resultant cost shifting have been increased premiums for indemnity plan policy holders; severely fluctuating dips in profits (called fund balances in the not-for-profit businesses); increased difficulty in making insurance sales; and increased case finding costs and competition among doctors and health care agencies to corral higher paying private insurance patients. There was a rush to deliver the "good paying" patient needed to fund all patients, and the marketing system began.

The managed care corporation was placed in a superior market position. The enrollees of indemnity plans were targeted for increased identification and service, and the only modes of recourse were higher premiums, and "*cherry picking*" (selecting new enrollees who are young, healthy, and physically active) based on more aggressive experience rating (actuarial tables defining the nonrisk, nonusers of health care services). Ultimately, the private insurers had to use capital, which in earlier times could be used to lower premiums and improve services, to purchase and establish HMOs.

Cost shifting drove health care costs up significantly while simultaneously making one of the culprits, managed care companies, more attractive (relative to price) to patients and the government. Inappropriately conceived HMO evaluation studies touted their capacity to hold down costs without factoring into the figures the portions of the costs which were being shifted to private insurers, controlled by limiting access, and which resulted from inappropriate services (overmedicalization, symptom oriented therapies, and other health care intervention cost shifting and delay tactics).

The government and certifying bodies began to integrate many of the managed care concepts for tracking, utilization review, doctor monitoring, and management information requirements into certification programs. Private facilities found themselves hiring nurse quality assurance clerks, physician administrators, specialist certified medical records clerks, administrators with masters' degrees in public health administration, and incurring significant secondary costs under the concept of "managing care." These costs, coupled with the increased case finding and marketing costs required to target privately insured patients, resulted in ballooning private health care prices.

It has been estimated that as much as 20 percent of the nation's health care budget is wasted on excessive administrative costs and unnecessary medical testing (Sperry, 1993). Hospitals were no longer managing their businesses: the government was. Hospital costs, along with physicians' salaries, soared. By the late 1980s it was not uncommon to spend

$50,000 to recruit a psychiatrist, another $240,000 per annum in salary, and another $40,000 in benefits and perks. The government busily promulgated and staunchly defended requirements that physicians perform all important patient functions. Even though more highly trained specialty disciplines were available in significant numbers and at more reasonable cost, the government insisted on physician control and supervision of all services and activities in hospitals and health care facilities (Social Security Administration, 1993).

Obviously, physicians with psychoanalytic or intensive psychotherapy proclivities (and similarly trained psychologists working with them) were eschewed in favor of biologically disposed doctors. The result was increased costs driven by overmedicalized approaches, mandates to use very expensive physicians for a broad array of functions, and low referral rates to intensive psychotherapy.

Prudent Managed Change

No reasonable and comprehensive studies assessing the impact of managed care on long-term mental health care costs exist. The control of intervening variables is difficult with regard to the effects of managed care which can be disguisedly spread to secondary and affected health care and correctional systems. Costs associated with the overuse of biomedical approaches; human potential and work force costs; effects on the structural resiliency of the family; violence secondary to untreated illness; child abuse and neglect; are difficult to measure. Research which comprehensively tracks the shifts of costs across systems must occur if we are to get a true analysis of the fruits of the managed care approach.

Managed care must therefore be considered an unproven and experimental approach with some potential for both good and harm. We do not know for a fact that it necessarily saves money, or that it is adaptable to all areas of health care. We do not know how to supervise and control for its weaknesses and potential dangers for patients and the society as a whole. Standards must be developed after careful description and measurement of positive and negative effects. Managed care philosophies and practices must be considered formative and evolving rather than congealed. It is certainly premature to be for or against something as ill-defined and little studied as managed care. It is also unreasonable to the point of naiveté to tout it as the "tool that will save the health care system" or even to assume that we know how to design and supervise managed care systems for the greatest public good.

Ron Fox, Ph.D., President of the American Psychological Association, has stated that "the house is burning, and we are fiddling" (Fox, 1994). However, I would say "the house is burning, and we are concerning ourselves with the joys of reconstruction plans."

Summary

As practitioner-scientists, we are in a unique position to use our dedication to patient advocacy to provide valuable leadership in health care planning and policy analysis. We must point out that a rush to adopt managed care as the solution to health care problems in America is premature and an oversimplification of a complex and as yet minimally defined problem. On balance we must point out that managed care as an approach is worthy of study and evaluation as a potential tool or set of tools in managing health quality and costs.

We can take part in comprehensive and longitudinal assessments of managed care approaches while keeping an open mind (scientific stance) about potential positive and negative effects which may ultimately be defined. We can illuminate global and long-term needs of patients and advocate for their rights to accurate diagnosis and access to appropriate mental health services. Some of these services will be short-term and others will be long-term and intensive psychotherapy interventions.

We can insist on treatments offered in the least restrictive modality. We can stand firm on access to differential lengths of treatment and approaches which include psychoanalytic and intensive psychotherapies based on the patient's private health care goals and the patient's right to access to nonmedical alternatives. We can diligently design research that assesses medical side effects, medical cost offset, cost shifting, and social and personal costs associated with palliative and prophylactic health care goals.

As psychologists we are behind. We must aggressively lobby Congress to fund important managed care and treatment outcome research and policy analysis. Alternative approaches such as area or local pilot projects with parallel models tested on a controlled and longitudinal basis should be undertaken.

Artificial barriers preventing the full development of nonmedical approaches and their cost and outcome testing in inpatient and outpatient facilities should be removed. In such a context, intermediate and long-term psychotherapy can be favorably conceptualized as a legitimate first resort, cost reasonable, and necessary health care intervention for appropriately diagnosed patients. Psychotherapy's goals must be broadly conceived as ameliorative and often curative. The cost of having or not having access to competent diagnosis and psychotherapy can only be evaluated in a system which appreciates the complexity and value of these issues.

Health maintenance organizations have increased their influence in the health care delivery system and the number of such organizations has nearly doubled every four years since the end of the 1970s (Levin and Glasser, 1992). A 1992 survey by Peat Marwick of more than 1000 companies with 200 or more employees indicated that 55 percent of the companies' employees were covered by managed care approaches as compared to only 29 percent in 1988 (Bengen, 1993).

Clearly, managed care approaches have been embraced by the United States Government and are here to stay. However, there is not a clearly defined managed care model with a well-developed set of ground rules and procedures. The models available currently are diverse, poorly supervised, lack the uniformity and specification which could allow for comparative and performance evaluations, and often discriminate against psychoanalytic and intensive psychotherapy regardless of the patient's needs or personal health care goals.

At the beginning of the 1980s evidence was emerging which indicated that HMOs could be cost effective in limiting the inappropriate overutilization of general medical services (Cummings and Vandenbos, 1981). However, it is just as possible that all of these things applied in an unbalanced and inappropriate fashion have created a part of the current problem and are driving the rush to universal coverage in order to control cost shifting.

These facets of managed care are largely unregulated by the government. Because of this lack of specificity in statute and regulation, the potential exists for abuse and short-term cost control based on limiting access, diluting the quality and availability of practitioners, poor quality utilization review, and the biomedicalization of all aspects of health care. The fact that abuses have already become common in the managed care industry is best illustrated by the necessity of Congress passing regulatory legislation in 1986 forbidding hospitals and doctors from using financial incentives to limit care.

If we are going to place our trust in the managed care movement, it is only reasonable to define what a quality managed care system is and how it must operate. The component parts, acceptable relationships between parties, and limitations on profits or fund balances, executive salaries, and percent of revenue which is allocated to overhead are just as important to define as the price of services. The fundamentals which make managed care work for the patient, such as freedom of choice of doctor; rational price goals maintained by competitive contracting; utilization review using peer appeal processes; the employment of a well-trained senior diagnostician; case management of unusual or high-volume cases; community rating; the use of least restrictive services; outcome based service menus; and investment in research and development must be specifically addressed in legislation.

Psychologists are practice and scientifically prepared to provide leadership in this time of managed change. We must insist, however, that change be based on proven effectiveness and on comprehensive and longitudinal analysis, and that we understand the side effects of proposed models sufficiently to build controls and remedies. We must insist that short-term, intermediate, and long-term and comprehensive psychotherapy be valued and evaluated within a comprehensive context and using reasonable and parallel cost–benefit comparisons with proposed alternatives. Above all, we must be the patient's chief advocate for access to nonbiological and nonmedical approaches.

References

Bengen, B. (1993), *Profiting from Managed Care in the Third Generation: Strategies for Providers of Behavioral Health and Substance Abuse Services.* Providence, RI: Manisses Communications Group.

Bittker, T. (1992), The emergence of prepaid psychiatry. In: *Managed Mental Health Care, Administrative and Clinical Issues*, ed. J. L. Feldman & R. J. Fitzpatrick. Washington, DC: American Psychiatric Press, pp. 3–10.

Code of Federal Regulations: Public Health (1992), 42, Subpart B—Qualified Health Maintenance Organization Requirements. 417.101, pp. 469–470, Office of the Federal Register, National Archives and Records Administration, October 1.

Commission on Professional and Hospital Activities Staff (1988), *Length of Stay of Diagnosis and Operation, North Central Region*. Ann Arbor, MI: Healthcare Knowledge Systems.

Congressional Research Services (1993), *Medicaid Source Book: Background Data and Analysis*. (Committee Print 103-A), pp. 939–940. Washington, DC: U.S. Government Printing Office.

Cummings, N. A., & Vandenbos, G. R. (1981), The 20-year Kaiser Permanente experience with psychiatric therapy and medical utilization. *Health Policy Quart.*, 1:159–175.

Dorwart, R. A., & Epstein, S. S. (1992), Economics and managed mental health care: The HMO as a crucible for cost-effective care. In: *Managed Mental Health Care, Administrative and Clinical Issues*, ed. J. L. Feldman & R. J. Fitzpatrick. Washington, DC: American Psychiatric Press, pp. 11–27.

Fox, R. (1994), President's Address to APA Council of Representatives, Washington, DC.

Health Maintenance Organization Act of 1973 (1973), Public Law 93-222. 87 STAT. 914.

Health Maintenance Organization Act of 1981 (1981), Public Law 97-35, 95 STAT. 572.

Health Maintenance Organization Amendment of 1976 (1976), Public Law 94-960, 90 STAT. 1945.

Kessler, L. G. (1984), Treated incidence of mental disorders in a prepaid group practice setting. *Amer. J. Pub. Health*, 74:152–154.

Levin, B. L., & Glasser, J. H. (1992), Comparing mental health benefits, utilization patterns, and costs. In: *Managed Mental Health Care, Administrative and Clinical Issues*, ed. J. L. Feldman & R. J. Fitzpatrick. Washington, DC: American Psychiatric Press, pp. 29–52.

Muszynski, I. L., Brady, J., & Sharfstein, S. S. (1987), *Economic Fact Book for Psychiatry*, 2nd ed. Washington, DC: American Psychiatric Press.

Seligman, M. (1993), *What You Can Change and What You Can't: The Complete Guide to Successful Self-Improvement*. New York: Alfred A. Knopf.

Social Security Act, Sec. 1861(f), 42 U.S.C. 1395x.

Social Security Administration (1993), Compilation of the Social Security Laws (Committee Print WMCP: 103-5). Washington, DC: U.S. Government Printing Office.

Sperry, P. (1993), High tech medicine's high cost. *Investor's Bus. Daily*, May 25:1, 2.

Stanton, D. (1989), Mental health care economics and the future of psychiatric practice. *Psychiatric Annals*, 19:421–427.

12

Ethics, Psychodynamic Treatment, and Managed Care

Norma P. Simon, Ed.D.

A short time ago I was at a working meeting concerned with ethical issues. The discussion was both highly charged and depressing. When at last a break was called, the colleague sitting to my left started to tell the group about a situation he had just suffered through with a managed care company.

His patient had been in treatment with him for a little over a year when she received a letter from the managed care company (MCC) which had recently been awarded the contract for mental health coverage for her company's employees. The letter informed her that her mental health benefit would be cut off after her next session with the provider because the MCC had determined that she had been in treatment too long for the condition for which she was being treated (DX major depression!) and that a support group would be adequate for her needs. Further, if she chose, she could seek treatment from one of the providers on the MCC's list of preferred providers.

She, of course, was furious: at the company, at the therapist, and at the situation. Interestingly, the therapist did not receive a copy of that letter or any other communication from the MCC. Coincidentally, he was in fact on this MCC's provider list, representing another employer, and was startled to discover that this did not place him on the MCC's list with respect to other contracts held by that MCC.

The therapist called the MCC to try to straighten out the situation with respect to this patient, a situation which had already become problematic, given the patient's degree of upset at the therapist (was he doing "proper treatment" in keeping her in treatment for a year? Was the MCC "correct" in telling her that she would be fine with a support group?). He hit a stone—or perhaps a paper—wall. Initially, the MCC advised him that he would have to be approved for each contract the MCC held; next he was told that his patient should have been sent to a psychiatrist for medication (actually, that had occurred, but she had refused medication after responding poorly to it), and finally he was told that the MCC had made its decision and that was that. He asked to be put in touch with the psychologist or psychiatrist who was responsible for this decision and was told that that person would contact him. In the meantime, he had to work with the patient who was understandably upset by the situation, which indeed included her fears of losing him before they were ready to terminate, her inability to "go it alone" at this time, and her anguish that the one person she had grown to trust was being taken from her as had "all the others" (abandonment was a big issue in her life).

The therapist agreed to see her without charge until she could be properly transferred to a provider "on the list," however long that would take, since the patient was unable to afford treatment without insurance coverage. He also agreed to help her choose an appropriate replacement. After this was agreed upon, and while the "working through" was taking place, the medical director of the MCC called and said they had never intended that he shouldn't be able to continue with the case. When the therapist asked for an explanation of the letter to the patient and all the rest, there was what amounted to a shrug at the other end of the wire, and an off-hand statement about getting the provider to appeal. By this time, obviously the damage had already been done both to this provider and to his patient.

This vignette highlights a few of the ethical issues for providers found with increasing frequency in the managed care situation. This article will cover such ethical issues as: informed consent, confidentiality, abandonment, and record keeping. It will also discuss: methods of dealing with the MCC, the MCC contract, appeals, and legal issues. Reference to all of these issues must include a citation to the ethical codes of our professional associations and the professional conduct codes to which we swear to adhere when we receive our licenses.

The Codes

There are three relevant ethical–professional conduct codes for psychology: The American Psychological Association's (APA) "Ethical Principles of Psychologists and Code of Conduct" (1992), The Canadian Psychological Association's (CPA) *Code of Ethics* (1991), and The Association of State and Provincial Psychology Boards' (ASPPB) *Code of Conduct* (1991).[1]

Although they are not identical, there are many similarities among these codes. The CPA Code, governing the practice of Canadian psychologists, is the most aspirational of the three. The APA code is both aspirational and, now, legally defensible. The third, the ASPPB Code, is a legal code originally developed to fill the gap left by APA and CPA codes

---

[1] The codes of ethics for other professions are available through the appropriate professional association.

which were originally only aspirational. Now the APA code has been revised and includes a legally sound code of conduct. State and provincial jurisdictions generally reference some or all of the sections of one of these codes or have developed their own state–provincial codes that cover virtually the same territory. There are, however, certain areas in which all of these codes are in complete agreement and most of the issues governing the behavior of therapists in dealing with MCCs fall into the agreed-upon areas (e.g., confidentiality). Because all of the codes are somewhat similar to the APA code, for purposes of this article relevant quotations will be from the APA code unless otherwise specified.

Changing Times

In the practice of psychoanalysis or analytically oriented psychotherapy, we have each been accustomed to setting our own standards for how we work: fees, referrals, consultations, and so on. But, with the advent of managed care along with a far more litigious public, we practitioners must learn to change in order to protect both ourselves and our patients. We must protect ourselves from charges that jeopardize our licenses or are made by our professions; and we must protect our patients from inappropriate care forced upon us and hence upon them by managed care companies, which in turn could result in the loss of our professional licenses.

Let us start with some questions: What have we done to protect our patients' confidentiality? What have we done to ensure that the MCC utilization reviewer is legally entitled to receive highly confidential information about the patient on the telephone? What protection or information should we provide our MCC patient to inform him or her with respect to: what is going to happen with confidential information about him or her; what is the meaning of the release he or she signs; and what will happen to the patient if the MCC denies payment?

How should the therapist proceed in order to protect a patient who needs long-term treatment when the therapist knows that the MCC will pay only for short-term treatment? What should we do if we firmly believe that the patient should be seen multiple times a week in order for treatment to be most effective and yet we know that such treatment will not be covered by the patient's MCC? What is the therapist's ethical responsibility as a provider to inform the patient of the limitations of the covered treatment prior to beginning such limited treatment? What will happen to the patient we start with, who thinks we will be able to continue as long as necessary, when the ax falls and the MCC turns off the money? Do we abandon the patient? If not, how do we make a living under these circumstances? All of these and many more are questions with which we will be dealing on a daily basis for the foreseeable future. And each of these kinds of questions pose ethical dilemmas for us as providers. Let us examine how these issues-problems fall under the Code of Ethics.

APA Ethical Principles of Psychologists and Code of Conduct

INFORMED CONSENT

    4.02 Informed Consent to Therapy

        a) Psychologists obtain appropriate informed consent to therapy or related procedures, using language that is reasonably understandable to participants. The content of informed consent will vary depending on many circumstances; however, informed consent generally implies that the person (1) has the capacity to consent,

(2) has been informed of significant information concerning the procedure, (3) has freely and without un-
due influence expressed consent, and (4) consent has
been appropriately documented [p. 1605].

The therapist has a patient who is able to come for therapy
at least partly because of the benefits he or she obtains from
a managed care company. The patient has signed all of the
usual forms and consented to waive confidentiality. What is
the extent of the therapist's responsibility? For some professionals, it seems to be filling out the forms, speaking to the
proper person on the phone, and ignoring the rest. What
we really should be doing, however, is going over in detail
and up front with the patient the precise significance to him
or her of using the managed care plan in terms of confidentiality and what the consent of the patient permits the MCC
to do. If the patient is, in fact, uninformed or even misin-
formed by the MCC (which is often the case) the provider
must fill that information gap. We cannot simply expect the
patient to know that we may be speaking on the phone to
an unknown individual with unknown training about the
most deeply personal aspects of the patient's life. The patient
may not be aware that treatment might be limited by the
MCC to only enough sessions for the therapist to be able to
begin treatment, which could be prematurely cut off by the
MCC. Let us posit that the patient, in good faith, starts treatment, begins to open up a "can of worms" that suggests
that the individual is going to be in need of continued treatment for a considerable time, and that the therapist also
knows that the MCC is not likely to pay for continued treatment for as long as the patient is in need of it. The treatment
has now been started, the MCC has ceased to pay for further
treatment, and the individual has very little in the way of
financial resources. Do we stop the treatment? Do we refer
elsewhere the patient who has trusted us to be the treating

therapist? We can see that the patient would have a valid reason to bring charges against the therapist before the licensing board or professional association for: (1) not properly informing that patient; (2) abandonment; and (3) speaking to a nonprofessional without any guarantee that the information about the patient will be treated in a confidential manner? Telling a licensing board that the therapist was only obeying the rules of the MCC will not be an adequate defense against charges of gross misconduct on the part of the professional. Our profession is now being driven by insurance companies, yet we have sworn to uphold the standards of the profession and the Code of Conduct of our jurisdiction. These two positions are not always in conflict; but, where they are, the psychologist's ethical and legal responsibility is to put the patient's welfare above financial considerations, which includes the dealings of the psychologist with a third-party payer.

CONFIDENTIALITY

5.02 Maintaining confidentiality
Psychologists have a primary obligation and take reasonable precautions to respect the confidentiality rights of those with whom they work or consult, recognizing that confidentiality may be established by law, institutional rules or professional or scientific relationships [p. 1606].

The client privilege is a legal right that belongs to the patient. Confidentiality is an ethical requirement of the professional. The patient may have signed an authorization for the release of information to the insurance company which technically breaks the confidentiality privilege and gets the provider "off the hook." If, however, the company insists as some do, that the provider telephone the information required by the MCC to a "voice" on the other end of the telephone, with whom he or she is unacquainted, and of whom the provider has no knowledge, and whose credentials may be nonexistent, what should we do? The patient signed the form. Are we excused? No, based just on that fact we are not excused. The patient's consent must be "informed consent," and this is where informed consent and confidentiality issues converge. If the patient is unaware of what signing the release form means, then someone has to be responsible for providing the patient with that information; otherwise, the patient is not making an informed choice. One speaker at a conference on this subject, a lawyer, suggested that the therapist not speak on the phone at all—and certainly not to anyone with whose credentials we are not thoroughly familiar. Get the name and address of the medical officer or the psychologist in charge of reviewing claims and *write* the report. Send the report marked "Private and Confidential" and review it with the patient prior to sending it. In this way, the provider has shared with the patient what is being said and is keeping the focus of the treatment on the patient and the patient's rights, wishes, and needs, rather than merely answering the summons of the MCC, regardless of how this might affect the patient—or the provider. If the MCC says we must do it their way or they won't reimburse us, we should ask to speak to someone higher in the chain of command so that we can explain the ethical problem inherent in talking to an unknown nonprofessional about a patient. The patient should be able to assume that the provider will not reveal personal information about that individual to an unknown person without getting assurance that the information will remain confidential and will be going to a locked file in the medical director's/psychologist's office. As a provider, we can insist on sending in the required report so that we have an opportunity to discuss our findings with the patient, and so that we can mark the file "Confidential" and "to be seen by X person ONLY." We are all being asked to be very trusting; however, if the information is misused, not only the MCC but the provider will be culpable.

ABANDONMENT

> Section 4.09 Terminating the Professional Relationship.
> a) Psychologists do not abandon patients or clients. (See also Standard 1.25e, under Fees and Financial Arrangements.)
> b) Psychologists terminate a professional relationship when it becomes reasonably clear that the patient or client no longer needs the service, is not benefiting, or is being harmed by continued service.
> c) Prior to termination for whatever reason, except where precluded by the patient's or client's conduct, the psychologist discusses the patient's or client's views and needs, provides appropriate pretermination counseling, suggests alternative service providers as appropriate, and takes other reasonable steps to facilitate transfer of responsibility to another provider if the patient or client needs one immediately [p. 1606].

In the example given at the beginning of this article, the provider was forced into an untenable position. He could not continue to see the patient for very long without being paid for his time; he could not transfer the patient without her consent; and he believed that the patient needed continued treatment for which the MCC would not pay. Given the relationship that had already developed between the patient and the therapist, transferring the patient before either the

therapist or the patient was ready for such a move presented
both of them with a very difficult dilemma. The patient was
justifiably angry, as was the therapist. The therapist believed
that he had helped this woman immeasurably and wanted
to continue until such time as it became appropriate to terminate. This became impossible given the circumstances,
however, so the therapist had to work with the patient to
accept a referral to one of the providers on the list. All of
us recognize that we are not the only therapist capable of
working with a particular patient, but there are certain circumstances that we all wish to avoid. Terminating an individual who has a history of abandonment, regardless of the
reason, has to be seen by the patient as not being in her
best interest. Her anger, hurt, and vengeful feelings would
all come to the surface in the event of such action. The
countertransference issues are equally as strong: rage at the
MCC for such unprofessional behavior, the loss of the patient (both the work and the income), and having to turn
over a patient to someone we might not know but who is
"on the list"—all are traumatic for the therapist.

In addition, a charge of abandonment is a very serious
charge against a therapist. It is important to make sure, when
the MCC-allocated treatment has run out, that the patient
has not been abandoned. This raises important issues and
requires preparation on the part of the therapist.

1. The therapist must decide whether to even begin treatment of a patient whom he or she believes would be
   harmed by the brief treatment available.
2. The therapist must determine what other sources of treatment are available in the vicinity where the patient can
   be seen for little or no cost.
3. The therapist should prepare the patient by discussing
   other options prior to starting treatment.

4. The therapist should ask the patient to sign a form indicating that the specific limitations have been explained by the therapist and understood by the patient.

THE MANAGED CARE PSYCHOLOGIST

What about the psychologist or other mental health provider who works on the staff of an MCC reviewing treatment plans? What ethical considerations might this individual need to be informed about? Try 2.01(b):

> 2.01(b) Psychologists' assessments, recommendations, reports, and psychological diagnostic or evaluative statements are based on information and techniques (including personal interviews of the individual when appropriate) sufficient to provide appropriate substantiation for their findings [p. 1603].

As any provider who has dealt on the phone with an MCC staff member can tell you, all too often the individual is ill-informed, has never seen the patient, has very limited knowledge of the patient, but nevertheless is making serious decisions concerning the treatment of the patient. The MCC will tell you that they are only concerned with "medically necessary" decisions. This translates to a decision regarding what will be the least treatment absolutely necessary to get the individual back to a moderate level of functioning in the workplace. By making such a decision and by trying to keep the costs down for the MCC, a professional working for such a company faces his or her own ethical dilemma. On the one hand, do these professionals meet the standard set by Section 2.01 and, on the other, are they properly serving the MCC that has employed them? Are they being financially rewarded beyond their salaries (by, for example, bonuses or promotions) for the amount of money they "save" for the

MCC by denying treatment to the patient? Cognitive disso-
nance comes in very handy in such a situation when we must
convince ourselves that what we are doing is being done in
the best interests of all the parties.

From the point of view of the provider, it is difficult to
distinguish "medically necessary decisions" from "clinical
decisions" when such decisions determine the number of
times the provider can see the patient or whether or not the
patient needs medication. The provider must develop the
skills necessary to hold his or her own in a dispute with
the MCC representative on the telephone or with the MCC
person-professional with whom the provider corresponds.
Being aware of the MCC's appeals procedures, for example,
is vital if the provider is to ensure decent care for the patient.
In fact, the provider may be required to appeal in order to
properly protect the rights of the patient.

In long-term treatment we have been used to not having
anything to do with the insurance company. We had a contract with our patients. They had contracts with insurance
companies. Now, the way MCCs want it, the patient is the
odd man out and the MCC wants only to deal with the provider. This is potentially infantilizing to the patient, as well
as a cause of the ethical dilemmas mentioned above.

What the Provider Can Do

What must the provider do to safeguard the treatment and
protect the provider from ethics charges that could jeopardize his or her license?

1. KEEP RECORDS

> Principle 5.04 Maintenance of Records: Psychologists main-
> tain appropriate confidentiality in creating, storing, ac-
> cessing, transferring, and disposing of records under their

control, whether these are written, automated, or in any other medium. Psychologists maintain and dispose of records in accordance with law and in a manner that permits compliance with the requirements of this Ethics Code [p. 1606].

How does this interface with the MCC? The MCC wants documentation for the provider's procedures and for his or her treatment plan. In order to convince the medical–psychological personnel of the need for the provider's services when there is a disagreement, we must be able to document the need for what we are requesting. Records are also our safeguard in presenting the treatment should we ever be investigated in the course of a professional conduct complaint. According to the new APA record-keeping guidelines, the following are recommended:

1. Content of Records

a. Records include any information (including information stored in a computer) that may be used to document the nature, delivery, progress or results of psychological services. Records can be reviewed and duplicated.

b. Records of psychological services minimally include a) identifying data, b) dates of services, c) types of services, d) fees, e) any assessment, plan for intervention, consultation, summary reports, and/or testing reports and supporting data as may be appropriate, and f) any release of information obtained.

c. As may be required by their jurisdiction and circumstances, psychologists maintain to a reasonable degree accurate, current, and pertinent records of psychological services. The detail is sufficient to permit planning for continuity in the event that another psychologist takes over delivery of services, including, in the event of death, disability, and retirement. In addition, psychologists maintain records *in sufficient detail* for regulatory and administrative review of psychological service delivery [APA, 1993, p. 985; emphasis added].

In the ASPPB *Code of Conduct* (1991), record keeping is more detailed than the above APA provision, so it might be useful to use this more detailed proposal as a model:

6. Maintenance and retention of records.
   a. The psychologist rendering professional services to an individual client (or a dependent), or services billed to a third party payor, shall maintain professional records that include:
   1. the presenting problem(s) or purpose or diagnosis,
   2. the fee arrangement,
   3. the date and substance of each billed or service-count contact or service,
   4. any test results or other evaluative results obtained and any basic test data from which they were derived,
   5. notation and results of formal consults with other providers, and
   6. a copy of all test or other evaluative reports prepared as part of the professional relationship [p. 8].

The section also requires that the records be kept for five years after the last date of service. Each jurisdiction has its own requirement for the length of time during which one must keep records and what must be done to dispose of records. Particularly in the psychoanalytic profession, we have been reluctant to keep records. I know of cases where no records were ever kept other than the payment schedule. Those days are gone forever. I have also known of cases where the MCC sends investigators to the office of providers to "inspect the records." The MCC investigator demands to see the records of the provider's patients, and I have been told that they sometimes even insist on seeing other patient records as well "to compare the quality of care." Obviously, as providers, we can and must require a release, and we can delay the "inspecting" individual, insisting that only a professional can review our records and that we must inform the patient that this has happened. This could decidedly jeopardize the patient's treatment as well as the therapist's ethical stance. The more this happens and the more that we accept these procedures without objection, the more the MCCs will continue to violate our belief in what is appropriate treatment and our determination to provide it. So, document everything!

2. PROVIDE CONFIDENTIAL TREATMENT REPORTS

Send treatment report forms to a professional in an envelope marked "Confidential." Keep a record of each such transaction.

3. KNOW THE LAW

Know the laws in your jurisdiction governing not only the professional conduct code but also laws regarding Child Abuse Reporting, AIDS Reporting, and Tarassoff-type laws[1] (requiring that confidentiality be breached in order to protect a third party). For example, some jurisdictions prohibit a provider from releasing information about the patient's human immunodeficiency virus (HIV) status. Even if the patient consents, this information may not be divulged. Such laws are very strict and are intended to protect the individual from possible harm by employers or third-party payors. If the provider does not know whether his or her jurisdiction has such laws, that really must be determined.

---

[1]In this case the treating psychologist and supervisor were held responsible (even though police were notified) when the patient killed his girl friend as he said he would. Laws sprang up across the country, requiring professionals to inform an endangered individual of the threat.

Do No Harm

1.14 Psychologists take reasonable steps to avoid harming
their patients or clients, research participants, students,
and others with whom they work, and to minimize harm
where it is foreseeable and unavoidable [p. 1601].

This is perhaps the single most important caveat. Unfortunately, here also is the root of many a dilemma. If one is a provider on the "list" of an MCC, one may be faced with an ethical obligation to behave in a manner one believes is best for the patient, while knowing that if one does behave in that manner one will not long be on the preferred provider list for that MCC. If one's livelihood depends on pleasing the MCC, what is one to do? Who is one going to call? MCC Busters? There are areas of the country where managed care contracts control 90 percent or more of the business. If the provider is to make a living he or she may have to be "on their good side." Yet often what they consider enough treatment, good treatment, or even any treatment, might be quite different from what the provider believes to be the treatment of choice or even what is possible. Each day a decision must be made that takes into account the patient's needs, the therapist's needs, and the wishes of the MCC. Our independent profession is no longer independent when we work within this system. Young professionals particularly are apt to be caught up in this since the fee paid by the MCC may be quite acceptable for someone starting out, although it would be low for the top professionals in the field. To the MCC, the amount paid is a predetermined fee regardless of the experience and the credentials of the provider.

Some contracts are very explicit in deprecating long-term treatment. One that came across my desk recently stated that therapists who were interested in enforcing dependency, regression, and the unconscious were not acceptable to the company.

A therapist can agree to do short-term treatment, become a preferred provider, make a good living, and not think about the issues discussed here. Quality of care, a basic tenet of our profession, does not even have a seat at the table. The MCC does not concern itself about quality. The company's primary interest is in making money—the "bottom line." These companies are most often for-profit companies, many of them traded on stock exchanges. It takes a certain amount of experience and strength to separate oneself from the decisions being made for us by the company that then holds itself harmless and places the onus for the treatment on the provider. The MCC contract holds the provider responsible for all "clinical decisions" as differentiated from "medically necessary" ones as mentioned above. The contract also holds the MCC harmless if a clinical decision is "incorrect." Both the MCC and our profession place responsibility for the "clinical decision" on the provider and rightly so. We *have* to decide what is best for our patients and we must fight for that. If our clinical decision is different from the "medically necessary" one acceptable to the company, then we are being placed in a situation where our needs are at odds with those of our patients and can place us, the professionals, especially new ones, in an intolerable bind. Do we proceed with a treatment model we do not believe will help? Do we fight with the MCC for what we believe will help?

Mental health has become an industry and we are the cheap labor. We and our patients are infantilized, we lose our sense of responsibility, and we lose our neutrality. Most of all, by doing these things we are open to censure and possible charges of professional misconduct. Maintaining the ethics of our professions and maintaining a practice are becoming more and more antithetical. The professional is put in an ethical bind at every turn. If we don't join MCCs, we seriously risk having little or no income; if we join, we very likely will be "coopted" by the MCCs and may be subject to professional misconduct charges. If we provide the information requested by the MCC we are probably in violation of the code of ethics; if we do not we will be removed from the provider list. If we inform the patient and the patient agrees to our speaking to the company in whatever form that takes, we will be "in good" with the MCC, but in a personal ethical bind; and finally, there is our responsibility of determining what we consider to be necessary and acceptable treatment and then finding it impossible to provide it for the patient.

I believe that in three to five years, if we continue down this path, there will be charges brought to professional associations, ethics committees, and licensing boards against professionals involved in managed care treatment in all of the areas mentioned above. If this does happen, we the professionals must be aware of our collusion with the MCC. Preventing such harm from happening to our patients requires each individual professional as well as our professional associations to work conscientiously with MCCs, with our patients, and with our colleagues to set a path for the future where our professional judgment is respected as it should be. Anything else could end in tragedy.

References

American Psychological Association (1992), Ethical principles of psychologists and code of conduct. *Amer. Psychologist,* 47:1597–1611.
——— (1993), Record keeping guidelines. *Amer. Psychologist,* 48:984–986.

Association of State and Provincial Psychology Boards (1991), *ASPPB Code of Conduct.* Montgomery, AL: ASPPB.

Canadian Psychological Association (1991), *Canadian Code of Ethics for Psychologists.* Old Chelsea, Quebec: CPA.

13

Legal Issues for Psychotherapy in a Managed Care Environment

Shirley Ann Higuchi, J.D.
Russ Newman, Ph.D., J.D.

In recent years, the growth of the managed care industry has given rise to various financing and cost-containment strategies. A resulting plausible definition of managed care during its "first generation" of development is any strategy designed to reduce price or cost by restricting choice or access. Assurance that quality care is being provided has received a much lower priority within a managed care context than developing business arrangements to provide care at a decreased cost.

One consequence of the business focus of managed care has been an erosion of the ability of practitioners to provide traditional psychotherapy. Psychological treatment, which relies upon an *ongoing* interpersonal process whereby a critical element of the intervention is the therapist's continual communication of empathy, understanding, and interpretation to the patient has been difficult to carry out in

Acknowledgment. The authors wish to thank Jeannie Coscia for her assistance in preparation of this manuscript.

239

a managed care environment. At the very least, arbitrary and abbreviated time limits placed upon treatment have presented significant obstacles to psychotherapy. This is particularly true for psychoanalytically oriented psychotherapy with an emphasis on helping the patient achieve some reorganization and/or restructuring of personality and characteristic ways of coping with the world.

Arbitrary limits to treatment aside, the strategy of utilization review—a review of proposed or existing treatment by the third-party payer to determine the "necessity" of the treatment—has proved to be a major obstacle to traditional psychotherapy. For the most part, the goals of personality reorganization or restructuring of defenses do not equate well with "medically necessary" or even "psychologically necessary." As a result, utilization review determinations of psychotherapy, in general, and psychoanalytically-oriented psychotherapy, in particular, have all too often terminated the psychotherapy process prematurely.

Even when psychotherapy is able to proceed, providing treatment of this type in a managed care environment encounters more subtle but significant obstacles. One specific problem is the breach of the therapeutic boundary and containment by forces outside of the patient–therapist relationship. This is perhaps best illustrated by the effects on confidentiality when the third-party payer is able to intrude into the psychotherapy process. The adverse effects on the therapy process are likely to go well beyond the need to provide relatively extensive information about the psychotherapy and the patient to a party outside of the therapeutic dyad.

One possible "solution" to obstacles of this type is demonstrated in the health care reform initiative to allow providers to independently contract with patients for psychotherapy services outside of the established financing system. This would allow an opportunity to provide the necessary length of treatment in an appropriately contained therapeutic environment, although it requires patients to pay completely out of pocket. Yet, providing services within the system that includes managed care techniques and strategies is a reality that cannot be ignored.

Legal trends in the last few years have offered some means of controlling the degree to which managed care techniques can emphasize the business of health care to the detriment of the quality of care. Utilization review laws, for example, are beginning to place limits on review processes, in contrast to earlier statutes which enabled all manner of review processes and cost-containment strategies. Also, the common law is beginning to assign some accountability and certain liabilities to managed care entities for the care they deliver. This is in contrast to a previous judicial perspective which viewed managed care as little more than a business arrangement where an attitude of *caveat emptor* prevailed. Negligent cost containment, negligent credentialing, and the application of the corporate negligence doctrine to managed care has begun to facilitate a better balance of cost control and quality assurance.

Despite some progress and hopeful future solutions, the practical reality necessitates that psychologists face the dilemmas created when providing psychotherapy in a managed context. This article presents the most typical dilemmas that occur and the related legal issues they raise. In addition, the article presents some emerging legal issues which, if appropriately dealt with, may potentially bring additional relief. Finally, a number of practical strategies are suggested for psychologist-psychotherapists when dealing with the obstacles presented by certain managed care cost-containment strategies.

The Utilization Review Process and Statutory Protections

All managed care entities and insurance companies have utilization review (UR) programs. Utilization review involves the evaluation of the necessity, appropriateness, and efficiency of the use of health care services and resources. According to proponents of UR (e.g., managed care entities and insurance companies), its purpose is to improve cost-effectiveness while maintaining high quality of care and reducing abuse of services. Many providers, psychoanalytically oriented psychotherapists in particular, would disagree, citing instances in which services are routinely denied without any real assessment as to whether the services are, in fact, medically or psychologically necessary. It is critical, therefore, that review criteria be based on *objective* clinical criteria with realistic treatment timelines reflecting well-known and highly predictable patterns of mental health services and mental health care service delivery and utilization (R. Newman, personal communication, February 3, 1994). To date, thirty-one states have enacted legislation to license and regulate UR companies. Although these laws are not comprehensive or perfect, they do serve to monitor many review activities while empowering providers to advocate on behalf of their patients as well as to implement their best clinical judgment.

A review of existing state UR laws reveals that several states' statutes do contain provisions that are generally favorable to psychology. For example, Georgia, Hawaii, and Texas all have laws which provide strict UR criteria involving the provider in the review process, restricting financial incentives, and including psychologists as health care providers for purposes of reimbursement eligibility. The American Psychological Association (APA) has created a draft model UR statute (APA, Office of Managed Care, 1992a) and several other national organizations, including the Utilization Review Accreditation Commission (URAC), a self-regulating body, have promulgated model provisions for both inpatient and outpatient UR (URAC, 1993).

STANDARD PROVISIONS

Almost all of the UR legislation evaluated contains standard provisions intended to promote the delivery of quality health care in a cost-effective manner. The statutes seek to protect patients by: (1) promoting public access to criteria and standards used in UR; (2) attempting to ensure the confidentiality of patients' medical records; and (3) ensuring that UR agents have the proper qualifications to perform UR. Many statutes also require that the UR entity establish a comprehensive appeals procedure by which the insured or the provider may seek review of an adverse decision.

A standard provision in UR laws requires that the UR entity provide the insured with a copy of the UR plan, including specific review criteria, standards, procedures, and methods to be used in the evaluation of proposed services (e.g., General Statutes of North Carolina, 1991; Annotated Code of Maryland, 1992; Annotated Code of Montana, 1992). Moreover, UR entities must provide for the confidentiality of the patient or insured's medical records and personal information in accordance with applicable state and federal laws (e.g., Annotated Code of Arkansas, 1990; Code of Indiana, 1992; General Laws of Rhode Island, 1993). Most UR statutes stipulate who constitutes a "health care provider" (e.g., Revised Statutes of Oregon, 1987; Annotated Code of Mississippi, 1990; Revised Annotated Statutes of Louisiana, 1991). Health care providers are subject to UR; have the right to appeal adverse decisions; and can perform initial URs and/or reviews on appeal. The statutes also typically require that the state insurance commissioner develop a formal complaint mechanism by which a provider may request that the commissioner conduct an investigation of the UR entity's review procedures in a particular case (e.g., Revised Annotated Statutes of Kentucky, 1990; Revised Statutes of Hawaii, 1991; General Laws of Rhode Island, 1993).

THE LIKE-PROVIDER PROVISION

In some statutes, the definition of health care provider is ambiguous in terms of who is professionally qualified to conduct UR (e.g., Code of Iowa, 1987; Annotated Code of South Carolina, 1991; Acts of Massachusetts, 1993). However, some statutes specifically mandate that the reviewer be a physician, excluding by qualification nonphysician providers—including psychologists—from performing UR (e.g., Annotated Code of Arkansas, 1990; Statutes of Minnesota, 1992; General Laws of Rhode Island, 1993). Some UR laws specifically require that mental health UR be performed by an experienced mental health professional (e.g., Statutes of Florida, 1992; Annotated Code of Maryland, 1992). This requirement is specified by a "like-provider" provision, and it applies to initial reviews, as well as appeal procedures. A like-provider provision mandates that only those health care providers who are trained and licensed in the specific area in which the review is being conducted may make final determinations regarding services rendered or to be rendered. In states with such a provision, psychologists have grounds for pressing UR or insurance companies to place psychologists on their review panels.

CONSUMER PROTECTION PROVISIONS

Most statutes require the UR entity to establish confidentiality provisions and procedures. Such requirements compel UR entities to comply with the confidentiality terms imposed by both federal and state law, including patient authorization for the release of records and limits on the amount of information that may be made available to third-party payers (e.g., Annotated Code of Arkansas, 1990; Annotated Code of Virginia, 1991; General Laws of Rhode Island, 1993).

Some states also have statutory prohibitions regarding disclosure or publication of individual medical records or any other confidential information obtained in performance of UR (e.g., Annotated Insurance Code of Texas, 1990; Session Laws of Arizona, 1993; Acts of Massachusetts, 1993).

A statute might also contain a provision specifying that a reviewing professional or agent may not have any financial incentive that is in any way connected with his or her decision to approve of health care services (e.g., Annotated Code of Georgia, 1990; Revised Statutes of Nebraska, 1991; Central Code of North Dakota, 1991). The UR entity may be required by law to provide the state's department of insurance with certification that there is no financial incentive, direct or indirect, that might influence the UR determination by the private review agent (e.g., Statutes of Florida, 1992; Statutes of Minnesota, 1992).

Review decisions must be based on criteria that take into account the patient's medical and/or psychological condition. Standards should also limit the frequency of specific case review so that interference with the patient's care is kept to a minimum. In this context, it could be argued that *any* outside review by a third party creates some interference to the psychotherapeutic relationship and process. At the very least, the existence of an outside review process lessens the therapist's ability to maintain the optimal containment within the psychotherapy; at most, utilization review can violate the confidentiality of the therapy and batter the therapy process with unwanted outside intrusions. Patient and psychotherapist alike may remain in a constant state of uncertainty as to whether the next session will be authorized.

Other important consumer protection provisions include those that establish mechanisms for both providers and consumers to file complaints and those that regulate reporting of complaints to the insurance commissioner (e.g.,

Annotated Code of Georgia, 1990; Annotated Statutes of Oklahoma, 1992; General Laws of Rhode Island, 1993). Reporting requirements ensure that the department of insurance receives results of the reviews and numbers and results of any appeals or complaints that have been filed. In this way, the commissioner can be fully informed about any prior complaints when contacted by a psychologist or patient with a similar complaint.

Reporting requirements also extend to health maintenance organizations (HMOs) and preferred provider organizations (PPOs). HMOs and PPOs have become increasingly regulated in an attempt by states to legislate in favor of protection of the consumer. Yet, these managed care models pose significant challenges to both practicing psychologists and consumers. Among the provisions favorable to psychology are the: (1) any willing provider provision which typically mandates that a plan must accept any provider willing to meet the terms and conditions of the plan (e.g., Revised Annotated Statutes of Louisiana, 1982; Annotated Laws of Michigan, 1988; Insurance Code of California, 1992); (2) freedom of choice statute which permits consumers to choose any health care provider practicing within the scope of his or her licensure and legislates that an insurer reimburse services provided by the chosen provider (e.g., Revised Annotated Statutes of Louisiana, 1982; Annotated Statutes of Kansas, 1983; Annotated Statutes of Illinois, 1992); (3) antidiscrimination provision which prohibits insurers from discriminating against classes of providers (e.g., Administrative Code of Iowa, 1991; General Statutes of North Carolina, 1991; General Annotated Laws of Massachusetts, 1992); (4) strict confidentiality requirements (e.g., Annotated Code of Arkansas, 1987; Annotated Code of Utah, 1988; Code of Maine, 1990); and (5) prohibitions against financial incentives (e.g., Regulations Code of California, 1990; Annotated Statutes of Illinois, 1992; Code of Pennsylvania, 1992).

Despite such legislation and regulations, mental health providers still face a number of problems in their efforts to treat patients within the managed care environment. Additional guidance for providers is emerging in the legal system where recent court cases have begun to hold managed care responsible for arbitrary reimbursement denials and other coverage decisions.

Recent Court Cases Pertaining to Managed Care

In a managed care system, practitioners may not always be able to provide or obtain the care they believe necessary for their patients, even when such care would appear to be covered by their patients' insurance (Appelbaum, 1993). If a UR entity concludes that the recommended care suggested by a psychologist is not medically necessary—the standard ordinarily applied—coverage may be denied, even if the patient has not exhausted available benefits.

In a 1991 article, Newman and Bricklin discussed case law in the area of managed care liability that creates significant parameters for the delivery of health care services and helps delineate appropriate from inappropriate cost-control techniques. *Wickline v. State of California* (1987; hereinafter, *Wickline*), is, perhaps, the most significant case to address health care liability in a managed care context. The case identified the legal responsibility of a third-party payer for harm caused to a patient when a cost-containment mechanism impedes the delivery of care required as determined by the provider's clinical judgment.

In *Wickline*, a MediCal (California's Medicaid program) beneficiary was hospitalized for an arteriosclerotic condition and underwent a surgical procedure to replace a portion of her artery with a synthetic graft. Because of complications, her physician requested from MediCal an 8-day extension to her originally preauthorized 10-day hospital stay. The Medi-Cal utilization reviewer, however, authorized only a 4-day extension. As the patient's physician did not request any additional hospital days, she was discharged after a total of 14 days in the hospital. Subsequently, the patient developed a blood clot that necessitated the amputation of her right leg. The patient sued the state of California, alleging that MediCal's refusal to grant the additional 4-day extension caused her injuries. The trial court held for the plaintiff and awarded $500,000 in damages and found the utilization reviewer negligent.

The appellate court, however, reversed the verdict and found that MediCal was not liable for the patient's injuries. The court's reasoning was twofold. First, because the treating physician did not protest MediCal's denial of the 8-day extension, MediCal was viewed as never having had the opportunity to override the physician's decision. Second, and most importantly, because it was concluded by the court that the blood clot and amputation would have likely occurred even if the patient had remained in the hospital another 4 days, MediCal could not be liable.

The court continued on, however, to discuss those situations in which third-party payers could be held liable for denial of care:

> Third party payors of health care services can be held legally accountable when medically inappropriate decisions result from deficits in the design or implementation of cost-containment mechanisms as, for example, when appeals made on a patient's behalf for medical or hospital care are arbitrarily ignored or unreasonably disregarded or overridden [*Wickline*, p. 1645].

The result, then, is that insurers, HMOs, other managed care entities that act as third-party payers, employers, and utilization reviewers may be liable for harm when defects in cost-containment procedures, such as utilization review, lead to patient injury. These entities must now conduct themselves with this potential liability in mind.

Perhaps more relevant for psychologist-providers is the portion of *Wickline* implying that a prospective denial of coverage may be viewed as a denial of care if the provider adheres to the payer's recommendation, *but only if the provider has first protested the payer's recommendation for length of treatment.* In effect, *Wickline* suggested that a psychologist must actively object to a utilization review decision if it is at odds with the psychologist's clinical judgment. However, in a recent California Court of Appeals decision, *Wilson v. Blue Cross of Southern California* (1990; hereinafter, *Wilson*), the court held that the provider need not protest the utilization review decision in order to trigger potential liability on the part of the utilization review entity; rather each party would be held responsible for their own negligence. In any case, it is important to note that the psychologist will not totally avoid treatment responsibility for the patient; both the treating provider and utilization reviewer can share responsibility for premature termination of treatment.

In *Wilson*, a patient was admitted to a psychiatric hospital while suffering from major depression, drug dependency, and anorexia. His treating physician determined that he needed 3 to 4 weeks of inpatient care. After 11 days of inpatient care, the UR company advised the insurer that it should not pay for more inpatient care. The patient was discharged, and 20 days later he committed suicide. The family sued both the insurer and the UR company. The UR company specifically asserted that it was not liable under *Wickline* (1987) and sought to put the entire responsibility on the attending physician, claiming that the provider did not protest the UR decision. The court rejected this argument. The court observed that, in most utilization management program cases, it is difficult to argue that a decision to deny coverage is not a substantial factor in the decision to discharge. Undoubtedly, there will be further litigation seeking to balance the obligations and resulting liabilities of managed care companies, UR entities, and providers as suggested by *Wilson* and *Wickline* with regard to an insurer's right to review medical-necessity determinations by attending providers.

In addition to liability stemming from utilization management and quality assurance issues, any third-party payer can be liable for "bad-faith" claim denials; i.e., denials of claims without justification (*Hughes v. Blue Cross of Northern California, 1989*; hereinafter, *Hughes*). Bad-faith claim denials can exist even when there is no allegation of negligence against the treating physicians or hospitals (Harbaugh, 1993). In *Hughes*, the plaintiff-patient successfully argued that certain relevant treatment records had not been reviewed prior to denial of the patient's claim for payment of hospitalization benefits for severe psychiatric problems. As a result, the denial was determined to be done in "bad faith" and inappropriately.

Relatedly, in a Louisiana UR case, the U.S. Court of Appeals, Fifth Circuit, ruled that a third-party payer abused its discretion by terminating inpatient psychiatric benefits for a patient when continued treatment was indicated (*Salley v. E. D. DuPont de Nemours & Company*, 1992; hereinafter, *Salley*). In *Salley*, the court held the plan administrator liable for failure to obtain certain records in order to make an informed decision regarding the insurance claim.

Liability for managed care entities has been further expanded under such legal theories as *respondeat superior*, ostensible agency, corporate liability, and breach of contract. Staff-model HMOs most frequently are subject to the theory of respondeat superior. This doctrine states that a higher authority or employer is vicariously responsible for the actions taken on its behalf by employees. Therefore, when providers are direct employees of an HMO, it is possible to find the HMO liable for employees' misdeeds. One example of this is the case of *Sloan v. Metropolitan Health Council of Indianapolis, Inc.* (1987) where the court ruled that a corporation may be held vicariously liable for the malpractice of its employee-physicians.

Schleier v. Kaiser Foundation Health Plan (1989; hereinafter, *Schleier*) is another case in which respondeat superior provided the basis for liability. In this case, the defendant, an HMO, was held liable for the actions of a physician who was a consulting specialist. Despite the absence of an employer–employee arrangement, the consulting physician had never directly informed the plaintiff that he was not an employee of the HMO. The court held that, if a consumer reasonably believes that the provider is affiliated with the business and relies on this belief, the business may be held liable for the consultant's misdeeds. In essence, when a provider is reasonably believed to be an agent of the HMO, the court will rely on the "ostensible agency" of the provider to find liability for the HMO.

A further expanding area of managed care liability is the corporate negligence or corporate liability doctrine. The corporate negligence doctrine, historically applied to hospitals in holding them liable for negligent selection and supervision of personnel, may also be used to hold managed care entities similarly accountable (Newman and Bricklin, 1991). A duty will be owed the patient by a managed care entity when provider selection results in limiting and restricting a patient's choice of provider (Hinden and Elden, 1990). Hence, the managed care entity must properly review and investigate the credentials and expertise of provider panel applicants. This view was expressed in *Harrel v. Total Health*

Care, Inc. (1989) where an HMO was held to have a responsibility to enrollees to select physicians carefully. Furthermore, the court indicated that an HMO could be liable where it did not personally interview the physicians or check their references.

Emerging Issues for Psychologists in Managed Care Settings

There are two evolving issues that affect psychologists who are either currently involved in a managed care practice or considering participation in one. The first issue is the exclusion of psychologists from provider panels. While such exclusions are, by definition, common managed care practice, there are certain steps that can be taken to determine whether "closed provider panels" potentially violate a state law or regulation, as when the exclusion or refusal of membership by the managed care company is outright discriminatory.

The second issue is the "no-cause" termination provision found in many managed care contracts. This provision stipulates that either the managed care company or the health care provider can terminate a provider's contract without having to justify the termination. Plan members who are patients of terminated providers must typically transfer to a new panel provider. Termination without cause may put the provider's patients unnecessarily at risk and deny the rights of the provider. At the very least, a forced transfer unnecessarily delays treatment and wastes resources, and, at worst, it may jeopardize the patient's progress and psychological condition.

EXCLUSION FROM PPO PANELS

Successful legal claims for excluding providers from panels are few and far between. In order to fully appreciate why a claim of exclusion from a provider panel would likely fail, one must understand some basic PPO concepts. According to proponents of managed care, a PPO provides health care in a more cost-effective manner than indemnity plans as a result of its ability to restrict or limit the number of providers on its panel. Panel providers are then reimbursed on a discounted fee-for-service basis in exchange for a guarantee of increased patient volume and quick reimbursement payments. A primary objective of the PPO is to provide financial incentives to its members to utilize the select group of preferred providers, thereby reducing costs. Although members are sometimes free to receive treatment from nonpreferred providers, higher copayments or deductibles serve as a financial disincentive to do so. Thus, PPO administrators contend that it does not make good business sense for a PPO to accept every provider who applies to the panel, when its objective is to foster competition among applicants for the best quality service at the lowest price. This cost savings is then passed on to the PPO members who utilize the preferred providers.

It has been argued by opponents of managed care that excluding providers from a panel is tantamount to an illegal restraint of trade or boycott. In practice, however, antitrust claims made against PPOs for exclusion from panels are usually unsuccessful. Managed care practices are typically perceived by the courts as actually being inherently procompetitive because of their commitment to containing costs and passing this cost savings on to the consumer. Since courts tend to balance the anticompetitive elements of the plan against the procompetitive ones in order to determine whether anticompetitive conduct exists, a managed care plan is usually held not in violation of the antitrust laws for simply restricting its panels of providers. Further, because consumers, rather than providers, must be disadvantaged to find an illegal restraint of trade, the fact that providers are adversely affected by closed panels is insufficient.

Courts routinely consider five factors when evaluating the reasonableness of a PPO's panel selection process. First, courts are likely to perceive PPOs to be inherently procompetitive as opposed to anticompetitive. Second, courts acknowledge that states' enabling legislation encourages the growth of PPOs. Third, because most PPOs permit their enrollees to utilize the services of nonpreferred providers, they do not directly inhibit clinicians from practicing independently. Fourth, courts perceive PPOs as stimulating more economic choices for health care consumers. Finally, courts have typically found that because PPOs do not have a sufficiently meaningful market share, they do not completely close the marketplace to providers. These five factors combined make it difficult for an aggrieved provider to win a claim against a PPO based on antitrust grounds.

WAYS TO CHALLENGE A DENIAL OF PANEL MEMBERSHIP

Although it is difficult to legally challenge a PPO's denial of membership to an applying psychologist on antitrust grounds, the following steps may prove useful in demonstrating some element of discrimination which may be actionable.

- Obtain in writing the specific reasons for the refusal. These reasons may help the psychologist to devise a strategy for use when reapplying for panel participation or applying to another entity's panel.
- Determine whether the managed care company is refusing the participation of psychologists altogether or has merely met its quota of panel psychologists. If the former situation exists, the next step is to determine whether the state's PPO law contains a willing provider provision (15

states currently do; see APA, 1992a). Such provisions have not been typically interpreted to guarantee panel membership to every provider who applies to a PPO panel, but can be used to protect psychologists as a class of health care providers from being discriminated against and excluded from a panel.

- Determine whether the state PPO law provides for recognition of nonpanel services. Some states require PPOs to cover the services provided by nonpreferred providers if an enrollee seeks their treatment. In such cases, the patient typically pays a higher deductible, copayment fees, or both. If the state law provides for recognition of nonpanel services and the PPO is noncompliant, the psychologist will have an excellent case to get the service in question covered even though excluded from the panel.
- Determine whether the psychologist's services are delivered under a plan governed by the Employment Retirement Income Security Act (ERISA, 1974). ERISA plans are typically not bound by state mandates.
- If no state law exists requiring that the PPO permit psychologists to serve on the panel, the decision is usually left to the discretion of the managed care company itself.

NO-CAUSE TERMINATION

In comparison to challenging panel exclusions, the prospects for successfully challenging a no-cause termination appear to be gaining support as the law affecting managed care practices evolves. It is important to keep in mind, however, that this issue has not been extensively litigated. Therefore, the information presented here represents potential theories upon which a claim may be successfully pursued.

No-cause terminations are particularly troubling for psychologists who contract with managed care companies. Because providers are often placed in a position of having to argue and negotiate with the company to allow for additional therapy sessions for their patients, there is concern that managed care companies could use the no-cause termination provision as a means of eliminating those psychologists who frequently contest the managed care company's decisions.

There are several potential arguments that can be used to challenge a managed care company's decision to terminate a psychologist without cause. It may be argued that termination of a panel provider is, in effect, a "decredentialing" process. Because inclusion on a managed care panel imputes certain economic benefits and rights to providers, removal of a provider from a panel should be accompanied by a certain level of "due process" to protect fundamental fairness and the provider's rights. Due process or fundamental fairness procedures for panel termination might include notice, opportunity to refute the termination, and the right to an appeal. This is similar to the protections which have evolved for health care providers who become members of a hospital medical staff. Because managed care companies, like hospitals, have legal responsibilities, certain due process rights currently afforded to providers in a hospital setting might also be guaranteed to managed care providers. As a result, the same obligations and liabilities which attach to a managed care company for credentialing providers may also attach to the removal of the credential or termination. Accordingly, it can be argued that managed care companies, like hospitals, should be required to provide basic due process appeal rights to a provider who is terminated (Curtis, 1990).

In addition, managed care companies have not typically been required to afford providers an opportunity to appeal or challenge their termination. As a result, to the extent that a managed care company simply terminates a provider without an appropriate review of the situation, any injury to the provider's patients could raise the issue of negligence related to the managed care company.

Several court cases can be used to strengthen the argument for the right to appeal no-cause terminations (e.g., *Pinsker v. Pacific Coast Society of Orthodontists*, 1969; *Hackenthal v. California Medical Association*, 1982; *Salkin v. California Dental Association*, 1986). Courts have recognized that medical professional associations and other entities related to the provision of health care are of "quasi-public" significance (Curtis, 1990); entities considered to have quasi-public significance cannot expel or discipline members, so as to adversely affect their substantial property, contract, or other economic rights, without fair proceedings. Because expulsion from a managed care plan also involves judgment by one's own profession and such plans serve the quasi-public function of providing health care, one could argue that in no-cause termination cases, certain property and economic rights are at risk.

It can also be argued that managed care companies have a duty to show good faith in terminating a contract. It appears that managed care companies believe that a contract between a health care provider and a managed care company should be treated by the courts like a standard business contract where no-cause termination provisions are prevalent. Although such provisions found in contracts have traditionally been held to be valid, courts have increasingly implied a duty of good faith that is intended to protect the "reasonable expectations of the parties" (Curtis, 1990). In effect, contracts with managed care companies should be treated as agreements to provide health services, rather than as simple business arrangements. Therefore, terminations must be handled in a manner that considers consequences for the health care being provided and consequences to the patient being treated.

WAYS TO CHALLENGE A NO-CAUSE TERMINATION

The following are some suggestions for steps that can be taken by a psychologist-provider who is terminated without cause.

- Carefully review the provider contract to determine the circumstances under which a managed care company can effectively terminate the relationship with the provider.
- If the managed care company is able to terminate the relationship, determine whether the company has complied with the termination procedures set forth in the contract.
- To challenge a termination, upon receiving notice, contact the managed care company's director of provider relations by telephone to explore what alternatives for redress exist. Be as congenial as possible; this is still a business process, not a legal/adversarial process.
- If the telephone call is positive and feasible alternatives exist, send a written confirmation of the conversation to the managed care company.
- In the event that the conversation with the managed care company is negative and the provider wishes to pursue the issue further, file an official complaint with the managed care company. Duplicate complaint letters could be sent to the state's department of insurance which is responsible for regulating the activities of most managed care companies.
- When appealing a termination decision in writing, the provider should cite specific reasons as to why he or she is uniquely qualified (e.g., cite a successful treatment history, successful working relationship with the managed care company, and additional experience or training).
- When consulting with the UR agent either to appeal a decision or to provide information to the managed care

company in support of a complaint, supply well-kept records and documentation of therapy.

● Be particularly sensitive to the use of the no-cause termination provision by the managed care company as an excuse to get rid of a provider whom it may view as a troublemaker; e.g., a psychologist who vigorously opposes adverse UR decisions.

A "good plaintiff" in a no-cause termination case is one who has historically had a good relationship with the managed care company, but whose relationship has soured because of the plaintiff's repeated attempts to appeal or complain about a decision made by a managed care company. Furthermore, evidence of a substantial caseload at some point during the relationship is significant, and the existence of solid documentation is essential.

Typical Dilemmas Faced by Therapists and Potential Strategies for the Practitioner and Patient Participating in a Managed Health Care Environment

Psychologists practicing within the realm of managed care frequently must do so without advance knowledge as to reimbursement for psychological services due to lack of information from managed care companies as to services covered, accessibility of services, and unjustified UR procedures and determinations. Many managed care entities, through contractual arrangements, limit reimbursement only to services that are deemed "medically or psychologically necessary." These entities typically do not provide a definition of what constitutes a medically or psychologically necessary service, and, as a result, neither the therapist nor the patient is given a sense, in advance, of what services are or are not covered.

Typically, the practices, policies, and design of managed care entities restrict access to the delivery of mental health care and other services to consumers. For example, difficulties are presented by the limits placed on mental health services through the use of caps on dollars spent and limits on number of visits allowed. Additionally, the quality and appropriateness of mental health services provided through some managed care entities may be considered by providers and consumers to be inadequate. Furthermore, consumers may not be provided full information about the operation of the benefit plan and the financial arrangements brokered by the managed care entity. Specifically, some managed care plans may fail to fully disclose information about cost-control mechanisms such as incentive plans that link a provider's decision to refer to a specialist—including mental health practitioners—to income that the provider will receive. Consumers and providers must ensure that they are adequately informed about the financial incentives, gatekeeping process, and services covered before entering into a legally binding relationship with a managed care entity.

Providers also frequently raise serious complaints about unreasonable requests for information by UR companies. Ethical and practice dilemmas arise when raw data, progress notes, and other information beyond what is considered reasonable are requested from psychologists. Additionally, both providers and patients complain about the lack of written or oral justification by UR entities when refusing to authorize additional coverage for services. As a result, psychologists are continually searching for guidance regarding ethical and practice dilemmas when delivering services in a managed care setting. As discussed, many states have begun to propose and implement legislation to help regulate UR activities of covered services.

There are a variety of ways that a practitioner and his or her patient can protect themselves and ensure approval of needed treatment sessions as well as adequate reimbursement for treatment provided. Unfortunately, *Wickline* and

Wilson do not provide clear parameters as to how far the provider must go in terms of providing treatment to a patient whom the provider believes needs more care, but for whom the UR entity has decided further treatment is not medically necessary (Appelbaum, 1993). This specifically becomes problematic when it is unclear whether the patient has the ability to pay. It may be that if a provider has not begun treatment, he or she is freer to turn away a case, provided that the case is not an emergency. However, most UR cases center around relationships already established between the provider and the patient. A termination of this relationship creates clinical, ethical, and legal concerns for the treating psychologist.

As a practical matter, termination of the psychotherapy relationship in a managed care environment should follow all the clinical requirements for termination of care in a nonmanaged care environment. To do otherwise runs the risk of being held liable for "negligent abandonment." The two elements helpful for avoiding a claim of negligent abandonment are (1) helping the patient to secure alternative health care services if additional treatment is necessary and it is not possible to continue treating the patient (e.g., at a community mental health center) and (2) giving written notice to the patient. In effect, providers must adhere to the customary standard of care for terminating treatment and/ or referring patients whether the treatment is provided through a managed care or traditional indemnity arrangement.

When UR denial applies to a truly elective procedure, there is generally ample opportunity for the provider to meet these requirements. However, when the patient is hospitalized or in an emergency situation, it will likely be much more difficult. In such cases, the issue of informed consent related to the utilization review process becomes a factor. In other words, it is important for psychologists to explain carefully to the patient, in advance of commencing treatment, the options and risks involved if the proposed treatment is denied by the UR entity. If treatment is denied at some point, *it is the patient who must then decide* whether to continue with the treatment at the risk of being held financially liable. The potential for added financial pressure on the patient may negatively impact the patient's progress and/or the therapeutic relationship. Potential denial of reimbursement increases the provider's need for sensitivity when carefully explaining the health care risks of foregoing treatment or paying for services rendered directly rather than through the reimbursement program of a third-party payer.

When a third-party payer denies a claim and a psychologist continues to treat the patient, that psychologist may assume some financial risk if he or she provides services without guarantee of payment from the payer. If a psychologist continues to provide benefits until the appeals process is resolved, it is best that he or she do so based on an express agreement with the patient as to who is responsible for charges not covered by the payer. Also, psychologists should review their contract with the payer to ensure that holding the patient financially responsible if the third-party payer does not honor the claim is not a prohibited option.

In advance of treatment, and as part of the informed consent process, the provider should review with the patient the proposed treatment and any procedures contractually agreed upon in the managed care contract signed by the provider (see Bennett, Bryant, VandenBos, and Greenwood, 1990). The information provided to patients should outline the various contractual provisions that could affect them, including, for example, limitations on benefits, financial incentives tied to the delivery of services, and the sharing of patients' records with the managed care entity. Providing patients with information during the initial phases of the professional relationship about the risks and limitations imposed by outside entities, particularly limitations on therapeutic confidentiality, has increasingly been cited as a crucial and necessary element of psychological risk management. (See Section 4.02 of APA's *Ethical Principles of Psychologists and Code of Conduct* [1992b].) At least two states now legally require informed consent as a standard of practice (Annotated Laws of Massachusetts, 1990; Oklahoma Statutes, 1991). Furthermore, there is at least anecdotal evidence that providing such information enhances, rather than diminishes, clinical effectiveness.

Practitioners should be aware of the specific limitations imposed by the managed care entities of which they are contracted members, and should be prepared to discuss them with patients. An informed patient is less likely to be disconcerted and the therapeutic relationship less likely to be disrupted when information is requested for UR purposes and/ or additional sessions are denied. A psychologist's practice of providing full information will help establish that he or she performs in a professional manner regarding disclosure of potential reimbursement problems. Standard disclosure would make an abandonment claim harder to substantiate although it would still be possible if the termination of treatment for nonpayment could be demonstrated to have damaged the client.

Informed consent is particularly important when the managed care entity, not the psychologist or the patient, has the power to limit the reimbursement available for psychological services and may require the release of confidential information in order to determine how much treatment is warranted. Often, patients are unaware of the requirements and limitations their plan imposes. The psychologist should clarify, for the patient's benefit, his or her responsibilities to the managed care entity. It is also advantageous for providers to notify patients when a plan imposes limitations on coverage so that patients can investigate those limitations before deciding to enter into treatment or to rely on their plan to cover the treatment.

The provider's responsibility to maintain the confidentiality of professionally obtained information becomes more complex in the current health care environment. While the responsibility is to protect the privacy of their patients, it is important to realize that if the patient chooses to waive that privacy, the psychologist is obligated to honor that choice. Yet, the provider is also obligated to inform the patient as to any foreseeable downside of waiving the privacy right and triggering a release of information. The basic right of insurance companies to obtain information that is deemed essential to determine whether services provided are within the benefit definition (i.e., medically necessary) is widely accepted within the insurance industry. However, insurance carriers require patients to sign a consent form that authorizes access for the insurance company to any information that it deems appropriate to evaluating claims as a condition of coverage. Issues have been raised regarding the appropriateness and voluntariness of such consent. Many states have laws to regulate how much information an insurance company can demand and what can be done with that information. In the absence of such regulation, from a practical standpoint, releases from patients are binding, and if a patient refuses to let a practitioner submit requested information, reimbursement may be denied.

Psychologists may also be responsible for assessing whether the particular management structure is conducive to providing appropriate professional services (APA, 1992b). If the system is not appropriate, a psychologist may have an ethical responsibility not to participate. If a particular plan imposes limitations on treatment, a psychologist has a responsibility to fully discuss those limitations with the patient.

For example, if a managed care plan provides reimbursement only for short-term, problem-oriented treatment and a psychologist feels that longer term treatment is essential, the psychologist should discuss the costs and benefits of both short-term and long-term treatment so that the client may make a knowledgeable choice.

Furthermore, psychologists can provide patients with information that enables them to advocate for their own interests with the plan manager. When an entity requests information from a psychologist, the psychologist may find it helpful to inform the patient and fully discuss the request with him or her, reminding the patient of his or her right to refuse to submit the information and to decline reimbursement. Psychologists should familiarize themselves with relevant state laws which impose any limitations on requests from insurance companies, and they should ensure that patients are aware of having access to the state's insurance commissioner if they feel aggrieved by the plan's procedures. If a patient feels that the information requested could be damaging, the psychologist should contact the entity and attempt to determine the necessity of such information and explore whether the information request could be satisfied in an alternative manner. The psychologist should not hesitate to speak with a supervisor if the benefits manager with whom he or she has contact is nonresponsive.

It is important to become familiar with internal complaint mechanisms available to beneficiaries and providers in a managed care setting. In the event of a denial of reimbursement, the psychologist should have access, as part of the appeals process, to obtain the basis for the UR decision to deny service. The provider should secure the basis for the UR decision so that he or she may respond adequately during the appeals process. Also, the UR appeals committee should prepare a written statement of its decision, which demonstrates a good-faith approach to the problem.

It is also important for providers to document conversations with the entity and to maintain any copies of correspondence sent by or to the entity so that a written file can be accumulated. Providers who are having difficulty resolving a complaint may wish to enlist help from a state psychological association and coordinate locally with association members. Generally, if providers join together, the managed care entity may be more responsive. Before reporting a problem to the department of insurance which is responsible for regulating the particular entity involved and/or enlisting the help of the state and national association groups, all the remedies present within the system should be exhausted. Once the practitioner has exhausted the internal grievance system, the practitioner then may seek outside help by filing a detailed letter of complaint with the department of insurance representative responsible for regulating the particular entity. Copies of correspondence should also be sent to the entity involved so that it is aware that a complaint is being filed. The practitioner may also wish to identify to the managed care entity the level of support enlisted by copying the relevant professional associations on all correspondence.

Psychologists should be willing to assume a similar role when they feel that benefits are being prematurely terminated. Psychologists can contact the case manager to formally request and discuss the rationale for the decision to terminate treatment coverage. Psychologists are more likely to be effective if they can refute the entity's rationale in a measured, professional manner, and less likely to be effective if they appear angry and generally resistant to the UR process. If reasoning on the part of the psychologist is not effective, the patient can be encouraged to appeal the decision by the psychologist willing to provide assistance in that process.

In conclusion, psychologists in today's health care market must have a greater understanding of the legal issues which impact the delivery of care to their patients. Psychologists with adequate knowledge of the legal limits of cost-containment strategies will be better able to provide needed care for their patients.

References

1992 Supp. Vol. 1, Florida Statutes § 395.0199.
1993 Arizona Sess. Laws 159.
1993 Massachusetts Acts 1812.
American Psychological Association (1992a), *Draft Model Utilization Review Legislation*. Washington, DC: American Psychological Association.
_____ (1992b), *Ethical Principles of Psychologists and Code of Conduct*. Washington, DC: American Psychological Association.
Annotated Laws of Massachusetts (1981), Mass. Anno. Laws ch. 176A, Sec. 10A. Eagan, MN: West.
Appelbaum, P. S. (1993), Legal liability and managed care. *Amer. Psychologist*, 48:251–257.
Arkansas Code Ann. § 20-9-901 (Michie, 1990).
Becker, J., Tiano, L., & Marshall, S. (1992), Legal issues in managed mental health. In: *Managed Mental Health Care: Administration and Clinical Issues*, ed. R. Fitzpatrick & J. L. Feldman. Washington, DC: American Psychiatric Press, pp. 6–8.
Bennett, B. E., Bryant, B. K., VandenBos, G. R., & Greenwood, A. (1990), *Professional Liability and Risk Management*. Washington, DC: American Psychological Association.
Boochever, S. (1986), Health maintenance organizations. In: *Introduction to Alternative Delivery Mechanisms: HMOs, PPOs, & CMPs*, ed. J. M. Johnson. Washington, DC: National Health Lawyers Association, pp. 5–10.
Curtis, T. (1990), Fair hearings for physicians denied participation in managed care plans. *Med. Staff Counselor*, 4:45–47.
Employee Retirement Income Security Act of 1974. 29 U.S.C. Section 1142 (1982).
Georgia Code Ann. § 33-45-1 et seq. (Michie, 1990).
Hackenthal v. California Medical Association, 187 Cal. Rptr. 811 (Ct. App., 1982).

Harbaugh, C. (1993), Courts all over the map on plan liability for allegedly negligent actions of physicians. *Manag. Care Law Outlook*, 5(2):10–11.

Harrell v. Total Health Care, Inc., 781 S.W.2d 58 (Mo., 1989).

Hawaii Rev. Stat. § 334B-1 et seq. (1991).

Hinden, R. A., & Elden, D. L. (1990), Liability issues for managed care entities. *Seton Hall Legislat. J.*, 14(8):1–60.

Hughes v. Blue Cross of Northern California, 215 Cal. App. 3d 832, Cal. Ct. App. (1989).

Indiana Code § 27-8-17 (1992).

Iowa Code §§ 514F.1, 514F.2 (1987).

Kentucky Rev. Stat. Ann. § 211.461-466 (Baldwin, 1990).

Louisiana Rev. Stat. Ann. § 40.2721 et seq. (West, 1991).

Maryland Health-Gen. Code Ann. § 19-1301 (1992).

Minnesota Stat. § 62 M.01 et seq. (1992).

Mississippi Code Ann. § 41-83-1 et seq. (1990).

Montana Code Ann. § 33-32-101 (1992).

Nebraska Rev. Stat. § 44-5401-5415 (1991).

Newman, R., & Bricklin, P. M. (1991), Parameters of managed mental health care: Legal, ethical, and professional guidelines. *Profess. Psychol.: Res. & Pract.*, 22(1):26–35.

North Carolina Gen. Stat. § 58-2-40(1); 58-50-60 (1991).

North Dakota Cent. Code §§ 26.1–26.4-.01 et seq (1991).

Oklahoma Statutes (1991). Okla. Stat. tit. 59, Sec. 1376.

Oklahoma Stat. Ann. tit. 36, § 6551 (West, 1992).

Oregon Rev. Stat. § 743.556 (1987).

Pinsker v. Pacific Coast Society of Orthodontists, 460 P.2d 495 (Cal., 1969).

Rhode Island Gen. Laws §§ 23-17.12-1 et seq. (1993).

Salkin v. California Dental Association, 224 Cal. Rptr. 352 (Ct. App. 1986).

Salley v. E. D. DuPont de Nemours & Company, No. 91-35-23 (5th Cir. 1992).

Schleier v. Kaiser Foundation Health Plan, 876 F.2d 174 (DC Cir. 1989).

Sloan v. Metropolitan Health Council of Indianapolis, Inc., 516 N.E. 2d 1104 (ind. Ct. App. 1987).

South Carolina Code Ann. § 38-70-10 et seq. (Law. Co-op, 1991).

Texas Ins. Code Ann. art. 21.58 (West, 1990).

Utilization Review Accreditation Commission, Inc. (1993), *Draft Revisions to the National Utilization Review Standards.* Washington, DC: URAC.

Virginia Code Ann. § 38.2.5300-5309 (Michie, 1991).

Wickline v. State of California, 239 Cal. Rptr. 805, 741 P.2d 613 (1987).

Wilson v. Blue Cross of Southern California, 271 Cal. Rptr. 876, Cal. App. 2 Dist. (1990).

14

Reflections on Managed Care, Health Reform, and the Survival of Dynamic Psychotherapy

Josef H. Weissberg, M.D.

During the past few years managed care has gained popularity dramatically as a means of limiting third-party reimbursement for mental health services. Often, managed care corporations have designed provider panels and medical necessity definitions to permit reimbursement for only the most rudimentary psychotherapeutic services. In areas where such plans have replaced indemnity health insurance, insured individuals must frequently bear the entire cost of psychotherapy themselves or accept the unfounded and capricious allegation of the managed care organization that psychotherapy is not an effective treatment and that a cheaper modality will be "better." Such contentions have been based on evaluation criteria that are applied to no other health care field. They have no basis or purpose other than to lower mental health reimbursement costs by irresponsibly eliminating an entire therapeutic modality.

Some areas of the country are more saturated with managed care plans than others, and not all managed care organizations are as arbitrarily restrictive as others. The situation

271

is complicated, however, by the likelihood that some form of health care reform will be enacted before long in most states. Most proposed health reform proposals contain provision for managed care. There is some question about whether it will be possible to contract outside the system. If it is not, and if managed care continues as unregulated as it has been, it might be impossible legally to provide intensive psychotherapy, let alone psychoanalysis, to anyone, no matter how compelling the indications.

Several states are considering legislation regulating managed care. Since managed care plans profoundly affect professional psychotherapists and their patients, we must be aware of the provisions that would make such supervision tolerable to us, rather than quietly observing the administering of intensive psychotherapy out of existence.

Confidentiality

While scrutiny of some sort seems to be a reality unlikely to disappear, steps can be taken to protect patients' privacy effectively. We should take a role in defining realistically the least amount of information necessary to make reimbursement decisions. It is rarely necessary to include specific potentially damaging data. Patients' names should not appear on review documents. Each patient should be assigned a number and the identity kept on a computer disk available only to a specified senior executive. Review documents of inactive cases should be destroyed after one year.

Provider Panel Composition

It is outrageous for managed care companies to declare arbitrarily that all providers are fungible and to include on their panels only nonprofessional therapists who receive lower fees. It should not be possible for managers to control practice patterns by "recredentialing" providers and eliminating those who use modalities, such as intensive psychotherapy, of which the managers arbitrarily disapprove. Point of service options, which allow patients to choose out of network providers for a small copayment increment, are desirable. Since such provisions interfere with control of practice patterns, it is unlikely they will be offered unless demanded by industrial clients. Patients should be free to choose any provider on the panel. Point of service options, which allow patients to choose out of network providers for a small increment in the copayment, are desirable. Since such provisions interfere with control of practice patterns, it is unlikely they will be offered unless demanded by industrial clients. Panels must be open to all professionals who meet published criteria and accept the contractual provisions.

Nature of Review

Reviews should be conducted by professionals, preferably of the same discipline as the provider. The purpose should be to reimburse the least expensive *effective* therapy. Emphasis on fiscal savings must be tempered by clinical responsibility. Initial review should identify "outliers" based on unindicated therapy, unusual duration, uncertain medical necessity, or lack of progress. These cases should be scrutinized more closely, not automatically denied reimbursement. An effective appeal mechanism must be in place, preferably including arbitration of disputes. Patients who choose to see out-of-panel providers should not be subject to prohibitive reimbursement penalties. Reviews should not be excessively frequent or time consuming. Choice of modality must remain a clinical, not an administrative decision.

Parity

The practice of reimbursing treatment for mental illness differently from illness of any other organ system is indefensible and perpetuates pejorative myths such as psychotherapy being designed for the "worried well." Legislation restricting parity to "serious" mental illness, ostensibly neurobiological in nature, is untenable, involving discrimination on a different but no less illogical basis. Besides the fact that diagnosis does not reliably indicate functional impairment, this restriction would have a negative influence on the whole field by creating pressure to secure coverage by slanting diagnosis in a more "serious" direction.

Independent Contracting

The right of patient and therapist to contract independently outside the system is of primary importance if patients are not to be deprived of whole therapeutic modalities by the arbitrary decision of nonclinical managers. Although this feature did not appear in the Clinton recommendations, it is strongly supported by all of medicine and has been present in most subsequent proposals.

Hold Harmless Clauses

Many managed care provider contracts still include "hold harmless" clauses, which release the corporation from liability stemming from reimbursement decisions. The individual provider is liable for damage resulting from inadequate treatment, even when reimbursement has been denied by the manager, if his appeal was not sufficiently vigorous. Not surprisingly, malpractice carriers either refuse to cover liability resulting from "hold harmless" contract clauses or charge increased premiums for such coverage.

Health Care Reform

With the failure of Congress to pass health care reform legislation in the 1994 session, the focus of attention has shifted to the state legislatures, and most are considering legislation modifying and regulating health care delivery. While congressional leaders continue to state their intention to enact reform laws, it seems unlikely that any comprehensive reshaping will take place on the federal level in the near future. State legislatures are under pressure from the insurance and managed care industries and it will be difficult to enact effective regulatory measures. However, our colleagues have been successful in several states and have proven that it is possible to reverse some of the more damaging effects of the past few years.

Discussion

American industry, in its headlong rush to reduce health costs no matter what the consequences, has found mental health services to be particularly vulnerable to wholesale cutting of reimbursement benefits. The reasons for this susceptibility have been explored elsewhere. They concern (1) the difficulty in verifying objectively the pathology of the patients we treat and the results we obtain; (2) the reluctance of our patients to complain about cuts because of the stigma of emotional illness; (3) the artificial adversarial dichotomy that exists between dynamic and biologic psychiatry; and (4) changes in our culture concerning the relative value of intellectual and technological endeavors. In addition, the special nature of intensive psychotherapy and psychoanalysis has made it unfeasible for us to ask former and present patients to lend their voices to our efforts to preserve the availability of these services.

The disability of emotional illness is as real as that of disorders of any other system. Recently published data show that the annual cost of depression alone is $43.7 billion, greater than that of heart disease (Greenberg, Stiglin, Finkelstein, and Berndt, 1993). *The New York Times* has claimed that the incidence of emotional illness in this country is significantly greater than previously thought; close to half the population will suffer from diagnosable mental illness sometime during their lives. Data are accumulating in studies comparing outcomes of patients treated in HMOs, those with indemnity insurance, and those who are uninsured. Preliminary findings show a significant difference in outcomes varying with the type of plan, the worst results occurring in prepaid independent practice associations (IPAs), the plan type that most resembles the Clinton blueprint for health care reform. Patients in this type of plan tended to receive medication immediately and very few visits. At follow-up, relatively few had continued medication and most had become more limited functionally.

Dynamic psychotherapy has been vulnerable to cyclical fluctuations in popularity over the years. Never before, however, has there been a real threat to legislate or administer an effective treatment modality out of existence. We are experiencing marked drops in applications to training programs and to psychoanalytic institutes. Many psychiatry residency training programs have drastically reduced the time devoted to instruction in dynamic psychotherapy. There are fewer active teachers and fewer students to teach. If the current climate were to persist, it would probably not take very long for dynamic psychotherapy to disappear. Since many patients presenting for mental health care will respond to nothing else, this must not be allowed to happen. The prospect of short-run savings must not be permitted to drive health care policy without clinical responsibility.

Mere survival, however, is not enough. We must also preserve an environment in which intensive psychotherapy and psychoanalysis can flourish. When mutagenic factors in dynamic psychotherapy are discussed, the relationship between patient and therapist, whether conceptualized as transference or alliance, is usually found at the top of the list. We do not know exactly what effect funding changes will have on this most sensitive ingredient. Clearly, the insertion of the managed care corporation into the therapeutic dyad will open the question of the allegiance of the therapist—does he work for the patient or for the third-party payer? Such possible problems as modifying diagnosis to favor continued reimbursement might seriously compromise the patient's perception of the therapist's integrity, complicating the therapeutic relationship in a possibly irreversible way. While concern about confidentiality can be used to support objections to any requests for clinical information, it seems likely that reasonable requests can be satisfied without affecting the therapeutic relationship adversely.

Some therapists have even found that the experience of responding cooperatively to third-party enquiries has facilitated and expedited the development of the therapeutic relationship. At any rate, we will face a challenge to develop new techniques to deal constructively with the many changes in the conditions under which intensive psychotherapy and psychoanalysis will be pursued in coming years. Fighting some of the destructive trends besetting us and our patients will require cooperation between groups that have been more concerned with protecting established turf. A comprehensive educational effort will have to be mounted, involving media, business executives, and unions. We must reconsider the ethical and therapeutic implications of inviting former patients to join our legislative and educational efforts. If our field survives the current crisis created by managed care and health care reform, its viability will, to a large extent, be measured by our effectiveness in handling this challenge.

References

American Psychiatric Association (1993), Clinton health care plan—Role of the states. *State Update* (APA Div. of Gov. Relations).

American Medical Association (1993), Analysis of the Clinton plan. AMA mailing. September 24.

Clinical Psychiatry News (1993), The Health Security Act of 1993. *Clin. Psychiatry News.*

Clinton Health Care Reform Proposal. H.R. 3600, S. 1757.

Doidge, N. An overview of empirical studies on the efficacy of psychoanalysis and psychoanalytic psychotherapy. Typescript.

Greenberg, P. E., Stiglin, L. E., Finkelstein, S. N., & Berndt, E. R. (1993), The economic burden of depression in 1990. *J. Clin. Psychiatry,* 54(11):405–418.

Grinfeld, M. (1993), Health care reform: The real debate begins. *Psychiatric Times,* 10:11.

National Advisory Mental Health Council (1993), Health care reform for Americans with severe mental illnesses. *Amer. J. Psychiatry,* 150:1477–1463.

Weissberg, J. H. (1992), The psychoanalytic envelope. *J. Amer. Acad. Psychoanal.* 20:497–508.

International Perspective

15

Psychoanalysis and Psychotherapy Under National Health Insurance Plans Around the World

Brent Willock, Ph.D.

Overview

Problems related to national health insurance and managed care are not unique to the United States (Willock, in press). Most industrialized nations have been grappling with these issues for some time. Each country has come up with its own particular system, and each has its assets and liabilities. Studying these diverse arrangements helps to place the particular circumstances in the United States within a broader context. In the table below, key features of the health insurance systems in several countries are listed so that readers can grasp at a glance the major aspects of each country's plan and also acquire some understanding of how that plan compares with what is available in other countries. We have selected an array of countries so as to provide a feel for the range of existing plans.

TABLE 16.1: Coverage of Psychoanalysis and Psychotherapy Under National Health Insurance Plans

Country	Frequency of Sessions	Duration of Treatment	Coverage for Psychoanalysis	Copayment	Acceptable Academic Background of the Analyst/Therapist	Alternative Arrangements for Excluded Analysts	Conditions
Australia (Martin, 1995; Waterhouse, 1994, personal communication)	Unlimited	Unlimited	Yes	Analysts tend to charge somewhat more than is reimbursed by the plan.	M.D. only.	Some private insurance companies provide (very) limited coverage for psychologists.	Patients pay for missed sessions. — Training analysis not covered.
Canada (Fayek, in press; Hanly, 1995; Pequeneza, 1995; Willock, in press)	Unlimited in most provinces. Restricted to twice a week in Manitoba, three times per week in Quebec. In provinces which limit frequency, analysts may not charge for extra sessions (though some apparently do).	Unlimited	In many jurisdictions but not all	None. Extra billing is illegal, but ways around the law are frequently found (charging for uninsured aspects of service).	M.D. only. Psychiatric training not required. Training in psychotherapy not required. G.P.'s can and do bill extensively (e.g., in Ontario approx. $156 million per year). In British Columbia, however, G.P.'s can only bill for the first 7 minutes of each session; the patient must pay for the rest.	Private insurance plans covering psychologists vary from minimal to generous, with the latter being rare. Social workers and psychologists also practice in hospitals on a salaried basis, providing generally free services. Intensive, long-term treatments are increasingly not encouraged in these institutions. In Quebec, psychoanalysis can be practiced in a small number of designated training hospitals.	

TABLE 16.1: Coverage of Psychoanalysis and Psychotherapy Under National Health Insurance Plans (continued)

Czech Republic (Ruzicka, 1994, personal communication)	Unlimited	Unlimited	Yes	None	Any psychologist or M.D. may provide up to 10 hours of psychotherapy per patient per year. — A clinical psychologist or psychiatrist may provide up to 100 sessions per patient per year. Social workers with appropriate training who have passed the mental health specialist examinations set by the Ministry of Health are covered. — Qualified analysts have unlimited coverage.	Medical referral needed except for patients in crisis or after trauma. (Previously patients could refer themselves. Therapists are struggling to restore this right.)
Finland (Sjodin, 1994)	Up to 3 per week. Patients may pay for additional sessions.	Up to 3 years. Patients may pay for lengthier treatment.	Yes		Whatever is acceptable to the psychoanalytic training program (e.g., psychiatry, psychology, theology) will be eligible for reimbursement upon completion of training and achievement of registration.	Psychiatric referral required attesting to "failing working capacity." — Annual checkup report required by psychoanalyst and psychiatrist.

70% of analytic treatments are financed by the National Medical Insurance or some other insurance system. 30% of patients pay for their treatment.

TABLE 16.1: Coverage of Psychoanalysis and Psychotherapy Under National Health Insurance Plans (continued)

Germany (Balzert, in press; Sjodin, 1994)	Up to 3 per week. Patients cannot pay for additional sessions, nor can they be provided free.	Up to 80 sessions at a time can be approved. Limit of 300 sessions. 15% of patients pay for continuing treatment after their limit has been reached.	Officially only "psychoanalytic psychotherapy" is covered. This has revived debate as to whether 3 sessions per week can be considered psychoanalysis.	Traditionally none, but government currently debating—could be up to 25%.	Psychology, psychiatry, and child and adolescent psychotherapists.	80% of psychoanalytic treatments are funded by the National Insurance Agency. 15% are funded by private insurance.	Only empirically validated treatments are funded. This includes psychoanalytic psychotherapy and behavior therapy but not Rogerian, Gestalt, or Art Therapy. ___ Treatment modality must be approved by panel of consultants appointed by National Insurance Agency.
Great Britain (Tarnopolsky, 1994, personal communication; Wallerstein, 1991)	One session per week in many National Health Service clinics. More intensive therapy must be financed privately by those who desire and can afford it. A few training facilities provide more intensive treatment (e.g., the Tavistock).	Unlimited	None	None			In the National Health Service clinics, in addition to the usual mental health professions, the independent profession of child psychotherapist is well established. Child therapists report that they used to have considerable freedom with regard to frequency and duration of treatments, but are under increasing pressure to see patients more briefly and less frequently.

TABLE 16.1: Coverage of Psychoanalysis and Psychotherapy Under National Health Insurance Plans (continued)

Netherlands (Abraham, in press; Groen-Filet, 1993; Prakken and de Noble, 1992)	Unlimited, but must be approved by a regional commission of colleagues.	Yes	90 sessions can be spread out over several months or years. If further treatment is required, patient must go to a clinic for at least a year, after which they may have another 90 sessions with a private practitioner. Patients are allowed to pay when their 90 sessions have finished. Some insurance companies assist patients wanting to continue beyond 90 sessions.	About $11 per session for the first 45 sessions in a year, free after that. If unemployed, it is free after about 9 sessions.	Psychiatrists; registered psychotherapists (mostly psychologists, some social workers and physicians). Separate budgets for psychoanalysis and psychotherapy.	Referral by G.P., psychiatrist, or mental health clinic.	Therapists must be under 65 years of age. — No therapist can have more than 6 45-minute sessions per day, for a maximum of 36 per week. — If therapist does not use all allotted sessions in a year, they are taken away forever and given to other therapists. The same happens to sessions of therapists who retire. These freed-up funds may be used to let new therapists enter the system, but at the moment, there is no mechanism to let new therapists in.

TABLE 16.1: Coverage of Psychoanalysis and Psychotherapy Under National Health Insurance Plans (continued)

Sweden (Birchard, 1994; Carlsson, 1993, personal communication; Sjodin, 1994; Stensson, 1993, personal communication)	Unlimited	Unlimited	Yes	$5 per session	M.D.	Government gives some money to local health authorities for patients of psychologists which are administered by local hospitals. Long waiting lists. Restrictions on frequency and duration. Must reapply after each year for continued treatment. Funding may only cover small portion of each visit, say 30%.
Switzerland (Condrau, 1994; Moser, 1992)	Federal Government recommends two sessions per week for up to 3 years, then one session per week for up to 3 more years. Common plan in actuality is 2 hours per week for up to 2 years, with extension under certain circumstances.	Varies depending on province (canton) and insurance company (usually 2–6 years).			M.D.	Psychologists recently approved to conduct "delegated psychotherapy" in M.D.'s consulting rooms, under physician control, at lower fee.

Problems in Maintaining Achieved Levels of Coverage

Just as conflicts about national health insurance and managed care have been heating up in the United States over the past several years, similar trends can be observed around the world. The global economic recession is a major factor in these debates. In Norway (Sjodin, 1994), for example, some psychologists and psychiatrists in private practice are paid partly by the National Medical Insurance and partly by the local community. Other practitioners, who do not have a contract with the local authorities, are paid by the National Medical Insurance and the patient. There is no private insurance. Recently, however, it was ordained that patients treated by therapists established after October 1992 would have to pay for their own therapy. This cutback is expected to have an extremely deleterious impact on the private practice of psychotherapy.

In Sweden (Carlsson, 1993, personal communication), certain state employees (e.g., at universities) used to receive assistance if they wished to engage in psychotherapy with a psychologist. The government might pay half to two-thirds of the fee. This support has been discontinued, a fact not unrelated to the economic downturn. Sweden, like other Scandinavian countries, used to be prosperous (Birchard, 1994). Unemployment, which was almost nonexistent as recently as five years ago, now stands close to 14 percent. Sweden has the highest per capita budget deficit of any industrialized country. From being one of Europe's largest spenders on health care, Sweden is now one of the lowest.

In Canada, one province, Manitoba, recently removed psychoanalysis from its list of insured services. Coverage for treatment in Manitoba is now limited to two sessions per week. Shortly after the Manitoba cutback, the government in Canada's most populous province, Ontario, actively considered a similar "delisting" of psychoanalysis. Vigorous lobbying by psychoanalysts and their patients succeeded in defeating this proposal. There is, however, a feeling that the same battle will have to be waged again some time in the future and that then, the outcome may not be so positive. The Dutch National Health care system also planned to stop reimbursing psychoanalytic treatment due to concerns about cost and efficiency. Similar concerns were raised in relation to psychotherapy. As in Ontario, political lobbying by analysts succeeded in preventing this cutback.

Opportunities Even in Difficult Times

While delisting and threatened cutbacks are the order of the day in many jurisdictions, it would be erroneous to conclude that all is doom and gloom. Even in these hard times, some improvements are being achieved with regard to coverage for psychoanalysis and psychotherapy in some countries. For example, until recently in the Netherlands (Abraham, in press) if a psychologist were to be reimbursed by the national health insurance plan for psychotherapy or psychoanalysis, the patient had to be reinterviewed by a psychiatrist in order to approve the diagnostic assessment and treatment recommendations. The psychologist had to continue working in association with the psychiatrist who would receive 20 to 25 percent of the psychologist's fee throughout the course of the treatment. These arrangements, known pejoratively as the "long-arm system," have now been abolished, except for patients whose treatments began before March 1994. Until recently, psychoanalysis in the Netherlands was defined legally as a medical procedure. Now that this is no longer the case, the Dutch Psychoanalytic Society changed its charter in 1990 to allow psychoanalysts from disciplines other than medicine to become President (Groen-Prakken and de No-bel, 1992).

In Switzerland, the health care system is organized along federalist lines, but is largely run on a canton level (as in the Canadian federal–provincial system). Traditionally, insurance payment was only for medical psychotherapists. During the past few years, some insurance companies have begun paying lower fees for "delegated psychotherapy" which is conducted in a medical doctor's consulting room, under physician control. Swiss psychologists have thus advanced to the position which their Dutch colleagues have just recently transcended. As a result of this progressive development in the funding system, the number of Swiss psychologists practicing psychotherapy has increased rapidly in the past few years (Condrau, 1994; Moser, 1992). In countries behind the Iron Curtain, psychology was officially devalued as bourgeois science. Psychoanalysis was usually illegal. A few analysts continued to practice underground (Sebek, 1993). Since liberation, the Czechs have developed one of the most rational, equitable, and generous systems of psychological health care in the world. Despite economically difficult times, Czech psychologists and other psychotherapists managed to win the public and political support necessary to make psychological health care a national priority (Ruzicka, 1994, personal communication).

In Germany (Balzert, in press), efforts by psychologists and other psychotherapists led to greater recognition of the importance of psychotherapy for the health of society. Discussions between consumers, providers, and the government led to the introduction of a bill in 1993, known as the Psychotherapist's Law. This legislation included, for the first time, two nonmedical professions as independent providers, psychologist-psychotherapist and child and adolescent psychotherapist. (Prior to this bill, physicians had to "delegate" patients to psychologists, as used to be the case in the Netherlands, and still obtains in Switzerland.)

Models for the Future

In revising its psychological health care system, Germany did not reduce the total duration of treatment allowed. They did, however, limit the frequency of sessions to three per week. Consequently, all psychoanalyses of traditional frequency (four to five times per week) must be conducted outside the system, as is the case in Great Britain (Wallerstein, 1991), the Canadian provinces of Quebec and Manitoba (Fayek, in press), Spain and Brazil (Sjodin, 1994), Argentina (Killam, 1994, personal communication), Denmark (Paikin, 1992), New Zealand (Muir, 1994, personal communication) and Hungary (Harmatta and Szonyi, 1992).

It is rare to find a country like Finland that both provides generous coverage for psychoanalytic treatment (three sessions per week for three years) and permits patients to increase the frequency or duration of the treatment by drawing on their own financial resources. It often seems to go against the grain of many health care managers' philosophy to have such a mixed public-private, or managed-"unmanaged" model.

As the global economic outlook continues to be rather bleak, many countries are thinking of cutting back, rather than improving programs. If the economic outlook were more promising, proponents of psychological health care would definitely want to advocate for more widespread modeling of the new Czech plan, which seems close to ideal. Even though one could, and should, make sound cost–benefit arguments, both economic and sociocultural, in favor of governments and insurance companies adopting plans similar to the progressive Czech model, it is difficult to find open minds these days in the insurance industry (private or governmental) willing to listen to anything other than proposals guaranteeing immediate and substantial cost reductions within the very sector under consideration (e.g., briefer treatments, less qualified providers, drugs instead of psychotherapy, etc.).

In such times, it makes sense to give serious attention to a model, like Finland's, which demonstrates the viability of good public coverage, with the possibility of augmenting it privately for those who would otherwise be frustrated by its outer limits. This is not to say that the Finnish model is necessarily the best in every way. Two sessions per week for four-and-a-half years might be a better way to allocate the same resources. The merits of the model favored by the Swiss government (intensive treatment for a couple of years followed by the possibility of less intensive therapy for a few more years) also needs to be studied. The essential point I am trying to make is simply that the Finns have demonstrated the viability of running a good plan, within the limits of their resources, that guarantees very good treatment for all their citizens and also allows those who have the time, energy, motivation, and financial resources to purchase even more intensive treatment. Unlike the Germans, and some Canadian provinces, the Finns have not found it necessary to create a rigid rule forbidding anyone to provide or receive more intensive therapy than their plan provides, unless they opt out of the system completely.

With regard to the acceptance of a Finnish style, public–private model, there are signs of such developments in Sweden (Birchard, 1994). The Swedish government has tried to give physicians more incentive to operate privately, while still receiving some public funding. Currently, 95 percent of Swedish physicians work for the state, mostly in neighborhood clinics, while 5 percent are in private practice. Similarly, in Canada, there is now intensive debate about whether citizens should be able to receive partial reimbursement from the government if they obtain health care services from private clinics.

These movements in Sweden, Canada, and elsewhere toward a more mixed, public–private model pertain to their health care systems as a whole, and mostly to physical health care. There is a great need to examine the applicability of such mixed models specifically within the psychological health care sector. Such blended models could provide a way for many countries to move beyond the constraints of their current plans which discriminate against patients who want the freedom to choose to receive psychological health care from the qualified practitioner of their choice and be able to determine the most suitable intensity and duration of that treatment, in conjunction with their chosen mental health care specialist.

Conclusion

The combination of such factors as prolonged economic recession and increasing health care costs (related to more sophisticated technology, aging populations, etc.) has intensified debates in many countries about what services should be covered under health insurance plans. In the psychological health care sector, there is considerable diversity of plans, ranging from those which are committed to such services as a national priority, to those which are minimal in extent. Some countries have responded to current fiscal challenges by dramatically reducing coverage for psychotherapy and psychoanalysis. Other nations have managed to preserve their plans despite these difficult times and some have actually improved their coverage (in terms of services and, more commonly, the range of qualified practitioners available to consumers).

The insurance systems in some countries (e.g., some Canadian provinces) are close to ideal, except that they discriminate against citizens who want the freedom to choose from among qualified mental health practitioners rather than having to go to a psychiatrist or perhaps to a general practitioner with little or no training in psychotherapy. The system in the new Czech Republic appears to be more thoughtful, and does not have any such blatantly discriminatory features. It demonstrates that, when a nation has the vision to establish psychological health care as a priority, an excellent system can be created, even in difficult times.

In countries that cannot see themselves reaching for the ideal standard of care, the nondiscriminatory Finnish plan provides an outstanding alternative model. The Finns believe they cannot provide unlimited coverage. They have concluded that they are able only to provide funding to enable their citizens to work with private practitioners up to three sessions per week, for up to three years. Unlike some countries, however, they do not forbid citizens to make private arrangements with their practitioners to have sessions more frequently, or beyond the three year limit. In this way, within what they perceive to be their fiscal limits, they encourage, and go a considerable distance toward creating the possibility of long-term, intensive, psychoanalytic treatment for their populace. While other nations might decide that they cannot afford such frequent treatment, or that they would prefer to offer lesser intensity but longer duration, the essential point is that the Finns have clearly demonstrated the viability of a non-discriminatory, public/private model.

The comparative study of existing health insurance plans, particularly the more enlightened ones, and of the progressive and regressive forces acting upon them, can furnish citizens' groups, health care managers, professional associations, and other bodies with the understanding necessary to advocate for improvements to the current plans in their jurisdictions. No plan is perfect. Some plans are far superior to others. Every country can benefit from studying other nations' systems, and working to replace unnecessary limitations and injustices in their own plans with some of the more progressive features which can be adopted from these other nations' plans.

References

Abraham, J. (in press), The latest developments in the Netherlands for the practice of psychoanalysis under national health care systems. In: *Psychoanalysis as a Health Care Profession*, ed. H. Kaley, M. Eagle, & D. Wolitzky. Hillside, NJ: Analytic Press.

Balzert, C. (in press), The experience of psychoanalysts in Germany. In: *Psychoanalysis as a Health Care Profession*, ed. H. Kaley, M. Eagle, & D. Wolitzky. Hillside, NJ: Analytic Press.

Birchard, K. (1994), States of health care—Global trends in health care reform: Sweden. *Can. Health Care Manager*, 1:16–18.

Condrau, G. (1994), Comment on the IFPS questionnaire. *Internat. Forum Psychoanal.*, 3:21–24.

Fayek, A. (in press), The effect of health insurance on psychoanalysis in Canada. In: *Psychoanalysis as a Health Care Profession*, ed. H. Kaley, M. Eagle, & D. Wolitzky. Hillside, NJ: Analytic Press.

Fillet, B. (1993), Transgressive social violence and the welfare state-repressive tolerance and the public organization of psychoanalysis. Paper presented at the 38th Congress of the International Psycho-Analytic Association, Amsterdam.

Groen-Prakken, H., & de Nobel, L. (1992), The Netherlands. In: *Psychoanalysis International: A Guide to Psychoanalysis Throughout the World*, Vol. 1, ed. P. Kutter. Stuttgart-Bad Canstatt: Frommann-Holzboorg, pp. 217–242.

Hanly, C. (1995), Canada. In: *Psychoanalysis International: A Guide to Psychoanalysis Throughout the World*, Vol. 2, ed. P. Krutter. Stuttgart-Bad Constatt: Frommann-Holzborg, pp. 55–73.

Harmatta, J., & Szonyi, G. (1992), Hungary. In: *Psychoanalysis International: A Guide to Psychoanalysis Throughout the World*, Vol. 1, ed. P. Kutter. Stuttgart-Bad Constatt: Frommann-Holzborg, pp. 173–187.

Martin, R. T. (1995), Australia. *Psychoanalysis International: A Guide to Psychoanalysis Throughout the World*, Vol. 2, ed. P. Krutter. Stuttgart-Bad Constatt: Frommann-Holzborg, pp. 27–39.

Moser, A. (1992), Switzerland. In: *Psychoanalysis International: A Guide to Psychoanalysis Throughout the World*, ed. P. Kutter. Stuttgart-Bad Constatt: Frommann-Holzboorg, pp. 278–313.

Paikin, H. (1992), Denmark. In: *Psychoanalysis International: A Guide to Psychoanalysis Throughout the World*, ed. P. Kutter. Stuttgart-Bad Canstatt: Frommann-Holzboorg, pp. 50–53.

Pequeneza, N. (1995), Psychologists react to G.P. psychotherapists. *Family Practice*, 7:50.

Sebek, M. (1993), Psychoanalysis in Czechoslovakia. *Psychoanal. Rev.*, 80:433–440.

Sjodin, C. (1994), Psychoanalysis, socio-medical security systems and the healing tradition. *Internat. Forum Psychoanal.*, 3:5–16.

Wallerstein, R. S. (1991), The future of psychotherapy. *Bull. Menninger Clinic*, 55:421–443.

Willock, B. (in press), An examination of the incredible variety of national health insurance plans under which psychoanalysts practise around the world: The good, the bad and the ugly. In: *Psychoanalysis as a Health Care Profession*, ed. H. Kaley, M. Eagle, & D. Wolitzky. Hillsdale, NJ: Analytic Press.

Epilogue

James W. Barron, Ph.D.

Aspects of managed care have been part of the health care environment for a long time. Experiments in prepayment and group practice go back to the turn of the century. But those early experiments, infused with social idealism, were flexible parts of the health care landscape. What is different now is that managed care, driven by cost concerns and the profit motive, has become the predominant model.

Cummings (personal communication [1991], cited in Winegar and Bistline [1994]) observes that we are witnessing the industrialization of health care in general, and of mental health care in particular:

The industrial revolution had three immediate effects. First, it reduced the number of workers needed. It organized labor more effectively avoiding duplication and waste; thereby, increasing the efficiency of the whole. Fewer workers were needed. Secondly, it drove down wages. More workers competed for fewer jobs. Increased efficiency and automation reduce the need for laborers. Finally, increased standardization was evident, making products more affordable and accessible for the mass of consumers. No longer were individual cobblers able to produce a unique pair of shoes. Instead,

many cobblers were organized together to efficiently produce the most satisfying product the market demanded. Basi-
cally, managed mental health care has had the effect on what
was once a cottage industry, the private practice of therapy
and counseling [cited in Winegar and Bistline, 1994, p. 5].

Cummings joyfully proclaims the imminent demise of
the private practice of psychotherapy which traditionally has
been the setting most congenial to longer-term psychodynamic treatments. Industrialization necessarily implies the
degradation of the patient–therapist relationship. Patients
and therapists become replaceable parts in a standardized
system of care. Not surprisingly, many psychodynamically
oriented clinicians are less celebratory of these trends toward
the industrialization and medicalization of mental health
care as they are enacted through the techniques of managed care.

Even thoughtful, ethical proponents of managed care
raise serious questions about its potential drawbacks. In their
excellent edited volume published by the American Psychiatric Press, Feldman and Fitzpatrick (1992) raise profoundly
unsettling questions: "Are these systems providing second-
class care? Treating long-term problems with short-term solutions? Are managed care clinicians caught in untenable
conflict-of-interest situations? Are capitated care or prepaid
arrangements unethical? Are alternatives to hospital care unsafe? Ineffective? Is utilization management intruding unduly into the practice of psychiatry? [p. xv].

Feldman and Fitzpatrick admit that they, along with
their colleagues who are among the most experienced and
sophisticated of mental health providers in managed care
environments, cannot definitively answer those fundamental
questions. Nevertheless, they remain sanguine about the future partnership of managed care and mental health services. They imply that early forms of managed care were

primitive but that now we are witnessing more sophisticated "fourth and fifth generations" which correct previous short-comings and abuses.

What is striking about these "fourth and fifth genera-tions" is the massive overlapping of administrative, manage-rial, and clinical concerns. This overlap is intentional. In their introduction, Feldman and Fitzpatrick note approv-ingly: "Every managed care clinician is a clinical manager. Administrative and clinical concepts are inextricably inter-twined. Since all mental health care is financed in *some* fash-ion, this confounding of economics and clinical care is universal, and not only attributable to managed systems. We hope that clinicians and administrators will be able to apply these concepts and ideas to other systems of care" [p. xvi].

While it is true that there has always been some overlap since ultimately all care has to be funded in one way or another, advocates of managed care are being disingenuous when they gloss over the huge differences of degree. The interpenetration of administrative-managerial and clinical concerns has profound impact on health care generally, mental health care in particular, and psychodynamic psycho-therapies most of all. Advocates of managed care are gener-ally more able to articulate the economic benefits of their model than they are able or willing to elaborate upon the clinical consequences. The underlying reason for this dis-crepancy is the inherent difficulty in squeezing human devel-opment, psychopathology, and treatment into modalities which fit comfortably within the managed care framework.

However well intentioned the therapist, the needs of the managed care system have a way of taking precedence over the needs of the patient. For example, focusing on the patient–therapist relationship, Feldman comments: "Often the therapist must educate the patient about the health care system in the midst of trying to evaluate or handle the pa-tient's acute crisis" (p. 20).

Clearly many of the contributors to this volume remain unconvinced that managed care in any of its incarnations represents progress or is compatible with meaningful psychotherapeutic treatment. As Allen and Morris both indicate, managed health care is not a philosophy of treatment, but rather is a set of interrelated business principles designed primarily to contain costs and maximize profits. By determining which services are reimbursable and under what conditions, these principles nevertheless greatly influence the form and substance of treatment.

When indemnity insurance was the prevailing model, managed care consisted primarily of retroactive utilization review of claims to rule out grossly inappropriate treatment or even outright fraud. This review process was minimally intrusive into the relationship and the mutual decision making of patient and therapist. Meehan points out that, under those conditions, the results of utilization review were more or less reliable and predictable, and patient and therapist could plan treatment accordingly.

As medicalization and industrialization of mental health care have marched hand in hand, health maintenance organizations (HMOs) and other variants have largely supplanted indemnity insurance. Managed care has increasingly adopted more active cost-control techniques of prior certification of treatments based on primary care physicians serving as gatekeepers, followed by case administrators determining the medical necessity, appropriateness, and cost-effectiveness of ongoing treatments. These techniques, responding to market forces, are having some positive effects: decreased hospitalization; creation of less costly and less restrictive alternatives along with vertical integration of services such as partial hospitalization, crisis intervention, and day treatment; utilization of short-term and group treatments in outpatient settings; and enhanced utilization of ancillary community resources. But, as both Simon and

Weissberg point out in their papers, managed care is leading to profound ethical dilemmas, and, as Higuchi and Newman note, flagrant abuses necessitating corrective legislation.

Managed care is also having a devastating impact on patients whose needs are best served by intensive psychodynamic treatment which extends beyond the confines of crisis intervention or brief psychotherapy. Vociferous proponents of managed care are stigmatizing patients who do not fit into the short-term/crisis intervention model. They label such patients as either too sick (consigned to psychotropic medication only) to benefit from psychotherapy or too healthy (derisively dismissed as the "worried well") to merit treatment at all. They also malign psychodynamic therapists as avaricious providers out of touch with progressive trends in health care. In his chapter, Pollack forcefully confronts and dispels those myths exploited by managed care companies to limit and deny appropriate treatment. Other contributors to this volume explore the negative impact of managed care on various aspects of the treatment relationship and of the therapeutic process.

The contributing authors leave little doubt that managed care, at least as it is currently conceived and executed, is inimical to psychoanalysis and psychodynamic treatment. Indeed it remains questionable whether managed care (even when its more flagrant abuses are curtailed) and psychodynamic approaches can coexist within the same framework. One conclusion is that, at a minimum, psychodynamic therapists should strive to protect the right of patient and therapist to contract privately with one another outside of systems of managed mental health care. With the collapse of large-scale national health care reform efforts (at least for the foreseeable future), psychotherapists will have to continue to monitor health care law carefully on a state by state basis. While protecting the right of patient and therapist to contract privately is essential, it is not enough. Many patients are dependent upon their health insurance to afford mental health treatment of any kind. Therapists should not abandon those patients, but should fight to make appropriately meaningful treatment, including intensive dynamically oriented psychotherapy, available to them as their needs require.

In addition to their fundamental concern of the quality of mental health care, therapists need to grapple honestly with the cost of such care. As Willock demonstrates, these attempts to balance quality and cost transcend our national boundaries. Governmental and regulatory bodies within each of the industrialized democracies are experimenting with rationing and managing care to varying degrees. These experiments will continue. There will be no return to the older system of indemnity insurance, but managed care as currently structured in the United States is not a "done deal" by any means. It will change, and other modes of health care service delivery and financing will evolve. Therapists who practice from a psychodynamic perspective need to participate actively in this ongoing evolution.

References

Feldman, J. L., & Fitzpatrick, R., Eds. (1992), *Managed Mental Health Care: Administrative and Clinical Issues.* Washington, DC: American Psychiatric Press.

Winegar, N., & Bistline, J. (1994), *Marketing Mental Health Services to Managed Care.* New York: Haworth Press.

Author Index

Subject Index

Abandonment, 137–138
  ethical issue of, 227–229
  of hospitalized children, 168
  negligent, 261
Access, obstacles to, 9–10
Administrative costs, 187, 211–212
Advocacy
  managed care impact on, 54–56
  patient, 265
AIDS Reporting, 233
American Psychological Association
  draft model UR statute of, 242
  *Ethical Principles of Psychologists and
    Code of Conduct*, 221, 223–
    230, 263
  Practice Directorate of, 55
Analytic situation, 136
Analyzability, of borderline patients,
    140–144
Appeal, of review process, 60, 243–246
"As if" personality, 134
Association of State and Provincial
    Psychology Boards, *Code of
    Conduct*, 221–222, 232–233
Atypical pervasive developmental dis-
    order, 160–162
Autonomy of practice, 36–37

Bad-faith claim denials, 250
Becoming a Constant Object (Cohen,
    Sherwood), 144–145

Behavioral medicine, 109–110
"Beyond the Pleasure Principle"
    (Freud), 195–196
Biological imbalance theories, 206
Biological markers, 109
Biological psychiatry, xiii, 275
Blue Cross/Blue Shield, 15
Borderline concept, 133–136
Borderline group, 134
Borderline patient
  attaining object constancy, 144–147
  characteristics of, 133
  countertransference reaction to,
    140–144
  efficacy of long-term treatment
    for, 149
  managed care of, 131–149
  structural treatment frame for,
    137–139
Boulder-model mental health organi-
    zation, 28–29
Bureaucracy, 182

Canada
  health care model of, 291–292
  health insurance system of, 287–
    288, 290
Canadian Psychological Association,
    Code of Ethics, 221–222
Case records, confidentiality of, 8
Case report, managed care, 66–70

309

Trauma
  passive experience of, 195–196
  trust in survivors of, 43–44
Traumatic Stress Institute, 28–29
Treatment
  authorization for, 37
  frame in, 136–139
  least restrictive modality of, 214
  managed care impact on, 132–149
  pyramid vs. multidisciplinary approaches to, 208–210
Triadic relationships, 190
Trust, 43–44

Unconscious processes, 190
Universal coverage, 77–79
Utilization
  changes in, 11
  management of, 73–74, 76
  problems related to, 207–208
  of psychiatric service, 120
Utilization review, 3
  arbitrary, 22–23
  basic concepts of, 18–21
  case examples of, 21–24
  case record requests for, 8
  complaint mechanism for, 243, 245–246
  complaint mechanisms of, 265–266
  development of, 17
  ethical issue of, 222–223
  of hospital-based clinicians, 169

informed consent and, 261–264
liability and, 247–250
medical necessity and, 184
nature of, 273
as obstacle, 240
professional responsibility for, 187–189
purpose of, 242
qualification of reviewer, 243
statutory protections and, 241–247
unreasonable information requests for, 260
Wickline case and, 247–249
Utilization Review Accreditation Commission (URAC), 242
Utilization review laws
  consumer protection provisions of, 244–247
  like-provider provision of, 244
  standard provision of, 243

Values
  issues of, 183–184
  professional responsibility for assessing, 187–189
Victim blaming, 44

Wickline v. State of California, 247–249, 250, 260–261
Wilson v. Blue Cross of Southern California, 249–250, 261
Woman Under the Influence (Cassavetes), 197